Teaching Thinking

Philosophical Enquiry in the Classroom

2nd Edition

Robert Fisher

continuum
LONDON • NEW YORK

Continuum

The Tower building,   15 East 26th Street
11 York Road   New York, NY,
London SE1 7NM   10010

www.continuumbooks.com

First published 1998
This edition published 2003 by Continuum
Reprinted 2004

British Library Cataloguing-in-Publication Data
A catalogue record for this book is available from the British Library

ISBN 0–8264-6804-7 (hardback)
    0–8264-6805-5 (paperback)

Typeset by BookEns Limited, Royston Hertfordshire, SG8 9PX
Printed and bound in Great Britain by CPI Bath

Contents

Contents

Acknowledgements

I am deeply indebted to the many people who have shared in the task of developing the 'philosophy for children' movement in this country, and who have given of their time and expertise in seeking ways to develop the teaching of thinking and philosophy in schools. In particular I would like to thank the following: Michael Whalley, who first demonstrated for me the potential of doing philosophy with primary school children; Will Robinson, Roger Sutcliffe, Karin Murris, Victor Quinn, Johanna Kiernon, Roger Prentice, Barbara Rae, Steve Williams and colleagues in SAPERE (the Society for the Advancement of Philosophical Enquiry and Reflection in Education); and to my research student Sara Liptai, for their many contributions to my understanding of the theory and practice of philosophy with and for children.

I am deeply indebted to the pioneering work of Matthew Lipman, Ann Margaret Sharp and their colleagues at the IAPC (Institute for the Advancement of Philosophy for Children) at Montclair University, and thank them for permission to quote from their Philosophy for Children programme; and am grateful for the work and advice of others in the international community of researchers including Catherine Mc-Call in Scotland, Phil Cam and Laurence Splitter in Australia,

Marie-Pierre Doutrelepont in Belgium, and Daniella Camhy in Austria.

I wish to thank the network of teacher researchers who have facilitated and contributed to my research in schools. Special thanks are due to Lizann O'Conor, Chris Johnson, Debbie Pacey, Nicole Lyster, Sophie Austin, Anne Watts, Karen O'Haire, Linda Harvey, Mireille Stanton and other teachers in west London schools who have been co-researchers on training courses and in the Philosophy in Primary Schools (PIPS) project.

Special thanks are also due to the many children in infant, junior and secondary schools who have shared philosophical discussion with me and constantly surprised me with the freshness of their thinking and depth of their philosophical interests, especially to those whose words appear in this book, including my sons Tom and Jake, who have demonstrated for me the value of philosophical discussion within the family. Thanks are also due to colleagues who have supported my research at Brunel University including Sarah Sandow, Bernard Down and Professor Linda Thomas. All these people have helped me in my understanding of the rich potential of doing philosophy with children. Their work has informed this book, the flaws and shortcomings in it remain my own.

Introduction

Philosophy for me means having adventures in ideas with children. I know it can be done. The problem is how to do it, and how to do it better!
Student teacher

This book is about teaching children how to discuss matters of importance in ways that help develop their thinking and learning. It is not about teaching children the subject of philosophy, but how to engage them in a special kind of discussion – philosophical discussion, teaching them in other words how to *philosophize*. It aims to show ways in which philosophical discussion can be used to add value to our speaking and listening with children at home and school. It is about what we do with children every day in talking and thinking with them, but trying to do it in better ways through an approach called philosophy for children.

The challenge to improve children's thinking, learning and language lies at the heart of education. It also lies at the heart of the world-wide 'philosophy for children' movement, which uses philosophical enquiry to enhance the thinking, learning and language skills of students of all ages and abilities in more than thirty countries around the world. This book makes a contribution to the theory and practice of philosophy with children, illustrated with work from children and teachers in schools in the UK. It explores ways to encourage children to think critically and creatively through philosophical enquiry, and offers ways to facilitate discussion with groups of children at home or school.

The book begins by exploring reasons why teaching thinking is so important, and the role philosophy can play in providing the means for developing more effective thinking. Chapter 1: Why Philosophy? seeks to answer such questions as:

- Why teach thinking?
- What kinds of thinking should be taught?
- What are the common faults in thinking?
- Can better thinking be taught?
- Why philosophy for children?

Philosophy is the only discipline which has as its subject matter thinking and the improvement of thinking. The problem teachers face is: How do we introduce our children to thoughtful discussion?

Chapter 2 provides an introduction to the Philosophy for Children programme devised more than twenty years ago in America by Matthew Lipman. This pioneering programme has been implemented in many countries, but has been little used in the UK. An overview of the programme is presented, illustrated with sample material and excerpts from classroom discussion. Philosophy for Children is not only a programme for developing reasoning skills through classroom discussion, it also aims to provide a context for moral and social education through a specific teaching strategy called 'community of inquiry (or enquiry)'.

Chapter 3 shows how a Community of Enquiry can be developed with any group of children to foster the moral and social aims of education, and how progress in creating such a community can be assessed. Later chapters in the book show how philosophical discussion can be applied to every area of learning, and try to answer the questions most often asked by teachers, such as:

- How do we plan for philosophical discussion?
- How do we facilitate philosophical discussion?
- How do we assess the benefits of philosophy with children?

Chapter 4: Stories for Thinking shows how philosophical discussion can be stimulated through story to help develop critical thinking and literacy (reading, writing, speaking and listening). The Stories for Thinking approach is illustrated through teaching ideas and examples of classroom discussion. Stories are shown to be a good way to stimulate philosophical enquiry and ways to facilitate discussion are suggested using a range of materials.

Chapter 5 explores ways of leading discussion through Socratic Teaching, and shows how Socratic methods of enquiry can be used to help meet some of the basic social, moral and cognitive aims of education.

Chapter 6: Philosophy in the Classroom summarizes the key elements of philosophy for children and explores ways of assessing the learning outcomes and benefits to be gained for individuals and for the community involved. Evidence of the success of philosophical discussion in developing aspects of thinking and learning is drawn from international research.

Finally Chapter 7: Philosophy across the Curriculum shows how philosophical discussion can feed into all areas of the curriculum and enrich all aspects of learning. At the end of the book are appendix materials to support the planning, teaching and assessment of philosophical discussion, a bibliography of recommended books and an index to key themes.

The book is illustrated with examples of philosophical discussion mainly derived from the author's research with teachers and children in school settings, in particular the Philosophy in Primary Schools (PIPS) project carried out in London schools 1993–6. These excerpts are intended to allow the voices of children and teachers to be heard, and to illustrate ways in which philosophical enquiry can be conducted with children of different ages and abilities. A list of the themes and questions which stimulated these discussions appears in Appendix 1 (p. 251).

It is hoped that the models of thinking and learning described here will provide an inspiration for your own discussions with children, and a spur for your own research.

Teaching Thinking Overview plan of chapters

1. Why Philosophy?	*focus of enquiry*
2. Philosophy for Children **3. Community of Enquiry** }	*general theory*
4. Stories for Thinking **5. Socratic Teaching** **6. Philosophy in the Classroom** }	*applied theory*
7. Philosophy across the Curriculum	*extended theory*

NOTE

The term 'philosophy for children' refers in this book to ways of introducing children to philosophical discussion through a community of enquiry approach, whereas Philosophy for Children refers to the programme created by Matthew Lipman discussed in Chapter 2.

CHAPTER 1

Why Philosophy?
Thinking about thinking

All which the school can or need do for pupils, so far as their minds are concerned . . . is to develop their ability to think.

John Dewey (1916)

Philosophy gives you something to think about.

Raymond, aged 10

Over the last twenty years we have seen the beginnings of a major new movement to promote intellectual development. This has been called the 'critical thinking' or 'thinking skills' movement.[1] Part of the aim of this movement is to create a 'thinking curriculum', placing the development of thinking at the heart of the educational process. But can we teach children to be more effective thinkers? And if so, how? Before we look at ways of teaching thinking we need to ask why a focus on thinking in education seems so necessary.

WHY TEACH THINKING?

Everyone thinks, or as a child recently put it: 'We all think . . . at least we think we do.' The quality of our lives and of our learning depends on the quality of our thinking. If we can systematically cultivate excellence in thinking then we should surely do so. One reason frequently advanced for the teaching of thinking is that thinking is intrinsic to human development and that every individual has a right to have their intellect developed.[2] Teaching thinking becomes an end in itself by the very fact that we are thinking animals, and have a right to the education of those faculties that constitute what it is to be a human individual. The development of our minds is part of what it means to be educated, because it is part of what it means to be human. According to this view the key function of education is to teach children to think critically, creatively and effectively. As David, aged 9, put it: 'What is school for if it is not to help you to think and become a better person?'

Another justification for teaching thinking is that we gain pleasure from the right sort of intellectual stimulus and challenge. Our brains are wired for problem solving, and we enjoy puzzles that we can solve. For the Greeks philosophy was a process of asking questions and solving problems, and it was a process that gave pleasure. They argued that the exercise of the human intellect produced both virtue and satisfaction. In the nineteenth century Mill developed this idea further by distinguishing what he called the 'higher' and the 'lower' pleasures of human existence. The higher pleasures of the mind he said were more profound and satisfying than the lower pleasures of the body. More recently philosopher John Rawls expresses this link between thinking and pleasure in a more general way when he claims that 'other things being equal, human beings enjoy the exercise of their rational capacities (their innate or trained abilities), and this enjoyment increases the more the capacity is realized, or the greater its complexity'.[3] We can see this in the popularity of puzzle books and television quiz programmes. Karen, aged 8, echoes this when she says that the reason she likes philosophy is that 'it is a kind of puzzle'.

Classroom research in schools supports the view that students are better motivated and more engaged in classes they find intellectually stimulating. They like those teachers who make them think. They prefer lessons in which they are for example 'asked to interpret, analyse, or manipulate information, or apply acquired knowledge and skills to novel problems or new situations'.[4] Intellectually challenging teaching has been identified as one of the key factors characteristic of effective teachers and of successful schools.[5] As Chris, aged 10, said: 'I like those lessons where the teacher doesn't tell you what you already know, but you have to think it out for yourself.'

What is philosophy about?

Some views on the pleasures of philosophy by children aged 9 to 10 years:

Philosophy is about . . .

. . . getting you thinking. It takes your thoughts higher. I like that, having something really hard to think about that you have never thought of before. (Carla)

. . . a lot of things like listening, reading and saying your thoughts, but most of all it is about thinking. It is the only subject that is thinking about thinking. There are many interesting things to think about which nobody has ever worked out before, like: 'When did time begin?' or 'Who thought the first thought?' (Jemma)

. . . solving problems. It is good because it gets you to use parts of the brain you don't use in other lessons. It's like a game. It can be fun listening to ideas and having your own ideas. (Karl)

Thinking can not only bring pleasure, it can be useful. Many of the reasons for seeking to develop thinking and learning skills are instrumental or pragmatic, and are to do with the success of individuals and of society. This view is set in the context of international concern about declining educational standards. 'Back to basics' movements are underway in many countries, including Britain, the USA and Australia. At the same time there are those who argue that the three 'Rs' of reading, writing and arithmetic need to be supplemented by a 'fourth R', namely Reasoning. This 'forward to basics' view claims that teaching thinking and reasoning is central to raising standards even in the most basic skills of the curriculum. It argues that the most important resource any society has are the intellectual resources of its people. A successful society will be a thinking society in which the capacities for lifelong learning of its citizens are most fully realized. If thinking is how we make sense of experience then being helped to think better will help children learn more from what they see, say and do. Critical thinking is needed to make sense of knowledge in any subject area. As Megan, aged 9, put it during one of her philosophy lessons: 'Philosophy helps me think, and I need to think well if I want to learn.'

Part of the perceived need to teach thinking skills has come from a growing awareness that society has changed and skills appropriate a generation ago may no longer prepare students for the world beyond school. The rate of change within society is accelerating so rapidly that it is difficult to assess what factual knowledge will be needed in the future, and this means that schools should be less focused on imparting information than on teaching students to learn and to think for themselves. Students faced with a future in an unpredictable world will need to gain the skills that will give them the greatest control over their lives and learning, and for this they will need to think critically and creatively at the highest possible levels, and to develop an awareness of global issues and problems. As Sandeep, aged 10, suggests: 'We don't know what problems there might be in the future, so we'd better start thinking about them now.'

Exercising the mind through intellectual challenge is not only a means for enjoyment and for success in a rapidly changing world, but can also promote moral qualities and virtues. Intellectual virtue can be seen as a complex set of attributes including curiosity, thoughtfulness, intellectual courage and perseverance in the search for truth, a willingness to speculate and analyse, to judge and self correct, an openness to the views of others and other elements, developed through practice. These are qualities that need to be practised through thinking for oneself and thinking with others. Philosophical enquiry with children can be a means whereby such qualities as open-mindedness, perseverance, respect for others and self examination can become embedded in human character. 'Thinking is what we are here for. Thinking can help you be a better person,' says Kirandeep, aged 8.

What is a good thinker?

The dispositions of ideal critical thinkers,[6] and some comments from children.

Ideal critical thinkers display a number of intellectual virtues. These include:

1. *Seeking truth*
   They care that their beliefs are true, and that their decisions are as far as possible justified.
   They show this by:
   a) seeking alternatives (hypotheses, explanations, conclusions, plans, sources, ideas)
   b) supporting views only to the extent that they are justified by available information
   c) being well informed, including being informed by the views of others
   'A good thinker is someone who is always trying to find out new things.' (Rachel, aged 9)

2. *Being honest*
   They care that their position and the positions of others are represented honestly.
   They show this by attending, by:
   a) being clear about what they mean
   b) maintaining a focus on the issue in question
   c) seeking and offering reasons
   d) considering all factors relevant in the situation
   e) being aware of their own point of view
   f) considering seriously other points of view
   'To be a good thinker you have to be honest with yourself, and with other people.' (Brian, aged 9)

3. *Respecting others*
   They care about the dignity and worth of every person.
   They show this by:
   a) attentive listening to the views of others
   b) avoiding scorn or intimidation of others
   c) showing concern about the welfare of others
   'A good thinker listens to what others say, even if you don't agree with them.' (Nicholas, aged 9)

Teaching children to be better thinkers is both a rational and a moral enterprise and can be seen as the fulfilment of the human nature of individuals through particular processes of education. These processes require more than an isolated set of 'thinking skills'. They are also a matter of developing attitudes and dispositions. Teaching thinking cannot be simply a matter of imparting certain skills, for if skills are not used they are redundant. All the finely honed thinking skills in the world will be for naught if they are not used for positive purposes. If teaching thinking is to be successful, we must consider what will motivate and strengthen the will to think. We must teach children not only the skills of thinking but also encourage the disposition to enquire, the attitude of commitment to enquiry, and encourage them to believe that their thinking is possible, permitted and productive. The skills we have do not say much about who we are because they make no reference to our character, needs or values. It is by virtue of these that we are persons of one sort or another.

Being a person means having a sense of oneself, including self as thinker and learner, and a sense of others through our interaction with them. A broad view of the purposes of education would include developing such intellectual virtues and dispositions as to attend, concentrate, cooperate, organize, reason, imagine and enquire. We need to develop the virtues of seeking truth, being honest and of respect for others. A central purpose of philosophical discussion with children is to develop these intellectual virtues. Rajiv, aged 9, seemed conscious of the need to *want* to think in his comment: 'I am good at thinking, but I don't always want to do it. In a philosophy (lessons) you want to think and you have to think.'

Another set of reasons for teaching thinking centres around the social nature of human life, and in particular the link between democracy and citizenship. A fully participative democratic society requires an autonomous citizenry that can think, judge and act for themselves. By definition, the education of a morally autonomous person requires the teaching of critical thinking. There can be no democratic liberty if citizens lack the skills to differentiate lies from truth. Democracy depends on shared understanding and the discriminating

use of language. What we need in an increasingly commercial-
ized world, as one 16-year-old said are 'well-developed bullshit
detectors'. As local, national and international issues become
increasingly complex, and as the voices of those who would
do the thinking for us become more persuasive, we need the
skills of critical thinking to help us to form intelligent judgements on public issues and thus contribute democratically to
the solution of social problems. Philosophical enquiry
involves enquiry into the moral codes and values of society,
and aims to develop in children the critical consciousness
which results from their intervention in the world as thinkers
in the world and as future transformers of that world

Democracy is the political expression of the human urge for
freedom, freedom of thought and freedom of expression. Education should be, as many Existentialist thinkers have argued,
a process whereby the child is gradually helped to recognize
the nature of human freedom and of human responsibility.
What children face at school is the ever-present danger of
setting aside what they really think in order to reproduce what
their teacher, or their peers, think. The temptation is for
children to rely on what Heidegger calls 'hearsay', that is what
is 'given' to children by way of second-hand ideas and experiences, without inviting them to evaluate and interpret what
they know and to make it their own.[7] In requiring teachers to
cater for individual needs in learning, curriculum planners and
inspectors sometimes ignore the most basic need – that of
encouraging children to think in ways which express their
authentic individuality. Being authentic means not caught up
in unthinking conformity of what others think, or subject to
the tyranny of hearsay, but being aware of a responsibility to
think for oneself and exercising the right to express oneself as
an individual. As Patrick, aged 11, said: 'If I can't say what I
think, why bother with thinking?'

One problem with the emphasis on authentic individualized
thinking is that it might lead to self-centredness. If everything
revolves around what I think then my thoughts will tend to
become self-referential, I will become part of what has been
called a 'me' society. G.H. Mead argued that the reasonable
person is one who can adopt the view of the 'generalized
other'.[8] If thinking for oneself is an important disposition then

11

surely also is the disposition to take account of the views of others. Thinking is expanded not only by thinking for oneself, but also by thinking with and through others. Part of the essence of who I am is my relationship with others and with their thinking. We are social as well as existential beings. Is not understanding others as important as understanding oneself? Teaching should be both individual-centred but also community-centred (a class being one form of community). Vygotsky claimed that it is through language used in social contexts that children learn to take control of their thinking and are helped to fulfil their intellectual potential.[9]

WHAT KINDS OF THINKING SHOULD BE TAUGHT? THINKING ABOUT THINKING

There is not yet common agreement or definitive explanation of the processes involved in thinking. It is therefore not surprising that there are many conflicts of opinion about the nature of reasoning and intelligence, and that many remain sceptical about the idea of teaching thinking. Even among experts definitions of thinking skills vary greatly. Many authors have created lists of thinking skills, sometimes running to hundreds of separate items. Matthew Lipman, creator of the Philosophy for Children programme, has pointed out the difficulties in defining thinking skills. Such a list would be endless, he suggests, 'because it consists of nothing less than an inventory of the intellectual powers of mankind'.[10]

While there is a problem in defining what it is in thinking we wish to develop, if we believe that a focus on teaching thinking has the potential to improve significantly the quality of education for all our students, then it is a problem we must try to overcome. Our first task then is to try to be clear in our thinking about thinking, before we attempt the ambitious project of defining a model of teaching that can help develop the intellectual powers of our students.

Thought is closely linked to language. According to Vygotsky linguistic communication is the primary vehicle for human thinking and learning. Not that all thinking depends on words. As Ryle said, an architect might try to think out his design for a building project by arranging and rearranging models on a computer screen; a sculptor might plan a statue by modelling and remodelling a lump of clay, and a child might draw her ideas. But what makes the human mind so powerful is the use of speech for learning, and in particular an elaborated syntax linked to a powerful symbolic memory which enables humans to elaborate, refine, connect, create, and remember great numbers of new concepts. One of the key aims of any thinking programme should therefore be to develop linguistic intelligence through enhancing in students their powers of communication and concept formation.

One way to begin encouraging children to think about thinking is for them to reflect on the question, 'What is thinking?' The more we can encourage children to think about thinking the more we can help them gain metacognitive awareness and understanding of their own minds. As one child recently said, 'If you really knew how your mind worked, it would work much better!'

What is thinking?

Some reflections on thinking by Anna, aged 10, an example of writing undertaken after discussion of the question in a philosophy class:[11]

Thinking is a state of mind. It is divided into two regions, Choice and Pleasure. Choice covers everyday choices, such as what to do at wet play, to serious choices like whether to go to college. Pleasure covers all other kinds of thinking. Guessing is *not* thinking. Thinking is life. We could not live without thinking. Dreaming is the only exception. The two regions of Choice and Pleasure do not cover it. Dreams are very strange because your body and brain do not control them. They are almost not thinking. What is a dream?

Vygotsky was one of the first to realize that conscious reflective control and deliberate mastery were essential factors in school learning. He suggested two factors in the development of knowledge, first its automatic unconscious acquisition followed by a gradual increase in active conscious control over that knowledge, which was essentially a separation between cognitive and metacognitive aspects of performance.

If we can bring the process of thinking and learning to a conscious level, and help students to become more reflective, then we can help them to gain control or mastery over the organization of their learning. On this view effective learning is not just the manipulation of information so that it is integrated into an existing knowledge base, but also involves directing one's attention to what has been assimilated, understanding the relationship between the new information and what is already known, understanding the processes which facilitated this, and being aware when something new has actually been learned. It involves not only thinking, but a metacognitive process: thinking about thinking.

What is your brain like?

Some children, aged 10, offer metaphors for the working of their brains:

My brain is like a massive forest, it's full of amazing ideas. But some of these ideas are like shy animals, they hide away in the middle of the forest. I don't think we can ever really understand how our brains work. (Richard)

My brain is like an anthill, with millions of tiny passage-ways. There is always something going on in my head, the ants in my mind never seem to rest. I just hope there aren't any ant-eaters! (Leigh)

My brain is like a naughty puppy. It never seems to do what I want it to. If I've got maths homework to do it wants to read a comic or watch TV. But like a puppy it can be trained. (Jemma)

Some researchers, like Flavell,[12] argue this metacognitive ability changes with age, and that older children simply become more successful learners because they have internalized over time a greater quantity of metacognitive information. Others, like Donaldson,[13] consider that development is not so much dependent on age but on experience, and that we can intervene to help even young children to develop some of the metacognitive strategies of successful learning. Like compound interest metacognitive strategies can be said to increase the learner's intellectual capacity. What are these metacognitive strategies?

Nisbet and Shucksmith[14] suggest a set of six strategies for successful learning, which involve:

- asking questions
- planning
- monitoring
- checking
- revising
- self testing

Such strategies, valuable as they are, do not go far enough. Learning depends on 'conversations', on the negotiation of personal meanings through dialogue with others, leading to improved understanding. These conversations can be internal, but are particularly effective carried out in pairs or groups where different ways of interpreting experience can be explored to mutual benefit. A number of 'teaching to learn' cognitive strategies have been identified in recent research, including 'discussing' and 'cooperative learning', as among those that help develop metacognition.[15] Philosophy with children is a process of cooperative discussion which according to Gary, aged 10, is: 'thinking about thinking times as many people as are there.'

For Anna philosophy is 'a way of solving problems when you talk about it together'. Problem solving is an area related to metacognition that has been much researched. The findings of such research indicate that an ordinary person rarely seeks to investigate and solve a problem systematically unless specifically educated to do so.[16] What then are the common faults in thinking that prevent us from being more effective in solving problems?

WHAT IS WRONG WITH OUR THINKING?
SOME COMMON FAULTS

There are those who believe that intelligence is developed not through processes of thinking but through acquisition of knowledge. But one of the dangers that learners face is what

15

de Bono calls the 'Intelligence Trap', or the illusion of knowledge, which is that the greatest obstacle to discovery can lie in what people believe they know or can do.[17] They become trapped in what they already know, and are not open to new ideas. Some knowledgeable students are remarkably unintelligent in their approach to learning. They do not generate new ideas but are blocked by old and familiar habits. Such learners need strategies for generating new ideas and for becoming open to the ideas of others. They need to become not only creative and critical thinkers but self-critical thinkers. Self criticism for Binet was the most important indicator of intelligence. For some the key benefit of philosophical enquiry is that it encourages self-correction in thinking. As Sarah, aged 9, said: 'In philosophy it is all right to change your mind . . . and sometimes you do.'

The capacity for self criticism is not something that is inborn, it must be nurtured through practice and education. Part of this education should be to help students become aware of some of the common faults that make their thinking and learning less effective.

One of the common faults in human thinking is that it is too hasty. We are impulsive and fail to take time to consider alternative plans of action. We do not think ahead to work through the consequences of our decisions, and we do not take time to review and learn from what we have done. 'It is not much good thinking of a thing,' said H.G. Wells, 'unless you think it out.' We see this in children who respond hastily to moves in a game, who respond to others unthinkingly, and who make impulsive choices. Perhaps the most common reaction to a problem situation is a random hunt for solutions and sometimes this results in success, but in school situations where there is usually a limited number of possible solutions frequent failure is likely. The need to avoid impulsivity, like the game of guessing what is in the teacher's head, and to take time to consider options and alternatives has been identified by Feuerstein as a key strategy in overcoming learning failure. The motto for all students should be: 'Stop, and think.' Philosophical discussion is one way that can help to overcome the tendency for haste by emphasizing the need to take time to think things through for oneself and to think about what others are saying. As one child expressed it: 'Philosophy . . . gives you time to think.'

Another common fault in human thinking is that it is too narrow. 'What is now proved,' said William Blake, 'was once only imagined.' We all have a need to expand out consciousness through the generation of ideas, and to be mindful about alternative possibilities. Through routine and force of habit human thinking tends to become mindless.[18] We become mindless when we rely on a fixed mindset and cling unthinkingly to the same view. We become trapped in premature cognitive commitments, familiar categories and well-worn tracks. We treat choices as inevitable between A and B, missing the possibility there may be other choices and better ways. Philosophy for children encourages the search for creative options, different viewpoints and ways of thinking. As one child put it: 'People are always saying the same things; in philosophy you are allowed to think something different.'

Another fault in human thinking is that it often lacks focus. When we lack a plan or strategy our thinking tends to become hazy. If we lack clarity about the targets we need to pursue we become haphazard and overlook what is important. Our thinking becomes random, disconnected, disorganized and fuzzy in our approach to problems. Philosophy helps us to focus attention on concepts and questions central to human understanding such as: Who am I? What is true? How do I know? As a child aged 10 said about her philosophy lessons: 'Philosophy gives you something important to think about.'

Philosophical enquiry provides an opportunity to stop and think, to identify problems and to engage in a systematic and sustained search for solutions. It also provides us with a means of thinking about thinking, and of engaging in metacognitive dialogue. Thinking about thinking is not something that comes naturally, but is developed through practice and through internalizing certain habits of mind. It is this ability to become conscious of our own thought processes which takes learning by the human species far beyond that of any other animal. The human brain's capacity to represent recursively its internal mental states allows us eventually to become poets, philosophers, physicists, and to achieve all the fruits of civilized life. One way to help students think about

17

thinking is to introduce them to the tradition whose subject matter is all about forms of thinking – philosophy. One simple definition of philosophy is that it is a process of thinking about thinking.

What is strange or puzzling about thinking?

Some questions about thinking asked by a group of 9- to 10-year-old children as topics for discussion:

1. What is a thought?
2. Where do thoughts come from?
3. Can you stop thinking?
4. How do you remember things?
5. What helps you to think?
6. Does your brain talk to you or do you talk to your brain?
7. Can you think someone else's thoughts?
8. Why are some people better than others at thinking up things?
9. Why doesn't your brain always work in the same way?
10. How do you get a better brain?

WHAT THINKING SHOULD BE TAUGHT?

Do traditional methods of teaching produce thoughtful and academically successful students? There is evidence that traditional methods are efficient in teaching what the Greeks called *tekne*, the 'technical' side of knowing how to do and make things, the basic skills and techniques which need to be introduced and practised by beginners in any area of learning. But traditional methods are less successful in developing what the Greeks called *phronesis*, that is practical wisdom or intelligence, the higher order thinking which enhances skill to the level of expertise. The following quote from a school inspection report of 1895 illustrates both the strength and weakness of traditional teaching in schools:

> The accuracy of the work in standards 1 and 2 is all that can be desired, and in many cases marvellous; at the same time the oral test shows that the children are working in the dark ... In these years, at least, far too much of the time is given to the mechanical sides of the subject. The result of this

unintelligent teaching shows itself in the inability of the upper years to solve very simple problems.

Systems of teaching and schooling have improved in many ways during the last fifty years, through an emphasis on curriculum development and 'student-centred' learning. However, many researchers argue that the results of contemporary schooling at both secondary and primary level are disappointing. Among the reasons cited is an absence of thoughtfulness and of cognitive challenge in classrooms. Official reports on schools have repeated similar criticisms of school practice. Among these are that:

• students are rarely required to use 'higher order' thinking skills such as inference, deduction, analysis and evaluation
• students are given insufficient opportunities to develop social skills and values of cooperation and communication through discussion and group work
• able students are not given work that is sufficiently demanding

There is a need for clearer and more definitive guidelines in helping children to think for themselves. Learning to think should not be left to chance. In national curriculum guidelines there is evidence of a growing emphasis on the importance of developing thinking in education. The Scottish Office Education Department National Guidelines (1991): English 5–14, for example, identifies four processes that underlie language and learning – communicating, thinking, feeling and making. When inspectors visit classrooms to assess teaching and learning they are looking for evidence of 'critical thinking, creative thinking and imagination'.[19] But which teaching methods best achieve these kinds of thinking?

What is needed is a theory of critical and creative thinking that is linked to practical methods in the classroom. This theory needs to be linked to curriculum goals and to the enhancement of educational standards.[20] It needs to recognize the role of thinking in the shaping of human feelings and behaviour. It needs to develop those attitudes and dispositions that will enhance moral, social, spiritual and cultural education. It needs to provide a framework for developing critical

19

thinking, creativity and imagination in the widest variety of contexts. It must provide both for the universal elements in reasoning and those which are subject and context-specific. It needs to offer procedures through which students can become more thoughtful, more reasonable and more humane. It needs to offer a discipline which models thinking of the highest order. It needs to offer tested teaching methods and materials through which the teaching of thinking can take place in any given classroom or community.

One comprehensive theory and methodology that meets these requirements is that of philosophy for children.

WHY PHILOSOPHY FOR CHILDREN?

Kirsty, aged 9, says: 'In philosophy you ask questions that you wouldn't ask in any other lesson.' One reason why philosophy is important is that it deals with the fundamental questions of human life, such as:

- What makes me who I am?
- How can I know anything for certain?
- How should I live?

These kinds of question about basic values and beliefs are in danger of being overlooked in a traditional subject-based curriculum. Philosophy begins by inviting us to examine what we think and what we believe. It suggests we should not lead unthinking lives. To do so is like owning a car that has never been serviced. You may be quite happy with the way it is running, but unless it is checked from time to time it may let you down. Similarly your beliefs and values may be entirely sound but unless they are examined you cannot be certain they are not faulty. Children can entertain the most unconsidered views, or live at a routine level without considered views at all. Philosophy invites children to move beyond routine thinking, and to interrogate actively their values and beliefs. Philosophy makes you think, as one child said, 'even when you don't want to'.

Philosophy is foremost a process of enquiry. It is a creative process rather than an imposed body of knowledge. It begins in wonder and the child's natural curiosity about the world. It uses questions as attention-focusing devices in a search for truth or truths. It uses 'Why?', 'How?' and 'What for?' questions to seek explanations of topics and problems of central concern. The following are the sorts of questions that are typical of philosophy:

What is truth? What does it mean? Can it be proved?	*Logical*
What is right and wrong? How should we live? How should we treat others?	*Ethical*
What is knowledge? How do I know? Can I ever be certain?	*Epistemological*
What is a person? What is time? Is there a God?	*Metaphysical*
What is beauty? What is a work of art? How should we judge a work of art?	*Aesthetic*

Philosophy is what happens when thinking becomes self-conscious. It offers the opportunity not only for young people to attempt to come to terms with a broad range of personal, moral, and social issues, but to become more conscious of themselves as critical thinkers. Children who do philosophy see themselves, and the world, in a new way. They gain access to ideas they might not otherwise have thought about, they begin to make connections which lead to deeper understanding. They become part of a tradition which is over 2500 years old. In so doing they are not constrained by the answers given by others, but are free to explore new possibilities and fresh ways of thinking. They develop a growing awareness of themselves as thinkers, summed up by one 11-year-old who said, 'Philosophy is a kind of exercise in which you train yourself to be a better thinker.'

Philosophy can help children to think together as a group or class, and to think for themselves as individuals. Philosophy with children aims to counter uncritical thinking, poor judgement, prejudice and apathy towards ideas. It can help to:

- encourage curiosity and the ability to ask questions
- strengthen judgement through the use of reasoning
- improve understanding of concepts under discussion

21

Should there be philosophy in schools?

Some reflections by children on whether there should be philosophy in schools:

I think philosophy should be taught in every school. You get to talk about all sorts of things and it makes you think before you talk. (Claire, aged 9)

Philosophy helps you to think about everything, and can give you lots of practice in expressing yourself. It should be used a lot in lessons, like it would help you debate things. The best way to do it would be in a philosophy club. Young children in infant schools should be given lessons in philosophy. You are never too young to start philosophy. (Peter, aged 11)

I think philosophy should be taught in secondary school as I believe it would add greatly to the understanding and logic of all. The 'love of wisdom' would be a good cross-curricular link. Philosophy can be taught on all levels. Some people are already 'doing' philosophy without knowing it. Whenever they have a discussion and are using reasons and argument to reach a logical conclusion they are being philosophical. 'Philosophy' might sound rather daunting or irrelevant or unfashionable, but it could be a great help to all. (Jake, aged 15)

- foster the ability to engage in reasoned dialogue and enquiry
- counter biased, stereotypical and unconsidered thinking
- encourage consideration of different viewpoints and being reasonable
- stimulate creative thinking and new ideas

Research into this approach is being undertaken in a growing number of countries around the world. Feedback from teachers and children has been encouraging and new materials for teaching philosophy are being developed.[21] Philosophical enquiry combines traditional methods such as whole-class teaching with creative kinds of mental challenge for children of all abilities. Philosophy introduces children to complex and abstract thinking. It can enhance the quality of teaching and learning in class or at home, by helping those who teach to become more sensitive to philosophical issues, better able to stimulate philosophical enquiry, and thus to engage children in thoughtful discussion. One 8-year-old child who had such a teacher wrote in her Thinking Book: 'I like my teacher. She is philosophical (sic). She makes me think.'

How does one become a 'philosophical' teacher? When asked what advice he had to give to teachers beginning philo-sophical discussion with children for the first time Matthew Lipman, creator of the Philosophy for Children programme, said:

> I would like to tell that teacher that you are going to be doing something quite different, and you are going to feel very uneasy, you are going to feel that you are not prepared. As a matter of fact no philosophy teacher feels prepared, no matter what their level of expertise, because you are dealing with more or less unpredictable matters. You are dealing with areas where the concepts are ill-formed, where prob-lems are unanswered, and your job is to get ready to do something which is of genuine educational importance.[22]

So how does Lipman seek to help teachers become more philosophical and children more thoughtful through his Philosophy for Children programme, and through the teaching method called 'community of enquiry'? This is one of the ques-tions we shall seek to answer in the next chapter.

NOTES AND REFERENCES

The quotations from children and classroom work in this article are drawn from the author's *Philosophy in Primary Schools* research project undertaken in London schools in 1993–6.

1. For a review of different approaches to teaching thinking see Fisher, R. (1995), *Teaching Children to Think*, Cheltenham, Nelson Thornes.
2. For discussion about the right of every individual to have his or her intellect developed see Machado, L.A. (1984), *The Right to be Intelligent*, New York, Pergamon Press; Siegel, H. (1988), *Educating Reason: Rationality, Critical Thinking and Education*, London, Routledge; Costa, A. (1991) *Developing Minds*, Association for Supervision and Curriculum Development (ASCD).

3. Rawls, J. (1971), *A Theory of Justice*, Oxford, Oxford University Press, p. 426.
4. Stevenson, R.H. (1990), 'Engagement and cognitive challenge in thoughtful social studies: a study of student perspectives', *Journal of Curriculum Studies*, Vol. 22, No. 4, pp. 329–41.
5. Mortimore, P. (1995), *Effective Schools: Current Impact and Future Potential*, University of London, Institute of Education.
6. Adapted from Ennis, R. (in press), *Critical Thinking*, Englewood Cliffs, Prentice Hall.
7. This existentialist view is discussed in Bonnet, M. (1994), *Children's Thinking: Promoting Understanding in the Primary School*, London, Cassell, pp. 97ff.
8. Mead, G.H. (1934), *Mind, Self and Society*, Chicago, University of Chicago Press.
9. Vygotsky, L.S. (1978), *Mind in Society*, Cambridge, Mass., Harvard University Press.
10. Lipman, M. (1983), *Thinking Skills Fostered by Philosophy for Children*, Institute for the Advancement of Philosophy for Children, quoted in Coles and Robinson (1991), p. 13.
11. I am indebted to Sara Liptai for this example from her classroom work.
12. Metacognition was a term introduced by Flavell in 1976 to refer to: 'The individual's own awareness and consideration of his or her cognitive processes and strategies'. See Flavell, J.H. (1977/1985), *Cognitive Development*, Englewood Cliffs, NJ, Prentice Hall.
13. Donaldson, M. (1978), *Children's Minds*, London, Fontana.
14. Nisbet, J. and Shucksmith, J. (1986), *Learning Strategies*, London, Routledge.
15. For a discussion of these strategies see Fisher, R. (1995), *Teaching Children to Learn*, Cheltenham, Stanley Thornes.
16. Newell, A. and Simon, H.A. (1972), *Human Problem Solving*, Englewood Cliffs, Prentice Hall.
17. de Bono, E. (1976), *Teaching Thinking*, Harmondsworth, Penguin.

18. Langer, E.J. (1989), *Mindfulness*, New York, Addison Wesley.
19. The OFSTED Handbook (1995), *Guidance on the Inspection of Nursery and Primary Schools*, London, Office for Standards in Education, HMSO, p. 68.
20. This call has also been made by Richard Paul, leading authority in the Critical Thinking movement in the USA. See Paul, R. (1995), *Critical Thinking, the State of Education Today, and the Goals of the 15th International*, Sonoma, Calif., Sonoma State University, pp. 9–10.
21. For classroom materials to support philosophical enquiry with children see Fisher, R., *Stories for Thinking* (1996) and *Poems for Thinking* (1997); Fox, R., *Thinking Together* (1996); and Cam, P., *Thinking Stories* (1995).
22. From an interview with Matthew Lipman recorded by the author at the International Conference on Critical Thinking held at the University of East Anglia, April 7th 1994, published in the *Centre for Thinking Skills Information Pack* (1995), Vol. 4, No. 3, pp. 5–8.

CHAPTER 2

Philosophy for Children: Teaching children to think

I began to think that the problem I was seeing at the university could not be solved there, that thinking was something that had to be taught much earlier, before thinking habits became entrenched, so that by the time a student graduated from High School, skilful, independent thinking would have become a habit.

Matthew Lipman

I think philosophy should begin at school. It is good because it gives you time to think. It helps you to ask questions. It shows you that there can be many answers to one question. It makes you think that everything must have a reason.

John, aged 10

One of the most successful attempts to build a coherent programme in teaching thinking is the Philosophy for Children programme, devised by Matthew Lipman and colleagues at Montclair University (USA). The programme has been developed to provide a curriculum for philosophical enquiry for children from nursery to college level, and is in use in an increasing number of countries around the world.[1]

Lipman was inspired to create such a programme because he thought that schools were failing to teach students to think. For him evidence of this lay in the low level of thinking skills exhibited by college students attending his courses at Columbia University, where he had a chair in philosophy. 'Why is it', he asks 'that while children of four, five and six are full of curiosity, creativity and interest, and never stop asking for further explanations, by the time they are eighteen they are passive, uncritical and bored with learning?'[2] If, as he asks, education is supposed to be about teaching young people to think, why does it produce so many unthinking people?

This view that habits of skilful independent thinking can become entrenched, or internalized, through practice and training became a central thrust of his programme. Lipman believes that children can be transformed by education, but to do this education must be transformed to make thinking rather than knowledge its guiding priority. Lipman proposes therefore to add a new subject to the curriculum – philosophy.

Lipman argues that children bring to school a burning curiosity and eagerness to learn, but that gradually this curiosity and impulse to know and understand fade. The reason for this Lipman lays squarely on the effects of traditional schooling. He says that we must capitalize on the natural gifts that children bring to school – their curiosity and hunger for meaning. It is the school's failure to nourish such needs, Lipman argues, which sets so many children against school. He proposes therefore a course in philosophy to teach children to think, because he believes such a course would develop reasoning skills, the missing element in the curriculum, and also a means of raising self esteem and developing moral values. What is needed, he believes, is a discipline that prepares us to think in other disciplines, and traditionally philosophy fulfilled this role. The challenge for Lipman was to create a teaching method and curriculum that could bring the discipline of philosophical enquiry into the experience of all children, at every grade level. Skilled reasoning for Lipman is more than just an intellectual bag of tricks picked up by chance along the way, it is best learned through the practice of disciplined discussion.

Since the days of Socrates dialogue has been recognized as a powerful means for seeking answers to the most fundamental questions about life, and Lipman chose to follow this tradition as a means of introducing philosophy into the school curriculum. Following Vygotsky he believes that language provides the essential tools for thinking and that children are able to function at an intellectually higher level when in collaborative and cooperative situations. The Philosophy for Children programme that he and his team devised has the overall aim of generating philosophical discussion through the formation of 'communities of inquiry (or enquiry)' in the classroom. We will look closely at this concept of 'community of enquiry',

WHAT IS THE PHILOSOPHY FOR CHILDREN PROGRAMME?

The main elements of the Philosophy for Children programme				
Age	**Children's novel**	**Teacher's manual**	**Philosophical area**	**Educational area**
3–6 yrs	*Doll's Hospital* (by A.M. Sharp)	Making sense of my world	Concept formation	Basic concepts – what is true, good, real, beautiful etc.?
6–7 yrs	*Elfie*	Getting our thoughts together	Reasoning about thinking	Exploring experience
7–8 yrs	*Kio and Gus*	Wondering at the world	Reasoning about nature	Environmental education
8–10yrs	*Pixie*	Looking for meaning	Reasoning about language	Language and arts
10–12yrs	*Harry**	Philosophical enquiry	Basic reasoning skills	Thinking and logic
12–13 yrs	*Lisa*	Ethical enquiry	Reasoning in ethics	Moral education
14–15 yrs	*Suki*	Writing: how and why	Reasoning in language	Writing and literature
16+ yrs	*Mark*	Social enquiry	Reasoning in social studies	Social studies

* The full title is *Harry Stottlemeier's Discovery.* [3]

and the claim that the programme will develop reasoning, self esteem and moral judgement in the next chapter.

Lipman left his post as philosophy professor at Columbia University and founded in 1974 the Institute for the Advancement of Philosophy for Children (IAPC) to research and develop the Philosophy for Children curriculum. The programme consists of specially written stories that act as starting points for philosophical discussion. The core of the programme consists of a number of short philosophical novels, accompanied by teacher's manuals, for use with children of all ages from three years to adult. It is the most widely used programme for introducing children to philosophy, and continues to be expanded and developed.

According to Lipman each novel has as a central theme the workings of the human mind, and a single purpose – to serve as springboards for intellectual debate. The great drawback to the novels is that they are not good stories in a literary sense. They do not hold the interest as stories. Lipman sees this as an advantage. The books and stories that children read do not contain a rich range of philosophical questions, nor do they necessarily provide models of children as enquiring thinkers. Much of children's literary experience is devoid of intellectual stimulation, and a disjunction between reading and thinking is established. Children can come to believe that reading is about following words in a book, not thinking about what those words mean for the story and for them. Lipman's 'philosophic novels', are seeded with puzzles, questions and problems of meaning. They have a clear didactic purpose – to stimulate questioning and philosophical discussion. They present models of reasonable and thoughtful discussion between children that Lipman hopes his readers will emulate in their own discussions of questions arising from the text.

HOW IS PHILOSOPHY FOR CHILDREN TAUGHT?

A Philosophy for Children lesson or series of lessons (Lipman recommends two one-hour sessions a week) might include the following elements – the reading of an episode from a Lipman

29

novel, followed by questions raised by students and discussion by the group of their chosen topic. The teacher might extend this discussion with questions from a Discussion Plan, or a prepared Exercise exploring a particular philosophical issue.

The following an excerpt from *Harry Stottlemeier's Discovery* by Matthew Lipman, abridged and adapted for use in Britain by Roger Sutcliffe as a stimulus to philosophical discussion:

> It was Friday, and Fran and Laura were spending the night at Jill's.
>
> 'There's a tune that keeps on going through my head,' said Jill. 'It's like I'm being haunted by it. It comes to me when I'm trying to do my homework or go to sleep.'
>
> 'Sometimes I have dreams like that,' said Laura. 'My grandmother was sick a long time, and then when she died, I kept dreaming about her, and I always had the feeling that she was making me dream about her. Yet how could that be when she was dead already?'
>
> 'Dead people can't do anything to you,' said Fran, but then added, 'Can they?'
>
> Jill gave Fran a funny look. 'Well the last time I heard my tune was a week ago, but it left a strong impression. So isn't it possible that Laura's grandmother's death simply made a strong impression on her, and that's why she's been dreaming of it ever since?'
>
> Laura shook her head. 'When I see the moon, it's because the moon is out there making me see it right? And in my mind just now I heard your voice because you were speaking to me. So I think that all the thoughts that are in my head are caused by the things outside my mind.'
>
> 'That's ridiculous,' said Jill. 'There are all sorts of imaginary things that are only in my mind, and there's nothing like them outside at all . . . pixies and vampires, for example.'
>
> 'Okay,' said Laura, 'it's true I don't believe in those sorts of things. Even so there are real people who make them up and tell us about them and make us think of them.'
>
> 'Laura,' Fran interrupted, 'you keep talking about what's in your mind and what's not in your mind. But what's a 'mind'? And how do you know you have one?'

One problem that the programme poses for teachers is the lack of literary style in Lipman's novels. This has led others to seek philosophical stimulus from traditional stories, picture books and from other kinds of writing. They argue that there is a range of children's literature that can offer philosophical interest and rich resources for intellectual enquiry.[4]

Another problem teachers face is their own lack of training in implementing philosophical discussion and difficulties in linking this work to the school curriculum. Before looking at ways of overcoming these problems, we need to see how the Philosophy for Children methodology works.

A typical session works as follows – a group of children or adults sit in a circle of chairs, with the teacher as part of the group. Part of the chosen novel is read aloud round the class or group. Poor readers are allowed to 'pass' and can choose not to read. After the reading is complete the teacher invites the group to look back over the story to pick out what they find interesting, puzzling or worth discussing. There is thinking time, and then time to share the discussion points that arise. The teacher (or pupil) writes each individual point in the form of a question on a wallboard – adding the name of the contributor as a sign of ownership of the question.

When there is a sufficient number of suggested topics, the teacher encourages the group to decide which topic will be the focus for discussion. Once a topic is chosen the teacher usually refers it back to the contributor, asking for a comment about the question. The aim is to explore the philosophical dimension of the topic – to question the text, to explore the meanings of words and concepts, to articulate views and give reasons for beliefs and judgements. But after the discussion of topics, what next, where does it lead?

Would-be teachers of philosophy, Lipman argues, 'need models of doing philosophy that are clear, practical and specific'.[5] The teachers' manuals that accompany the novels are filled with discussion plans and exercises for extending leading ideas and thinking skills relating to the story. A philosophical discussion plan consists of a group of questions around a central concept or problem. The questions may form a series, which either build upon each other, or which circle around a topic so that it can be seen from many angles. Such a series is in a sense Socratic, since it models the kind of systematic and sustained questioning that Socrates used, as reported in the dialogues of Plato. This planned use of leading questions aims to stimulate the creative response of the student, to think more deeply, more widely and more systematically about the key topic of discussion.

Thinking and having thoughts

Discussion plan from *Looking for Meaning* by Matthew Lipman and Ann Margaret Sharp, the instructional manual for teachers to accompany the novel *Pixie*.[6]

1. Do you think all the time, or just some of the time?
2. Do you think while you're asleep?
3. Can you think without thinking of someone or something?
4. Do you think in words? If so, do you think in sentences?
5. Can you have thoughts without actually thinking?
6. Can you think without having thoughts?
7. Can you think of something, without it making you think of something else?
8. Can you think of more than one thought at a time?
9. Can a thought be divided, the way pies are divided?
10. Can thoughts be beautiful?
11. Can thoughts be beautiful, even if they are not true?
12. Can thoughts be beautiful, even if they are true?
13. Which would you rather have: lots and lots of thoughts, or just a few nice thoughts?
14. If your body is the same age as you are, does that mean your thoughts are the same age as you are?
15. Can other people let you think their thoughts?

Note to the teacher: One way of handling this and similar discussion plans is to go around the room, asking one question at a time, and discussing each question in turn. Another method is to assign each person a question, give the class time to reflect, then call on individuals as they volunteer to discuss their answers.

Follow-up activities may include specific questions for discussion, concept-mapping, creative writing or art-work. They are for teachers to adapt and develop as they wish, but their focus as for the initial discussion is to give close attention to context (for example by interrogating the text for meaning), and to relevant criteria (for example by considering reasons for belief). In so doing the group will be developing their judgement and their creative thinking, and a special sense of community – what Lipman calls a 'Community of Inquiry'.

A weakness of the programme for many teachers is that there seems to be no clearly defined developmental progression within the great number of skills and topics presented in the teacher's manuals. It would be possible to construct a developmental taxonomy of reasoning skills through the programme, but it would be a challenging task (the teacher's manual for *Kio and Gus*, for example, runs to 559 pages!).

What is real, and what only seems to be real?

An exercise that aims to foster conceptual understanding of what is real and not real, as well as the reasoning and a sense of community.

From *Looking for Meaning*[6]

Prepare cards for four different desks or tables. This is what the cards read:
1. Things that seem real, but aren't.
2. Things that seem to be real, and are.
3. Things that don't seem to be real, but are real.
4. Things that don't seem to be real, and are not.

Now, each person is to bring an item to class and put it on one of the tables. Here are some suggestions:
a. an artificial flower
b. a toy automobile
c. a book of fairy tales
d. a coke bottle filled with water
e. a potato carved in the shape of a cat
f. a paper aeroplane
g. a photograph of a member of class
h. a small mirror

Go around the room and each person, in turn, must challenge someone else to give the reason for putting that person's object on that particular table.

One of the aims of this exercise, central to all philosophy, is that of concept development. One way to help children develop a concept is to map the boundaries of the term. Through grouping a term with its synonyms, the resulting set of terms will help to establish the boundary of the concept. For example by constructing three concentric circles (Figure 2.1) or a Venn diagram of overlapping circles, we can put the synonyms and antonyms in outer circles, and in the intermediate space borderline terms which may be problematical, controversial or contestable. With young children we might want to give them the terms to classify. Older children can

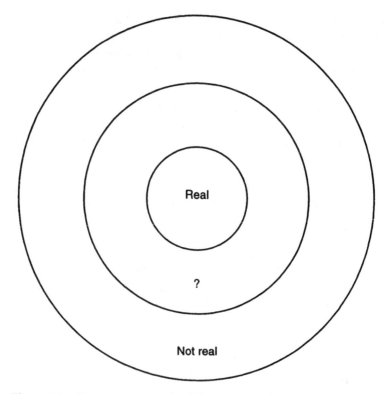

Figure 2.1   Concept map: real and not real

brainstorm, classify and discuss their own concept map of terms. Such an exercise will help to cultivate a number of skills, such as:

- concept definition
- classification
- generating alternatives
- distinguishing differences of degree and kind
- giving reasons or evidence to support views

Such an exercise can stimulate discussion of concepts, word meanings and definitions, particularly if it is a group activity, but is secondary to the central process of enquiry which is the philosophical discussion of questions and issues posed by the students themselves. 'The reason *I* like philosophy,' said Greg, aged 9, 'is because we get to choose what to talk about. That doesn't happen in any other lesson.'

A PHILOSOPHICAL DISCUSSION:
IS YOUR BRAIN THE SAME AS YOUR MIND?

The following dialogue with a group of 11-year-olds was prompted by reading part of *Harry Stottlemeier's Discovery* by Matthew Lipman. After raising several questions from the reading, one was chosen by the children for discussion:

RF: Is your brain the same as your mind? Let's see if we can get a bit closer to an understanding of that. Tom, why did you ask that question?

Tom: Well is it, I mean your brain controls your heart and your arms and everything that goes on in your body, but does your mind really think 'Okay I'll move left,' and do you think 'Okay brain send messages down to the muscles to move'?

RF: So are you saying because the brain has its messages that the mind is not aware of that it means that the mind cannot be the same as the brain?

Tom: Yes. It isn't the same as the brain, because . . . it's part of the brain but it isn't the brain.

(This age-old question in philosophy prompted a number of comments from children, agreeing, disagreeing, suggesting or building on ideas . . .)

Mark: I think I'd agree with Tom that your mind is part of the brain. But . . . if you'd like to put one inside the other you'd put the mind inside the brain.

RF: So if the mind is inside the brain . . .

Tom: Or inside part of it . . .

RF: Part of it. How do you think it's *different* from the brain? If not the same as the brain it must be different, mustn't it?

Tom: Well the brain controls everything about us, the mind as well, but the mind only controls our thoughts . . . and contains our thoughts.

Jamie:	Memory . . .
Tom:	I think the mind is made out of memories and thoughts . . . it's a thinking bank.
RF:	So is the mind the same as the brain, but the brain just bigger than the mind, or is the mind different from the brain?
Melanie:	Different.
Isabel:	Yes.
Melanie:	Because it doesn't control anything . . . the mind just thinks.
Camilla:	The mind I think is our thoughts more than controlling our body. I mean our brain sends messages everywhere round our body all the time to nerves and everything, or they are sending messages to the brain but the mind isn't part of this, I don't think. I think the mind just contains your thoughts.
Jamie:	And memories.

(The discussion moved on to what happens when you die . . .)

Paul:	I think when your brain dies it's like a shut down, and it shuts down your body. And I don't think your mind does carry on really, it just shuts down every system and your brain has to work your mind really because I don't think your mind would really work if your brain had shut down.

(The children went on to discuss what happens in the mind when you dream, and were then encouraged to think of analogies for the mind . . .)

RF:	Would you agree with someone who says the mind is a bit like smoke in the brain . . . a sort of strange ghost?
Jamie:	Yeah.
RF:	If it's like a strange ghost then could it live outside the brain?
Maria:	Not like a ghost.
Peter:	The mind's not like that . . . it's not very good.
RF:	Not a good way to describe the mind? A lot of thinking goes on in what are called analogies.

	We've got to liken it to something else to understand it better. What would you say the mind is like?
Peter:	Like a big warehouse . . . with things on the back shelves of your memory . . . and things being moved around in your thoughts.
Jamie:	Yeah.
RF:	So part of the warehouse is called the mind? The active part . . .
Tom:	No, the warehouse is your mind.

(Discussion continued on how the mind was like a warehouse . . .)

RF:	If the mind is like a warehouse what is the brain like? Can your to continue this analogy . . .?
Maria:	A brain is like a . . . a . . . beehive.
Peter:	A dock . . . containing lots of different warehouses for doing different things.
Mark:	An ants' nest!

(The topic ended with children being offered a 'last word', and the chance to sum up their thoughts . . .)

RF:	So if we come back to Tom's question – 'Is your mind the same as the brain?' – we could now formulate a much better answer to that, couldn't we?
Tom:	Yes.
RF:	How would you sum up your answer now, Tom?
Tom:	Your brain is like a dock and your mind is like a warehouse in it containing all your memories and thoughts on lots of different shelves . . . and your brain sends lots of different messages around and across the dock.[7]

A philosophical discussion with children relies on several assumptions. One is that children are naturally disposed to wonder and to think about ideas, in ways that many adults may have long since forgotten. Another is that such discussions can help children to perceive, construct and interpret their world in ways that help their understanding of themselves and of the world of which they are a part. A third is that adults can facilitate this process by helping children to discuss their questions philosophically. Not only is this kind of philosophical discussion rewarding for children, but can be seen as giving them access to an important part of their intellectual heritage. Why is the right of young people to do philosophy so important?

WHAT KINDS OF THINKING DOES PHILOSOPHY FOR CHILDREN DEVELOP?

Lipman defines Philosophy for Children as 'philosophy applied to education for the purpose of producing students with improved proficiency in reasoning and judgement'.[8] Philosophy for Children is a kind of applied philosophy, but not in the sense that it is a programme where the ideas of philosophers are used to clarify and resolve problems faced by non-philosophers, but with the aim of getting pupils to philosophize and to do the philosophy themselves. Because of the absence of the names, dates and technical vocabulary of traditional philosophy children are free to think about philosophy and the practice of philosophy which relate to their own ideas and interests. The aim is to help children move from the routine to the reflective, from unconsidered to considered, from everyday thinking to critical thinking.

The following table contrasts some of the elements of everyday and critical thinking.

Elements of thinking		
Everyday thinking	➡	*Critical thinking*
Guessing	➡	Estimating
Preferring	➡	Evaluating
Assuming	➡	Justifying
Associating/listing	➡	Classifying
Accepting	➡	Hypothesizing
Judging	➡	Analysing
Inferring	➡	Reasoning

This improvement in thinking can be viewed as a move from unconscious to conscious thought, from everyday to critical thinking, moving from the surface of things to the structure of things, from what Socrates calls the 'unconsidered life' (Plato: *Apology*) to a considered view which backs claims and opinions with reasons.

The work of the American philosophers Peirce and Dewey provided important theoretical foundations for the Lipman approach to philosophy for children. Peirce introduced the concept of a 'community of inquirers', by which he meant that scientific progress depends on the shared enquiry of a larger community of thought, a community that extends beyond the individual thinker and ultimately beyond the boundaries of time and place.

In Dewey Lipman found a pedagogy for philosophical discussion that could help teachers convert their classrooms into communities of enquiry. Partly this was derived from Dewey's insistence that learning comes from reflection on experience. Lipman wanted to give children the *experience* of being philosophers and of thinking philosophically in the supportive community of the classroom. Experience for Dewey was not just about doing things but involved the active processes of reflective thinking. Learning through experience should include both the experiences that students bring to the classroom, and the experience of imaginative and reflective thinking they get in the classroom.

Dewey defines reflective thinking as the

> active, persistent and careful consideration of any belief or supposed form of knowledge in the light of the grounds that support it, and the further conclusions to which it tends . . . it is a conscious and voluntary effort to establish belief upon a firm basis of reasons.[9]

Dewey seems here to be describing a persistent act of enquiry, where there is an ordering of thought which builds towards a considered judgement. Reflective thinking for Dewey is a process by which we examine the grounds and consequences of our belief in order to investigate an area of imperfect knowledge or to solve a problem. Life is a problem-solving process. In many areas of life we encounter problems, face obstacles or dilemmas, questions trouble us and the meaning of events and reports of events can be ambiguous and confusing. It is when we feel puzzled, perplexed, confused or uncertain that our thinking needs to become reflective. It is then that we need a plan, an explanation, or a judgement of some kind. We look for reasons and causes. We marshal facts, look for evidence and make inferences from the clues that we have. Routine thinking means we come up with the same answers, reflective thinking involves a search for better answers.

Dewey's conception of reflective thinking has influenced many of the leading theorists of critical thinking. For example Robert Ennis, a pioneer of the critical thinking movement, says: 'Critical thinking is reasonable, reflective thinking is focused on deciding what to believe or do.' Harvey Siegel defines critical thinking in a simpler fashion when he says: 'To be a critical thinker is to be appropriately moved by reasons.'[10] Whatever else belongs to critical thinking and to the practice of philosophy in the classroom *reasoning* seems to lie at the heart of the concept. As Rajiv, aged 10, put it: 'In philosophy you have to give reasons for everything you say, so you get better at giving reasons.'

The trouble with the terms critical thinking and judgement is that they have both positive and negative aspects. I may be skilled at thinking and expert in judgement but for selfish ends. Paul[11] proposes two definitions of critical thinking, a 'weak' sense in which the thinking is skilful but selfish, used in the pursuit of egocentric ends, and a 'strong' sense in which reasoning is allied to fair-mindedness. 'Weak sense' critical thinkers tend to pursue 'monological thinking', that is thinking exclusively from one point of view or within one frame of reference. Such thinkers use their intellectual skills selectively, using argument to serve personal and vested interests. They are able to use reasoning to defend any point of view. Many politicians would serve as examples of critical thinkers in this 'weak sense'. By contrast critical thinkers in the 'strong sense' are able to engage in 'multilogical thinking' by which Paul means seeing issues from more than one point of view, thinking that is responsive to others and consistent in its intellectual standards. Critical thinking on this view embodies a number of values and attitudes, it rejects dogmatism and indoctrination, allows intellectual dissent, and encourages reflective questioning in an effort to achieve fair-mindedness and intellectual integrity. It is being open to self-criticism and self-correction. In the words of Elaine, aged 10: 'Philosophy lets you change your mind.'

Being uncritical includes features that are easy to identify, such as being unthinking, unquestioning, undiscriminating, undisciplined, without reference to reasons, evidence or criteria, basing argument on unstated assumptions and so on. Identifying the elements of reflective thinking is less easy. Peters speaks of the need to develop the 'rational passions' necessary to prevent our intelligence becoming the tool of our egocentric emotions, while McPeck talks of the need to develop 'informed scepticism' as a defence against false claims and hidden persuasion in a consumer society.[12]

Being a critical thinker is perhaps as much a matter of who I am as of the skills I possess. Wittgenstein echoed this point when he wrote, 'I wish I were a better man and had a better mind: the two are really the same thing.' A good thinker is reflective in the sense of exercising his/her own powers of thinking, and being responsive to the thinking of others. Reflective thinking in this sense unites reason with empathy, and closely resembles what Lipman calls 'caring thinking' – the linking of emotions with thinking.

For Lipman there are three kinds of thinking that Philosophy for Children aims to improve – critical, creative and caring thinking. These he says are different modes of thinking, linked to different expressions of judgement which equate to the Greek ideals of Truth, Beauty and Goodness, to Aristotle's divisions of enquiry, to different branches of philosophy with different cognitive objectives, as indicated in Figure 2.2.

Lipman and his co-researchers at IAPC divide the thinking skills developed by Philosophy for Children into the following categories, each with my own short summary:

- Concept formation skills
  Guided by questions such as: 'What do we think?' and 'What do we know?', these involve developing conceptual understanding through defining, classifying and extending conceptual links and frameworks.

41

	Truth	Beauty	Goodness
Mode of thinking	critical	creative	caring
Mode of judgement	saying	making	doing
Division of enquiry (Aristotle)	theoretic science	productive science	practical science
Branch of philosophy	epistemology	aesthetics	ethics
Cognitive objectives (Bloom)	analytical	synthetic	evaluative

Figure 2.2 Divisions of philosophical enquiry

- Enquiry skills
  Guided by questions such as: 'What do we want to find out?' and 'How do we find out?', these involve seeking to question and explore issues in a community of enquiry, learning how to observe, describe and question.
- Reasoning skills
  These can be said to be guided by the questions: 'How do we know? 'Is it true?' and involve the skills of logic and argument, of deductive and inductive reasoning (critical thinking).
- Translation skills
  Guided by questions such as: 'How can we interpret and communicate it?', these involve comprehending, interpreting and communicating the meanings of one's own and others' ideas.

Skills alone are not enough and Lipman argues that what must be added to these to make them effective are the dispositions to use them. These involve three sets of attitudes or dispositions which Philosophy for Children aims to foster:

- Critical dispositions
  Guided by the question: 'What do I think?', these involve attitude of thinking for oneself, seeking reasons, judging with criteria, of questioning and challenging any given idea.

- Creative dispositions
  Guided by the question: 'What other ideas are there?', these involve the attitude that values the search for new ideas, hypotheses, viewpoints and solutions.
- Co-operative dispositions
  Guided by the question: 'What do others think?', these involve learning to cooperate with others in a community of enquiry, building self esteem, empathy and respect towards others.

The philosopher Kant believed that the rationality of formal logic and maths were transcendental and existed before language took shape, but he also believed that the abstractions of reason were not sufficient to guarantee knowledge and that judgement was necessary to make sense of them. Knowing the rules, such as 'Thou shalt not steal', is not enough, what is required are continual acts of judgement to make sense of them (what is 'stealing'?) and come to know them (what counts, or does not count, as stealing?). Judgement for Kant is a peculiar talent which can only be practised, it cannot be taught like a form of knowledge. It is practised through what Kant called the 'method of enquiry', which for students should involve 'learning to philosophize'.[13] This Kantian view of judgement, summed up in his famous phrase: 'Percepts without concepts are empty, concepts without percepts are blind', underpins Lipman's approach. A central aim of Philosophy for Children for Lipman is to 'strengthen judgement', which he identifies with the Greek notion of phronesis or 'practical wisdom'. He talks of 'sharpening' judgement, 'developing' judgement and 'exercising' judgement, as if it were some identifiable faculty or element of the mind. He argues that in 'strengthening' my judgement I am strengthening myself as a person. What Lipman is identifying is the necessary link that must be made between thought and action, between reasoning and contexts, between pure and applied wisdom. Essentially judgement is concerned with critical evaluation (the highest in Bloom's taxonomy of thinking skills[14]). In talk of developing reasoned judgement we should focus not only on the judgement of arguments, but also encourage critical self-evaluation. Judgements or evaluations should be disciplined by reasons and be always open to question or challenge. As one child put it in the middle of a discussion on the possibility of the existence of angels: 'I may be right. I think I'm right. But I could be wrong.'

THINKING AND REASONING IN CLASSROOM DISCUSSION

The following is an excerpt from a transcript of a discussion by 12- to 13-year-olds in a philosophy class at Christ's Hospital School using Lipman's novel *Harry* as a stimulus for discussion, with annotations (in brackets) to show some of the elements of thinking, reasoning and discourse being used in each contribution to the discussion (see Appendix p. 262 for more on ways to evaluate group discussion).[15]

Is there such a thing as the most interesting thing in the world?

(question chosen for discussion)

Nick W.: Well, I thought this could be a very hard task, choosing the most interesting thing in the world, because there are so many things that we don't know about, different people's opinions, and I actually think that it would be impossible, which is why I put the extra bit on the end: is it actually possible? I think I'd like to go to Mark. *(Reasoning by explaining, questioning an assumption, collaborating by nominating another)*

Mark: Well, I don't think it's really possible to actually find what the most interesting thing in the world is because it's all a matter of personal preference, really – the individual, what they find interesting. *(Reasoning, giving a reason)*

Kate: I think it's possible so long as you're only deciding for you personally, but if you're trying to work out for a group of people, I don't think it is. *(Extending the discussion, questioning a generalization)*

Emma: I agree with this thing about, you know, personal preference. I mean, but if there was a group of people and they were all one religion, or they all did the same thing together, they could agree, say 20 or so people, could agree that this one thing was the most interesting thing. *(Extending the discussion, hypothesizing, giving an example)*

Facilitator: Can we just take that back to Kate, and say if you go with that? *(Questioning, collaborating, extending the discussion)*

Kate: Well, I think they might be able to agree on maybe the most important thing, but I don't know about the most interesting. *(Countering/qualifying by drawing a distinction)*

Matthew: I agree it's down to personal preference, but even then, does that make it the most interesting thing in the world even for you? I mean, you need a straight definition of 'interesting'. *(Collaborating, questioning, initiating an appeal for definition)*

Facilitator: Okay, can anyone take on board that question straightaway? It was a question ... Nick, you want to come back? *(Questioning, organizing/ collaborating)*

Nick W.: I'll have a go. I think interesting is, the most interesting, is the thing which would draw your personal attention the most ... But it's questionable. *(Extending, giving a definition, judging)*

Facilitator: Come back on that, Matthew, and then nominate someone, could you? *(Organizing/collaborating)*

Matthew: Yeah, maybe, but would that then make what you found, the thing that attracts your attention to it most, the most interesting in the world? Because there's nobody that's seen everything or heard everything or done everything. So I mean, it possibly would make it the most interesting thing in the world for them, unless you're talking about their own world, the world that they have knowledge of. *(Reasoning, explaining, countering by raising possible objection)*

45

Damien: I think, as he said, in your own world. I think it would be quite nice and I think it would probably help if we could, sort of, in a way define 'world', whether you're relating it to the whole world as in the earth or whether you're relating it to the world of knowledge that particular person has. *(Collaborating, reasoning by explaining definition)*

Facilitator: I see a nod there. Can we make an agreement about that? Does anyone have anything to say directly to that point? We'll just take Matthew's point and then we'll see if we can reach an agreement. *(Collaborating, questioning, organizing)*

Matthew: I think if you're talking about the most interesting thing in the world, you're talking about the thing that's actually in the book, and I think that means the most interesting thing in the world, as in the earth. *(Extending by giving example, reasoning by explaining and defining)*

Facilitator: In the whole world. Does anyone disagree with that? *(Responding, organizing/questioning)*

Matthew: I think that's what it's saying in the book. *(Extending)*

Facilitator: Yeah, Okay ... Nick? Sally, you come in now. *(Collaborating/organizing)*

Sally: I think it's the interest ... most interesting thing out of anything that you just ... I think you can't actually say there is a most interesting thing in the world, 'cos even I can't! I can't think of what the most interesting thing in the world for me is. It would take ages to think of it, and I think I wouldn't be able to come to a conclusion. There might be something that, you know, more people find intriguing than something else. I mean, I think there isn't a one most interesting. *(Countering, reasoning – generalizing, hypothesizing and comparing alternatives)*

Facilitator: Okay. Now, we need a 'last words' session now, but let's try and use that as a platform for the continuation next lesson. So, put up your hand if

	you just have anything to say now about what we've already talked about, and ... right ... so Hannah to start, and then we'll take Emma. *(Organizing/collaborating)*
Hannah:	I think the interesting thing, I don't think anyone can ... I think there might have been some scientists that tried to find out maybe, but I don't think they ever came ... I think it's about like thinking. You can't definitely define it, you know, you can't define what you're looking for. So I think you can, if you really try, you might be able to find the most interesting thing in your world, but not in the big world. *(Reasoning – seeking definition, probable explanation)*
Emma:	I just want to continue the thing about what kind of world it is, and they were talking about your personal world of knowledge, but what about your world in your mind? And if you go to work, you'll have, like, a different world and a different situation around you when you come back, and they're two different things. *(Extending, questioning, reasoning – comparing/drawing distinction)*
Diana:	Yeah, I mean I'd just like to say because if I went up to my science teacher and said, 'Sir, what do you think the most interesting thing in the world is?', he'd probably say 'Science'. So it depends, it depends what your career is, or something. A vet would probably say animals and their bodies and the way they think and everything. *(Extending by giving examples, reasoning – explaining, comparing and generalizing)*
Annie:	Surely your own world is the whole world to you, and you don't have any knowledge past your own world, but that is your whole world, to you as a person. *(Extending – making connections)*
Daniel:	Well, I think that in terms of what you like best, I think, you can reach a conclusion, because you can say, 'Oh, I like swimming the most, and that really interests me more than anything else,' but in terms of the whole world, I don't think you

can. *(Countering/qualifying, reasoning by justifying and noting a criterion)*

Tom: I think that when you're saying about interesting, sometimes you could say something like a feeling you have, when you think it's really interesting and you want to find out about it, or you could say the most interesting thing is the thing that you want to do and that, sort of, like makes you feel good, and you think it's interesting how it makes you feel good. It's sort of, like, two different ways. Also, on the whole world, maybe when it says the most interesting thing in the world, it doesn't say your world, so you couldn't define it, because everybody has a different opinion, and it could also cause fights, you know, like, If you try to say, 'I think this is the best' . . . 'No, no, this is the best'. *(Qualifying, assessing arguments, hypothesizing, judging between viewpoints)*

Matthew: Emma said there's a different world at work, but, surely, or wherever you go, but surely it's your own . . . it's still your own personal world. I think if we use 'world' as like, I don't know, a collective noun, and all your experience, your *philosophy*, that might be a good word, I don't think it's a different world at all at work. I mean, you could still say, 'Oh well, that's the way that the machinery works at work, it's more interesting than the way I make toast in the morning.' I still think it would be your whole world. *(Countering, reasoning – explaining and justifying, drawing an analogy)*

Nick O.: I'd just like to refer back to, sort of, the medieval ages when there were many hundreds of small villages around the country, and the villagers, they knew nothing apart, or very little, apart from the village life, sweeping, cleaning up and looking after Granny. They wouldn't have a vague knowledge of foreign lands or animals unless it's brought with a messenger. *(Extending, reasoning – explaining)*

Nick W.: Going back to what Emma said earlier, she said that people don't agree on what they think is the most interesting thing, but if, say like, you get loads, like a whole cricket team, yeah, and they think, like, oh yes, this is really interesting, I'm really enjoying this, this is really important to me, they could agree that cricket is the most important thing in the world to them. *(Recounting, extending the discussion, reasoning – justifying by example)*

Tom: If you asked someone to define what it was in their particular world, it would be a lot easier for a, say, adult, or a middle-aged adult, who's got a job, say an Olympic athlete, it would be a lot easier for him to define the athletics. But for a child at school there are so many different things in your life. It would be very difficult, and if you thought of one, you're bound to think of another one that's even more important straight afterwards. And it's also difficult to define what is more interesting. There's not, sort of, a big gap. *(Hypothesizing, assessing factors, identifying problems of definition)*

Rupert: I just want to say something to Diana. How do you know your science teacher would say that science is the most important or interesting thing in the world, because he might have a different opinion? And about the vet as well, I don't think that a vet, just a vet has a job with animals. I don't think ... he might, might just go for the money, to get a good, well earned life. *(Responding, countering – raising objections with counter-argument)*

Kate: I think you can maybe define more important and more interesting, but I don't think you can get most important or most interesting. *(Countering, extending by noticing differences of degree)*

Kirsten: How can there only be one most important thing in the world when everyone's different? *(Extending, questioning)*

49

What Philosophy for Children does provide, as the above example shows, is a means for developing various skills in reasoning through the stimulus of a story. If questions for discussion by the community are embedded in their own concerns it allows for both universalizable argument and the expression of personal experience. To that extent the discussion can be both rigorous (through appeal to reason) and open-ended (through the creative exploration of ideas), providing a space where a range of viewpoints, including masculine and feminine, and cultural and culture-critical can be equally heard.

What is needed for effective philosophical discussion as this example illustrates is the exercise of reason, reflectiveness and responsibility (that is the moral responsibility exemplified in the attitudes and dispositions characteristic of the collaborative working of a community of enquiry). It is these moral dispositions that Paul says characterizes critical thinkers in the 'strong sense' and which Lipman says are characteristic of caring thinking. We will look at how a community of enquiry can foster moral education in the next chapter. We need also to consider the question most commonly asked by teachers – does it work?

Chapter 6 looks at research which shows that Philosophy for Children can be successful in developing reading ability, verbal reasoning and other skills. Its methods and materials have been developed, as later chapters will show, so that it has become now more than a programme for developing thinking. During discussion at one of the international seminars on Philosophy for Children held at Montclair University (USA) a Canadian teacher said: 'Philosophy for Children is not so much a programme as a vision of the child.' It is a vision that extends beyond the results of reading and verbal reasoning tests to a fulfilment of the child's human capacities – moral, social, cultural and spiritual realized in the social setting of a community or classroom. According to Sandeep, aged 10: 'Philosophy helps to make you a better person.' The moral context for this is the method called Community of Enquiry. We will now examine this method to see what it is, how it works and why teachers have called it 'the heart' and the 'secret of the success' of philosophy with children.

NOTES AND REFERENCES

1. Philosophy for Children is particulary strong in South America, where it is estimated that 30,000 children are studying Philosophy for Children in Brazil alone (other countries include Peru, Columbia, Guatemala and Chile). Mexico has six Philosophy for Children centres. In Canada there are centres in Quebec and Montreal. The strongest centre in Africa is Nigeria, where Philosophy for Children is used in teacher training (other centres include Zimbabwe and Botswana). There is much Philosophy for Children activity in Australia, and in Taiwan. There is growing interest being shown in Eastern Europe, especially in Russia, Armenia, Poland, Hungary and Bulgaria. Other European centres include Austria, Belgium, Spain, Portugal, Malta and Iceland. Researchers from many countries attend annual Institute for the Advancement of Philosophy for Children (IAPC) training conferences, run by the founders of Philosophy for Children, Matthew Lipman and Ann Sharp, to research ways of implementing the Philosophy for Children curriculum. The International Council for Philosophical Inquiry with Children (ICPIC) exists to promote, co-ordinate and disseminate research in developing philosophical enquiry in both primary and secondary schools throughout the world, and holds regular international conferences. In this country a national organization called the Society for the Advancement of Philosophical Enquiry and Reflection in Education (SAPERE) exists 'to enrich the personal and social lives of people of all ages, and especially children, through the promotion of philosophical enquiry in communities'.
2. Lipman, M. (1982), 'Philosophy for Children', *Thinking: the Journal for Philosophy for Children*, Vol. 3, p. 37.
3. A version for use in Britain has been produced by Roger Sutcliffe (1993), which combines the pupil's novel with exercises from the teacher's manual. There is also an adult version of *Harry*, called *Harry Prime. Harry Stottlemeier's Discovery* was the first philosophical novel of the series, first published in 1974 and the most widely used. It aimed

to introduce 10- to 12-year-olds to some philosophical topics and elements of logic in a fictional context. The plan
was to use the story to initiate discussion in the classroom
so as to develop reasoning skills. Through discussing the
ways in which Harry and the other characters in the novel
try to question, reason and unravel the mysteries of thinking, the aim is that the children will thus engage in thinking about their own thinking and explore ways to improve
it. It was found that the story itself did not offer teachers,
unused to philosophical method, enough support in initiating philosophical discussion in the classroom, and so a
teacher's manual was produced, providing extensive back-
up material to aid discussion. The book and manual have
since been translated into many languages and have been
the basis of much research literature (Sharp and Reed,
1991). A growing number of publications has been
produced to extend this programme (see Bibliography).

4. See for example Murris (1992), Fisher (1996).
5. Lipman, M. 'Philosophical discussion plans and exercises',
   Critical and Creative Thinking, Vol. 5, No. 1, 1997, pp. 1-17.
6. Lipman, M. and Sharp. A.M. (1985), *Looking for Meaning:
   Instructional Manual to Accompany Pixie*, Montclair:
   IAPC, p. 4.
7. Fisher, R. (1995) *Teaching Children to Learn*, Cheltenham:
   Nelson Thornes, pp. 52–4.
8. Lipman, M. (1991), *Thinking in Education*, Cambridge:
   Cambridge University Press, p. 112.
9. Dewey, J. (1909/1933), *How We Think*, p. 6.
10. Siegel, H. (1988), *Educating Reason: Rationality, Critical
    Thinking and Education*, London: Routledge and Kegan
    Paul, p. 32. Ennis, R. and Norris, S. (1989), *Evaluating
    Critical Thinking*, Pacific Grove, CA: Critical Thinking
    Press.
11. Paul, R. (1993), *Critical Thinking: How to Prepare Students
    for a Rapidly Changing World*, Santa Rosa, CA:
    Foundations for Critical Thinking.
12. Peters, R.S. (1972), 'Reason and Passion', in Dearden, R.F.,
    Hirst, P.H. and Peters, R.S. (eds) *Education and the
    Development of Reason*, London: Routledge and Kegan
    Paul. McPeck, J.E. (1981), *Critical Thinking and*

Education, Oxford: Martin Roberson. See also McPeck, J.E. (1990), *Teaching Critical Thinking: Dialogue and Dialectic*, London: Routledge.

13. Cosentino, A. (1994), 'Kant and the pedagogy of teaching', *Thinking*, Vol. 12, No. 1, pp. 2–3.
14. Bloom, B. *et al.* (1956), *Taxonomy of Educational Objectivies*, Vol. 1: *Cognitive Domain*, New York: McKay.
15. I am indebted to Roger Sutcliffe for this example of classroom discussion.

CHAPTER 3

Community of Enquiry: Creating contexts for moral education

What matters at this stage is the construction of local forms of community within which civility and the intellectual and moral life can be sustained.

Alisdair MacIntyre[1]

Sometimes you're afraid to say things, but in philosophy lessons you can say what you really think and sometimes you change your mind.

Michelle, aged 10

Children and their teacher sit in a circle to share some reading and listening. The children take some thinking time to devise their own questions and then discuss them. The group meets regularly in this thinking circle. The questions they ask become more frequent, more searching and more thoughtful. Their discussions become more disciplined and focused, and also more imaginative. The process by which this is achieved is called a Community of Enquiry. This chapter describes what a community of philosophical enquiry is, and how it can contribute to the moral and social development of participants. Or how, in the words of David, aged 9: 'In a thinking circle you have to listen and care what people say.'

Human beings are characterized by conflicting natural tend-
encies: to care and not to care, to be generous and to be selfish,
to be competitive and to be cooperative, to love and hate and
so on. As one 8-year-old put it: 'The trouble is people are
telling you to do different things, and sometimes your mind
tells you to do different things too!' In trying to teach our
pupils to be thoughtful and reasonable persons, with the
capacity for resolving conflicts in themselves and in society,
we must try to provide school and home environments that
are thoughtful and reasonable. This means treating children as
rational beings capable of reasoning about conduct, and providing the opportunity for them to practise thoughtful and
caring behaviour. One way to do this is to create a community
of enquiry in the classroom, which embodies social forms of
reasoning and of respect for others. Through participating in a
community of enquiry children cultivate the social habits
required for good moral conduct. 'In philosophy you have to
follow the rules,' says Carla, aged 10, 'but you also set the
rules.'

WHAT DOES A COMMUNITY OF ENQUIRY AIM TO ACHIEVE?

For some teachers philosophy undertaken in a community of
enquiry is not so much about developing language and thinking skills, its value lies in its contribution to personal and
social education. A community of enquiry can help children
develop the skills and dispositions that will enable them to
play their full part in a pluralistic and democratic society. It
boosts self-esteem, intellectual confidence and the ability to
participate in reasoned discussion. It achieves this by creating
a caring classroom community where children learn to:

- explore issues of personal concern such as love, friendship,
  death, bullying, and fairness, and more general philosophical issues such as personal identity, change, truth and time
- develop their own views, explore and challenge the views
  of others

55

- be clear in their thinking, making thoughtful judgements based on reasons
- listen to and respect each other
- experience quiet moments of thinking and reflection

How is it best to solve a problem?

An excerpt from a discussion with 14- to 15-year-old children:

RF: What are the best tactics for thinking when you are trying to solve a problem?

Tom: If you want to solve a problem, like say whether to do something or not, the best tactic is to weigh up the pros and cons on each side of the argument and see the difference between them.

Nick: You need to find out as much as you can first to understand what it's all about. You need a fair amount of information before you make a decision.

Tom: One way is to write things down, like a list 'for' and 'against'. That's good because sometimes you forget things. You could decide by adding up the pros and cons and see who wins.

Nick: That won't work because some of the things and arguments are more important than others.

Tom: Yeah, well you could put them in one list of importance ... and then ask other people what they think. They may have important points that you have not thought of. If it's a social problem, like mugging or something, you need to look at the long and short term effects before you make a decision. You need to get everyone's opinion.

Philosophical enquiry initiates children into public discussion about meanings and values. It encourages them to think what it is to be reasonable and to make moral judgements.

Such discussions are not just 'talking shops' but help to create a moral culture, a way of thinking and acting together that cultivates virtues such as respect for others, sincerity and open-mindedness. In a community of enquiry children are encouraged to find their own path to meaning through sustained discussion with others. We cannot control the responses children will have to the dangers and temptations they will face on the streets and in their private lives. We can, however, in classroom or home, try to establish a safe place in which to share what they think, feel and experience, a place where their thoughts will be heard. A community of enquiry aims to provide a safe space for thinking, a creative context for moral and social enquiry. 'Philosophy,' says Salome, aged 10, 'gives you the chance to take out your thinking and share it with others.'

The concept of community of enquiry is not new, nor is it unique to philosophy for children. Various forms of 'circle time' have been developed to create a supportive environment in which to explore feelings and build self esteem. A community of enquiry offers a circle approach aimed at developing thinking and personal growth. But what is this 'community' it seeks to create, and how does it foster moral development?

WHAT IS A COMMUNITY?

The concept of 'community' has been the focus of lively political and philosophical debate in recent years. One strand of this has been Hegel's notion that communities emerge out of conflict-filled situations, as a synthesis emerges out of opposing theses. The problem lies in deciding how conflict and argument should be resolved. There are differing views about the role of argument in the formation of communities. Should a community (or a relationship) always seek to establish a shared viewpoint, or should it recognize and allow different viewpoints? Should the guiding principle of a community or relationship be to seek to resolve conflicts of argument through a synthesis of views, or should there be a recognition that differences of opinion and varied viewpoints are inevitable?

There has been much interest recently in the notions of 'community' and communitarian theory. These echo Hegel's ideal of a community which is rationally organized and founded on individual freedom. For Hegel critical thought and reflection are the key to developing freedom within an organic community.[2] This concept of free enquiry as a constituent of community began with Socrates, as recorded in the Platonic dialogues. Typically Socrates would engage in dialogue with some worthy Athenian who thinks he knows what it is to be good and just. This 'knowledge' turns out to be merely the ability to echo some customary concept of morality. Socrates through questioning this view has no difficulty in showing that this received view cannot be the full story. For example against the common idea that justice consists in giving to each what is owed to him, Socrates suggests the case of a friend who has lent you a weapon but has since become deranged. Should you return him the weapon? The questions raised by Socrates lead his audience to reflect on the conventional morality that they have uncritically accepted. This critical reflection pursued in a spirit of free enquiry makes reason, not social custom, the arbiter of right and wrong. The unconsidered acceptance of received wisdom is not true wisdom, and can lead to errors of judgement. Or as Kelly, aged 8, put it; 'If you always do what other people tell you to you're bound to end up in trouble.'

This Socratic view that a community should be founded on principles of freedom of expression and recourse to reason has its problems. What happens when there is a conflict of interest between the needs of individuals and the democratically expressed interests of the community? Socrates was after all condemned to death by democratic Athens. One way of overcoming this problem of clash of interests is for the relationship between individuals and community to be organic and reciprocal. Communities should develop through adapting to the individual needs of its members. Hegel argued that communities must be organic in the sense of having their conventions open and adaptable to reasoned argument. He believed that all communities are, and should be, in a state of evolution. What is constitutive of the moral order in a community, such as a classroom or a family, should always be open to review and reason. Liberal theory provides a means for ensuring this openness to change in response to the needs of individuals through the process of democracy, by embodying the rights of all to a voice and a vote.

The elements of community identified so far are that it:

- embodies as a principle the freedom of expression of individuals
- makes critical reasoning not convention the arbiter of moral judgement
- is organic in the sense that its working procedures and values are open to adaptation
- is democratic in ensuring that all its members have a right to a voice and a vote

When two or more people come together, they not only respond to the institutional and social order they find themselves in, but they also in a sense are co-constructors of that order. They are involved in the process of socialization into a specific way of life that constitutes the community. This process is made possible by the symbolic resources provided by language and the shared meanings provided by communication. We learn standards of normative behaviour, whether expressed in talk or action, by observing how others respond to us, anticipating responses and developing our own repertoire of responses. This process is not only crucial to the development of our ability to communicate in groups, but also to the development of self esteem and socialization. Nor does it end once the child is socialized to the norms of a community. For the child as participant also becomes constitutive of the community, influencing the response of others, and thereby the nature of the community, by their interactions. 'During philosophy', says Darren, aged 9, 'you really feel part of the class, because everyone listens to you and you listen to them.'

Discussion plays a central role in the development of a community, because it requires speakers to put themselves in another's place in order to know how to communicate information (syntactically, semantically and pragmatically) so as to be comprehensible to others. This ritualization of speaking through a shared discussion, involving the practice of 'speaking for another to understand', can be seen as part of an interactive process that creates both a linguistic and moral relationship, and the blending of the self into the community. Learning how to speak to others and the conventions of discussion are central to the successful functioning of a community of enquiry. As one child commented: 'Once you follow the rules you can forget them.'

HOW DOES A COMMUNITY OF ENQUIRY DIFFER FROM ANY OTHER COMMUNITY?

The 19th-century sociologist Ferdinand Tonnies made a useful and much cited distinction between natural and artificial communities – *Gemeinschaft* and *Gesellschaft*.[3] A natural community is one united by a common knowledge and shared experience, whereas an artificial community was an association created for a common goal such as a factory or school. A natural community has a voluntary nature, it is characterized by a self discipline, by 'unwritten rules' and by purposes that are intrinsically meaningful. A family can be regarded as a natural community intermediary between the individual and the state. An artificial association is one that is bound by rules and by purposes that are extrinsic to its members. A community of enquiry aspires to the condition of a natural community, united by the following characteristics:

- shared experience
- voluntary communication
- shared understanding of meanings

What differentiates any learning community made up of individuals from a community of enquiry is the notion of shared enquiry. A community of enquiry can be said to have been achieved when any group of people engage in a cooperative search for understanding. In so doing each member benefits from the ideas and experience of everyone else, and each person feels a valued part of the whole community. This collegial structure shares characteristics of all effective thinking groups, from political 'think tanks' to university research groups, from industrial research teams to school staffs, from families at home to classes in school.[4] This sense of community has a dual aspect: a *rational structure* for maximizing effective thinking, and a *moral structure* of mutual respect and shared democratic values. In this way philosophical enquiry becomes the context for a powerful kind of moral conversation.

The philosopher Habermas argues that moral judgement is best developed through a kind of idealized conversation. He claims that the distinctive idea of moral discourse is not to find universal laws but a general law which will be agreed by members of the community to be a universal norm. In this way it is possible to escape from mindless acceptance of given rules and from a mindless relativism which suggests there are no moral norms at all. 'The only norms that can claim to be valid,' says Habermas, 'are those that meet (or could meet) with the approval of all affected in their capacity as participants in a practical discourse'.[5] Habermas is here referring to an idealized conversation through which moral agreement is reached and is accepted by all. It is this idealized conversation through which a group discussing contestable and problematical matters of real concern exercise reason and so come to better judgements and (sometimes) a consensus which is the ultimate aim of a community of enquiry.

Another notion that underpins the idea of community of enquiry is that of distributed intelligence. This argues that human thinking is at its richest when it occurs in ways that are socially shared and distributed. In common parlance it is the view that in solving problems two heads are better than one. The classic view of intelligence is that it is bounded by what lies inside individual heads. Vygotsky, however, reminds us that our intellectual range can always be extended through the mediation of and interaction with others, by the social distribution of intelligence. The value of this was summarized by Jane, aged 10, when in a discussion on the best ways to solve personal problems she said: 'When you are trying to work something out, it's best to get as many heads working for you as possible.' But how do you do that in a busy and crowded classroom?

HOW IS A COMMUNITY OF ENQUIRY CREATED IN THE CLASSROOM?

The following summarizes the elements that create a community of enquiry for philosophical discussion in the classroom. Fuller discussion of this process will be found in Chapter 6.

- a community setting, such as a circle
- a shared stimulus to think about, such as a story
- an invitation to question
- a group or whole class discussion
- activity to extend thinking

Community setting

Sit so that all can see and hear each other, with the teacher as part of the group, using agreed rules: for example – 'Only one speaks at a time', and 'Everyone listens to the speaker'. These rules can be established by the discussion leader or agreed through discussion by the group.

What should be our rules for discussion?

The following were rules for discussion agreed by a group of 10-year-olds:

1. Give everyone a turn at speaking.
2. Don't interrupt when someone else is talking.
3. Give support and help them add things.
4. Don't say anything mean, stupid or unpleasant.
5. If people don't want to say anything they don't have to.
6. Don't laugh unkindly at something someone has said.
7. Think before you ask a question.

A shared stimulus to think about

If it is a story, each member may have a turn to read, and the option not to read, a chosen text. The stimulus is a point of entry to the consideration and discussion of key concepts and questions identified by the group. The stimulus could for example be a story, poem, work of art, experience or open question that invited response.

An invitation to question

Time is given to think about the stimulus or story for individuals, pairs or groups to raise questions, problems or ideas stimulated by the story. These questions are written up for all to see and consider as a possible subject for enquiry.

Discussion of a chosen question

Each member of the group is given the opportunity to express their own opinions and feelings about the question or issue chosen for discussion or what has been said, and each must listen to others, and consider their points of view and ideas.

Activity to extend thinking

Before, during or more usually at the end of discussion the thinking of the group may be extended through the use of activities, exercises or further discussion that apply and extend leading ideas.

A community of enquiry has therefore both a cognitive and a moral dimension. It is a progressive means to achieve traditional ends. Learning to listen to and respect the opinions of others is part of the caring for others that is central to the values of many schools and communities. But how are moral values developed through a community of enquiry?

WHAT CONTRIBUTION CAN COMMUNITY OF ENQUIRY MAKE TO MORAL EDUCATION?

> *For our discussion is no trifling matter but on the right way to conduct our lives.*
>
> Plato, *Republic*, VIII, 352d

There is growing concern in many countries about the problem of teaching values. And in this country hardly a week passes without some public agonizing over a fresh example of lack of moral judgement. The important role that education can play, at home and school, in the moral development of children hardly needs emphasizing. Recent discussion papers and the setting up of the National Forum for Values in Education and the Community highlight the challenge schools face in educating for democracy, and in core values such as respect for self, respect for others and respect for the environment.[6] It would be difficult to find fault with the call for pupils to develop the ability to make judgements on moral issues by applying moral principles, insights and reasoning. The problem emerges when the question is raised about how moral judgement is to be taught.

The simple answer is that schools should teach what is 'right' and 'wrong'. On this view teaching consists in upholding certain core values, such as truth-telling, care for others and following socially prescribed rules. But moral education must be more than teaching these core values, no matter how commendable these values may be. Values taught didactically may not be internalized, may not become part of the beliefs and values of individual children. The point is that children need to learn that all moral acts have reasons, and they need the skills that will help them to deal with the moral conflicts that they will face in an uncertain world.

'We should think what we do, and do what we think, so long as it's right,' said an 8-year-old. But what makes an action 'right' or 'wrong'? How should I treat other people? What sort of person should I be? What does it mean to be 'fair'? What is justice? What rights and responsibilities do we have? These are some of the general moral questions we all face as individuals and as citizens. One of the central problems of moral education is that terms like 'right' and 'wrong' are not unique to morality. The moral senses of 'right' and 'wrong' need to be distinguished from their legal use, or when applied to answers to factual questions. Like 'good' and 'bad' they also feature as basic words of commendation or disapproval, and have different functions in different contexts. How do we help children develop moral resilience and understanding in a confusing world?

The aims of moral education can be summarized as helping to develop:

- knowledge of the language and ideas of morality through engaging students in moral discussion
- understanding the nature and purpose of moral beliefs through discussion and reflection on moral issues
- a set of personal values with reference to oneself and others, through helping students to decide what they hold as right and wrong, why they do so, and how they should act in accordance with their moral beliefs
- moral dispositions to act in accordance with personal values and beliefs, to *be* 'moral'

But what does it mean to be moral?

Broadly speaking there are two types of answer that moral philosophers have given to this question. One view can be called the *moral principles* approach. To be moral is to be guided by principles, that can be universalized as a set of rules. These principles can be derived from the exercise of reason, as Kant and his followers have tried to do. Or they can be derived from authority, for example from religious doctrine. To be moral on this view is to follow a code of rules or universal principles. Moral education would be seen therefore as the development of a set of moral principles that would inform belief and action. In its earliest stages moral development would entail following the rules of others, and later develop into moral autonomy where rules become rationally based self-accepted principles (as in the theories of Kohlberg and Piaget below). We need principles but we also need the contexts in which moral action occurs. We are motivated by stories, by what happens to particular people, not by rules. Stories are used to motivate discussion in a community of enquiry and these provide a vehicle for moral discussion.

The problem with principles or rules is that they do not necessarily show you how to act in particular circumstances. Are they to be applied in all circumstances? Are there to be no exceptions? Is being moral just about what we do and the rules we follow, or is it more about the sort of people we are and the way we feel about and respond to other people? Is being moral about principles, or virtues?

Another view regards morality as *development of the virtues* that characterize 'good' persons. This is a view that derives from Aristotle and his followers who are concerned to define the characteristics and virtues of the moral person. Moral education is seen as the development of dispositions and virtues such as tolerance, respect and care for others. Feminist philosophers have argued that reasoning and principles should not be detached from the human contexts of care and compassion. They say that moral emotions and personal relationships should be central to morality. Important questions to consider here would be:

- What qualities do we want to develop in our students?
- What qualities do our students think make up a good person?

What is a good person?

An excerpt from a discussion with 6- to 7-year-olds:

RF:	When we say someone is good in a story or in real life, what makes someone a good person?
Jody:	A good person you say is someone who does what is right.
Charlotte:	Someone who is kind.
RF:	What does 'being kind' mean? Can you give an example?
Tony:	A kind person helps you. Like helping an old lady across the road, that sort of thing, or giving you something you need.
Jane:	A helping hand.
RF:	Is everyone who is kind or helpful a good person?
Tricia:	A person could be kind one day and be horrible the next.
Robert:	No one could be good all the time.
Clare:	Except Mrs Jones. *(Note: Mrs Jones is the class teacher)*
Mrs Jones:	I try to be good, but I'm not good all the time.
Paula:	A good person is someone who is good inside, but doesn't always do good things.

One of the problems with the view that morals is a matter of developing certain virtues is deciding what virtues these should be. There are different concepts of what a 'good' person is, and we would not necessarily agree with, for example, Aristotle's list of virtues. Do rules have no part to play in moral judgements? Are there to be no guiding principles of action? Is morality simply a matter of being well-motivated, or are some acts right or wrong whatever the circumstances?

These views sum up what might be seen as the two key aspects of moral education, the need to develop both principles and virtues. Principles provide reasons for belief and action. They provide a basis for personal autonomy and accepted social codes of public life – but what principles should they be? We do not live in a moral vacuum, moral decisions are interpersonal, and also depend on the consequences for others. Virtues are needed to provide the disposition to act on judgements, the imagination and empathy to guide our understanding of the needs and feelings of others, and to foresee the consequences of actions. But what virtues are needed, and how are they to be developed? Do they develop in stages?

Piaget and Kohlberg have argued that moral education should be informed by an understanding of the psychological stages of moral development. In their research they explored children's responses to moral judgements through the use of stories, and used these findings to construct theories about the stages of moral development.

Piaget used stories, for example about a child who broke cups that were on a tray behind a door. Was the child to blame? Piaget found that many young children thought the child was to blame as he had broken the cups. Older, more autonomous children argued that the child although objectively responsible for smashing the cups should not be blamed. Another story was of a child who broke a cup while trying to steal a jar of jam by climbing up in a larder. From children's responses to such story problems Piaget argued that moral development could be viewed as two distinct stages:

1. *authoritarian* morality – the belief that moral codes are given by others, they exist outside people and are nonrational, morality seen as obedience to a given code
2. *autonomous* morality – where fairness in moral actions takes account of motive and individual needs, and is open to reasoning

Kohlberg also used stories such as the story of a boy whose father says he can go to camp if he earns $50. Later the father says the boy must hand over any money he earns. The boy lies, he earns $50 but says he has only earnt $10, taking $40 to camp. He tells his younger brother. Should his brother tell his father? From responses to stories such as this Kohlberg argued for three broad stages of moral development, summarized as follows:

1. *Pre-moral* – where rules are obeyed to avoid punishment, or to get a reward (instrumental hedonism)
2. *Conventional morality* – where rules are obeyed to avoid disapproval ('good boy' morality), or to avoid censure or guilt (obedience to authority)
3. *Self-accepted principles* – a contract morality where the rights and duties are reciprocal, or where principles conform to individual conscience

Critics of this view have argued that moral decisions and moral development are more complex. All the above factors can relate to a person's response to any one moral situation. There is also no evidence that moral development occurs along a linear track, we do not progress up a neat hierarchy of moral responses. It is, however, widely agreed that the goal of the development process is to achieve moral autonomy.

Moral decisions have a dual focus, the *self* (what are the consequences for me?) and *others* (what are the consequences for them?). Development in moral thinking can be seen as a move from the egocentric ('What's in it for me?') to the sociocentric ('Is it right for all?'). This involves moving from simplistic notions of self interest to the complexity of considering other points of view, it involves the use of moral imagination and of empathy. Moral concern should not be exclusively about myself, but inclusively involves consider-

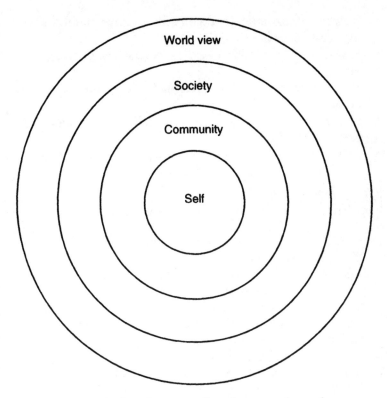

Figure 3.1   Moral education: extending the range of moral concern

ation of the interests of others (see Figure 3.1). This empathy or understanding of others has an affective or feeling element, which might be called sympathy or care, but also has a cognitive aspect involved in understanding the reasons why people think, feel and behave in certain ways. The development of moral intelligence can be seen in the growth of awareness and understanding. Morals are not simply a matter of following rules, either conventional or self-accepted rules, but relate also to the outcomes we want to achieve including the sort of person we want to be and what sort of place we want the world to become.

Moral education is complex and involves developing:

- attitudes – that others are equally important, and principles are therefore universalizable

- insight – imagination and empathy to understand the feelings and needs of others
- knowledge – to predict likely consequences for oneself and others
- ability to communicate – feelings, needs and interests to others
- to make rational judgements – to make moral judgements based on good reasons
- dispositions – to act on judgements, to do what is right

Should animals be killed?

An extract from a discussion with 6-year-olds:

Linda:	I don't think animals should be killed.
RF:	Why not?
Graeme:	Animals haven't done anything to us, why should we kill them?
RF:	Sometimes animals are killed because people want to eat them, like cows or rabbits.
Rachel:	We shouldn't kill cows . . . they give us milk and that's good for you.
Craig:	If we kill animals we shouldn't eat them. You wouldn't want to be eaten, would you?
Rebecca:	It's not fair to kill animals to eat them. There are plenty of other things to eat.
RF:	Some animals are killed and eaten because they taste nice.
Ivan:	That's not fair.
Holly:	Sometimes you have to kill animals when they are very ill.
Inga:	Or if it's hurt, in an accident or something.
Teacher:	Some wild animals kill people, should animals be killed if they are dangerous?
Wesley:	Like tigers – they can kill people.
Neal:	I think we should only kill animals when they have killed six people or more.
Teacher:	Should an animal be killed if it has only killed one person?
Juliet:	No, because it doesn't know what it is doing.

Moral development would seem to depend on a broad education, but it becomes difficult and debatable to identify the specific gains in knowledge and understanding that should be the focus of teaching. In order to develop moral qualities schools will need to provide well-regulated communities founded on principles of justice and fairness. But they will also need to act within the curriculum to develop knowledge, understanding and care about the effects of human decisions on others and on the environment.

One aspect of development to focus on is *attitudes*. How do we develop positive moral attitudes? The following are some questions that could help act as guiding principles for developing attitudes of moral awareness:

- Is this (does it fit in with) the sort of person I want to be?
- Do I want people to behave to me like that?
- Does it help or harm other people?
- Could I (he/she/they) have done better?
- Does this make the world a better place?
- Is this a constructive or destructive thing?
- What would others think of this?

Is morality taught or caught? A Russian proverb says: 'It takes a whole village to educate a child.' Much of moral education is indirect and depends on the influence of external models in the culture or community, and on what has been internalized as the norms of ethical behaviour. There is widespread agreement that young people must first be taught appropriate behaviour by conforming to rules and conventions – and that the reasons for abiding by certain rules should be clearly articulated. But if morality is essentially the product of a way of life is it possible to teach moral reasoning?

Aristotle thought that moral philosophy was not for the young, for two key reasons – their inexperience and their lack of rational principles. Piaget and Kohlberg argue that it is the egocentricity of young children that prevents moral development before 7 or 8 years. But although young children have little reflective understanding of moral knowledge there is a growing body of evidence that even young children of 4 and 5 years can answer questions about moral rules and can consider the consequences for others. Young children have a keen sense of fairness and this can be developed through discussion stories and real-life situations. Even young children, within the limitations of their experience and of their powers of reasoning, can become engaged in imaginative and provocative moral thought.

Gareth Matthews gives an example of this – Ian, aged six, one of three children, when his parents' friends monopolized the choice of television programme, asked in frustration: 'Why is it better for three people to be selfish than one?'[7] Young children face many dilemmas in their lives, and these can often provide the yeast for moral discussion.

Moral education: what do the key terms mean?

Some of the key terms in moral education can be defined as follows:

ethics (from the Greek *ethos*, character) The study of the codes or systems of morality and the concepts involved in practical reasoning such as good, right, fair, justice, virtue, freedom and choice. A branch of the study of philosophy.

morality (from the Latin *mores*, manners or customs) A broad term referring to the codes, customs and conduct of individuals or groups, including the goodness or badness of character, principles of right and wrong, moral habits, actions and virtues. Sometimes used as equivalent to ethics.

values In ethics that which has intrinsic worth. More generally the principles or standards used in judging what is valuable or important in life. Some believe values are subjective and open to individual choice. Others that there are objective standards established by reason, human nature, God or some other authority.

virtues A trait of character that is to be admired, making the person better either morally, intellectually or in the conduct of their affairs. For Aristotle virtues of character were the essence of moral goodness. Different cultures have different conceptions of virtue, e.g. Christian virtues. For Kant virtue lay in duty, for utilitarians in the pursuit of the greatest happiness.

HOW ARE MORAL AND SOCIAL VALUES TO BE TAUGHT?

There are various ways in which moral and social values can be taught. Different approaches include:

- Indoctrination
- Religious authority
- Common sense approach
- Values clarification
- Moral dilemmas
- Philosophical/ethical enquiry

Indoctrination

For some moral education is best taught as a form of moral training, that is through the thorough teaching of a set of moral rules. This involves children being told what they should know and what they should do. It prescribes a set of adult values to be accepted without choice or question. But a 'Do as I tell you' approach will not help children develop a set of personal values, nor a care, concern or respect for others. It may provide the necessary social boundaries and conditions for education to take place but is not in itself educative, whether the indoctrination comes from a parent, a teacher or other source – such as a book. Philosophy for children is about an open, challenging and questioning enquiry into the meaning and relevance of fundamental values, it is not therefore a form of indoctrination. As Charmaine, aged 11, said: 'Philosophy doesn't tell you what to say or do, you must work it out for yourself.'

Religious authority

Many derive their moral and social values from religious authority, and from being members of a religious community. Discussion of religious values and beliefs in a community of enquiry should help young people from whatever faith to gain personal and social skills in dealing with moral issues. Exploration of values can be important in helping children understand how religious values can enrich their own lives and the lives of other people. Omar, a Muslim aged 9, put it this way: 'Philosophy gives me a chance to share my religion and what I really believe and think.' Further discussion of the use of philosophy in religious education is in Chapter 7 (p. 239).

Common sense approach

For some people moral education is a matter of common sense and agreed conventions. Personal morality is seen as a utilitarian matter of deciding what is sensible in any situation, or of following social conventions such as school rules. The trouble is that this approach can become *laissez-faire*, with children being assumed to know what concepts like 'right', 'wrong', 'fair', and 'truth' mean, but left confused, and the concepts unexamined. Morality cannot simply be left as a matter of uninformed personal choice, or as a set of mindless assumptions. Children need to know the codes, conventions and conduct expected by society, but they also need to understand the concepts and criteria involved in making moral judgements, and to develop moral principles that will be resilient in the face of external threats and pressures. In a community of enquiry common sense notions are subjected to close scrutiny. 'In philosophy,' says Justin, aged 7, 'you have to know why you are saying things.'

Values clarification

Values clarification involves students talking about and sharing values in a neutral and non-judgmental setting, and reflecting on the implications of their values. One problem with this approach is what to do when values conflict. The approach can show that any value is defensible (it is possible to find arguments to support any moral viewpoint). But if all values are regarded as of equal worth then children are left in a mindless relativism. If values are equally valid, just different, there can be no certain or necessary basis for moral life. Clarifying moral values, by giving reasons and evidence in support of our beliefs, is important but is not a sufficient basis for moral education or for a community of enquiry. A community of enquiry embodies certain fundamental values such as truth telling, equality of opportunity and respect for others, which are essential to its working and to its moral ethos. Children soon become aware that certain basic values or rules need to be in place for the community of enquiry to work. As Daniel, aged 9, says of discussion: 'There are some rules that everyone has to know or it doesn't work.'

Moral dilemmas

What moral choices do people face? One way of stimulating moral discussion is through the use of dilemmas. Moral dilemmas such as those used by Kohlberg and Piaget can provide case studies through which moral principles can be discussed. It may be helpful with young children to discuss everyday or imaginary dilemmas that involve decision-making first. Picture books can provide a stimulus for this sort of discussion.[8] Other possible introductions to dilemmas include posing questions which offer alternative choices such as:

- Where would you rather live, in ...... or ......?
- Would you rather have a friend who ...... or ......?
- Would you rather have a teacher who ...... or ......?
- When you grow up would you rather become a ..... or ......?
- Would you rather have a gift of ...... or ......?

Open questions can be as fruitful as dilemmas in stimulating discussion and argument. These can be generated from news items in the papers or from TV, they can come from the lives of students (for example through having a 'problems box' in the classroom where students can anonymously report problems for discussion) or from open questions of a general nature, for example:

- Is it more important to be happy or to be rich? Why?
- Is it better to be a child or adult? Why?
- Are boys and girls treated differently? Should they be?
- What is bullying? What should be done about it?
- Do children have rights? What are they?

The aim here is to encourage flexibility of ideas, and to consider the creation of real choices. Follow-up questions can include: Are some dilemmas easier to decide upon than others? If you have a choice to make who can help you decide? Have you ever faced a dilemma (difficult choice) in your life? If so, how did you decide what to do?

Real-life dilemmas of course face us with many of our most important decisions. We all need the resiliency that thinking for ourselves, and being able to defend what we believe is right to others, can give. Examples of moral dilemmas that can provide a focus for discussion include:

- You see your best friend steal a packet of sweets from a shop, what should you do?
- A friend lends you a toy, and you lose it. Should you buy them a new one? What should you do?
- You have promised your mother not to eat crisps on the way home from school, but you do. Your mother finds a crisp packet in your pocket, and asks where it has come from. What should you say? What would you say?

The following was a real-life dilemma facing a child one morning. On his way to school he found a £5 note in the street. He picked it up. No one had seen him. What should he do? Perhaps a more fruitful question to ask children is: What *could* he do? Consider the alternatives, or in the words of one of de Bono's 'thinking tools': CAF – Consider All Factors. The essence of creative thinking about problems is conditional thinking – trying to analyse all the conditions, factors or schoices in a situation. In the discussion about finding a £5 note a junior class was asked to discuss: *What choices does the finder have?* then to prioritize choices: *Which is the right choice?* and then to move from the particular and personal to a general rule: *Which choice would you make – what would you actually do? Why? What general rule applies here?*

Moral dilemma: If you find something should you keep it?

An excerpt from a discussion between 9/10-year-olds on the following dilemma: If you found a £10 note on the way to school, what could you do with it, what should you do with it and what would you do with it? In answer to the question: 'What *could* you do? What choices has the person who found the £10 note got?' the children list seven possible lines of action:

Anthony:	Leave it there, don't pick it up.
James:	Pick it up and spend it.
Mandy:	Pick it up, take it to school, and give it to your teacher.
Richard:	Take it, keep it and save it.
Daniel:	Take it to the police station. Because if someone claims it you might get a reward.
Ben:	Take it and give it to charity.
Darren:	I'd pick it up and share it with my mates.
RF:	Thank you. You've chosen seven possibilities. Which of these do you agree should be the right choice?
Nadine:	I agree with Anthony, I think you should leave it.
RF:	Why?
Nadine:	Because it might belong to someone, and they might come back when they realize they've lost it.
Ashley:	I disagree, I think you should take it to the school. You shouldn't take it to the police station. It might belong to someone in school.
Garry:	I think you should put it in your own drawer.
Daniel:	You should take it to the police, because if no-one claims it after five days it could be yours.
James:	I agree with Daniel. You should take it to the police station, because it's not yours to spend, and they might find the real owner.
Isaac:	I disagree with Ashley. If you take it to the school, the person you give it to might keep it, or your friend might say it's theirs and you'd have to give it to them.
Donna:	I agree with Isaac. If people in school see it they might say it's theirs. Or they might try to steal it.
Richard:	I think you should keep it because the person who dropped it should be more careful, otherwise it wouldn't be there in the first place.
John:	You should keep it and invest it.

Sharon: You could keep £5 and give £5 back.

Lee: I agree with Richard. Suppose if you dropped it, someone else would pick it up. So if they drop it, then you should pick it up and keep it.

RF: OK. Can anyone remember and sum up the different views about what you *should* do? Yes?

Simon: Hand it to the police, give it to the teacher, keep it and spend it, or leave it, and take it and share it.

RF: You've told me what you could do and what you should do. Now I wonder what you *would* do if it happened to you?

Lee: I would keep it.

RF: Why?

Lee: Because that's what someone else would do if they found it, other people would just pick it up and spend it.

RF: OK. If other people do it, is that a good reason for you doing it?

Isaac: If other people do it why shouldn't you?

Mandy: I disagree. Just because other people do it is not a good reason for you to do it. You wouldn't like them to take what's yours would you? Well, would you?

It is not just moral dilemmas that give rise to moral puzzlement and the need for careful thinking. We need to provide students with opportunities to sort out the subtle and complex features of situations that call for moral reflection. Real life is a complex affair and only rarely are the choices clear-cut. The challenge for moral education is to provide opportunities for students to engage in meaningful reflection and discussion of issues that are going to support, challenge and engage them in complex moral thinking. A community of enquiry provides the opportunities in the words of Kiran, aged 8: 'to puzzle what to believe'.

Philosophical/ethical enquiry

There is an important link between moral development and intellectual development. This can be seen in the very different capacities that young people have for articulating a moral position and reflecting upon it. Some students are able to justify a moral viewpoint in informed, coherent and reasonable ways. Others are less able to articulate what they think, in particular those whose attitudes are dependent on habits of deference and respect. Moral development is partly to do with the development of the capacity to reason. It follows that the best of moral education should be intellectually challenging and rigorous. It should be Socratic in the sense of questioning, demanding reasons and open to honest enquiry.

What is a bully?

An excerpt from a Community of Enquiry discussion with 7- to 8-year-olds:

RF:	What is a bully?
Nicole:	A bully is someone who is nasty to someone else, on purpose, like when they gang up on people and call them names.
Ellie:	A bully is someone who's nasty to someone smaller or younger than themselves.
RF:	Can a bully be someone smaller or younger than the person they are bullying?
Ellie:	No. A bully is someone bigger or older who bosses you around or hits you or calls you names.
Beth:	I disagree with Ellie, I think it's not how big or old you are, it's what you do that makes you a bully.
RF:	How do you mean? Can you explain why or give an example?
Beth:	Well ... take the story of David and Goliath. Goliath was a bully because he chopped off people's heads and things, but David could have been a bully. He could have bullied bigger people if they were scared of him.
RF:	Who agrees or disagrees with that?

Tony:	I agree with Beth. My sister tries to bully me and she's smaller than me.
RF:	What do you say Ellie?
Ellie:	I still don't think someone smaller could bully you. They could *try* to bully you, but it wouldn't really be bullying unless they hurt you and you couldn't do anything back at them.
RF:	I see. Who else has got a view on that?
Zara:	Well, bullies often go in groups. That's why they feel big and strong [and] able to say nasty things.
Beth:	A wasp can bully you. That's something smaller.
Tony:	A wasp doesn't know what it's doing, it's just being a wasp. A bully is someone who's nasty on purpose. They want to hurt you. A wasp just wants to . . . frighten you away or something like that.
RF:	OK. So who can now say what a bully is?
Nicole:	A bully is someone who is nasty to you, like hitting you . . .
RF:	Do they have to hit you?
Nicole:	No. They can call you names, stuff like that. They do it on purpose . . . to hurt or frighten you, like ganging up on someone. Usually they are bigger or older but they don't have to be. They can be bigger or smaller, older or younger than you.
RF:	Thank you. I don't think everyone agrees with all of that. Ellie, can a bully be bigger or smaller than you?
Ellie:	I think I've changed my mind a bit. It's not how big you are, it's what you do to other people that makes you a bully.

EDUCATION FOR DEMOCRACY

For many teachers, especially in countries that have been liberated from dictatorship, the value of the community of enquiry is primarily seen as a form of education for democracy. How, they ask, can you teach children about democracy unless they experience democratic processes and see the value of democracy in practice? This view that democracy is best learnt through experience echoes the view of J. S. Mill,[9] who wrote:

> We do not learn to read or write, to ride or swim, by merely being told how to do it, but by doing it, so it is only by practising popular government on a limited scale, that the people will ever learn how to practise it.

The argument for moral education through philosophical discussion in a community of enquiry can be summarized as follows:

1. Democratic ideals require educational practices that avoid indoctrination and promote the ability of people to judge for themselves.
2. Therefore in moral education we should avoid moral instruction and concentrate on developing children's reflective moral judgement.
3. Developing children's reflective moral judgement requires a programme of moral education through which children come to think critically and responsibly about moral and social issues.
4. Philosophy through a community of enquiry promotes moral thinking within a democratic social context.
5. Therefore children's moral and social education would benefit from the experience of a community of philosophical enquiry in the classroom.[10]

Democracy involves the belief that mutual understanding across differences of opinion and diversity of interest can only be achieved through genuine dialogue and discussion. Since the time of Aristotle ethics and politics have been seen as public concerns, as a kind of practical knowledge best fostered through critical discourse in self-governing communities. A community of enquiry is an experience of dialogue whereby participants are encouraged to use each other's ideas as building blocks to increase understanding.[11] For many children it is a unique experience in the exploration of ideas and in the reasoning out of problems together. Through it they can learn to discuss logically and creatively such fundamental moral issues as freedom, fairness, and friendship, and social issues like law and order and the nature of government.

What is government for?

The philosopher David Hume was asked: 'What do you consider the object of Government?' Unhesitatingly he said: 'The greatest good for the greatest number.' 'And what is the greatest number?' he was asked. 'Number one,' he replied.

The following is part of a discussion on the same question with 9-year-olds:

Lisa:	Governments exist to provide things like roads and schools.
RF:	What happens if governments don't provide them?
Lisa:	If they don't provide them you choose a new government.
Joe:	Governments are there to do things you couldn't do by yourself, like defend yourself against enemies and crooks. That's what the police are for.
Annette:	Yes but the police aren't the government. That's parliament. Parliament controls the police . . . I think.
RF:	OK. So, what's the most important job that a government has got?
Fergus:	To protect people. From burglars and suchlike . . .
Miranda:	They're there to look after you . . .
Joe:	. . . when you can't look after yourself.

But what form should this community of enquiry take? Victor Quinn emphasizes the role of provocation and challenge, the strategy of the teacher playing 'devil's advocate'.[12] To a class of primary children he says: 'Look, I'm bigger and stronger than you, and I can shout louder. So if we have an argument I'll win, won't I?' One child replies, 'No you won't win, 'cos you wouldn't be right . . .' and the discussion takes off. For teachers he throws out this challenge: 'If you believe in free speech then it's right to give a platform in school for the Nazi Party to explain their case.' If a moral education programme is not to be regarded as indoctrination should it not allow the expression of all moral viewpoints? Should a democracy allow the expression of undemocratic views? Should the teacher be 'up front' with his or her own views on what is right and wrong? Should we seek to counter-balance every moral argument? Should we play 'devil's advocate'? Or are there better ways of encouraging moral resiliency in children and of encouraging them to reason about what is right?

Teachers of philosophy in the classroom might differ on their answers to these questions but agree that discussion in a community of enquiry can encourage and support children in the search for meaning and purpose in life, and for values by which they live, and can promote both the search for individual identity and a sense of community. One of the keys to understanding is good communication. Common to the theory and practice of philosophy in the classroom is the aim to develop the skills of speaking and listening. But more it is a means of promoting the curiosity, the inclination to question and the exercise of imagination which are vital for the motivation to learn. There is a close connection between the nourishment of the moral dimension and the development of reason. For children, and for us all, it is not just the question of knowing what is good that is important, but the ability to answer the question 'Why *should* I be, or do what is, good?' Any moral renaissance will be best served by the cultivation of careful thinking in communities of enquiry.

EVALUATING PROGRESS IN A COMMUNITY OF ENQUIRY

There are problems in trying to evaluate the development of any moral culture. Certain indicators such as levels of bullying, disruption or theft might be available. Other observable features would include the evidence of reciprocity in the behaviour of individuals and groups. Reciprocity is shown in the 'give-and-take' of discussion, in the cooperative nature of a community of enquiry. These reciprocal relations link our self-directed thoughts, feelings and actions with the thoughts, feelings and actions of others. Moral development means

Skills of moral reasoning, to help to develop a moral point of view	
Thinking skill	Key question
Imagination – considering all factors, motivation, consequences	'Have we thought of . . .?'
Empathy – thinking of others, reasoning through analogy	'How would you feel if . . .?'
Universalizing – testing the implications of a rule	'What if everybody . . .?'
Anticipating consequences – ends and means	'What if you do . . .?'
Sensitivity to context – special circumstances, instances	'Does it matter when/ where . . .?'
Hypothetical reasoning – considering alternative possibility	'What alternatives are there?'
Giving good reasons – supporting judgements with reasons	'Is it a good enough reason?'
Testing for consistency – re actions and beliefs	'Is the action consistent with beliefs?'
Projecting an ideal world – moral/social/cultural ideals	'Is it a world you'd like to live in?'
Projecting an ideal self – a moral view of oneself	'Is that the person you want to be?'

enabling children to develop a set of values that are both personal, relating to self interest, and public, relating to the interests of others.

Self

One of the key elements of ethical living is autonomy. Autonomy is the capacity for self government. It is indicated by evidence of a child thinking for themselves, for example in taking a minority viewpoint, or in challenging the viewpoint of others. Children are autonomous to the extent that their thinking and actions are truly their own. For some philosophers this freedom from external control is a necessary condition for being truly moral. Others argue that such freedom is an illusion, and that all action is determined by social and personal factors. However, although we may not know all the factors, personal, social or cultural that affect a child, we can observe evidence of progress in a capacity to reason, argue or state a case. We can see evidence of independence in thinking and learning. Children show independence in judgement by taking responsibility for their thoughts and actions. Evidence of this might be seen in the capacity to sustain an argument and to self correct, to show resilience in reasoning in the face of opposition and the openness to admit mistakes.

Autonomy can be shown in children when there is evidence that they are thinking for themselves, when they try to understand their own character, strengths and weaknesses. It shows itself in a developing sense of self esteem, and in the willingness of children to take responsibility for how their lives should be lived. Autonomy can be exemplified in questions such as:

- What do I really think?
- What do I feel about myself (or about the situation)?
- What sort of life do I want to lead?
- What sort of person do I want to be?
- What are my values and my priorities?

Comments from teachers that indicate a growing sense of autonomy in children include:

That is the first time I have heard Jasbir volunteer her own opinion.

Kirsty showed she was able to self correct when she changed her mind and corrected her earlier opinion about what it means to be a friend.

Paul really showed confidence when he stuck out to his opinion against the others . . .

Others

Another sign of reciprocity is empathy, that is the state of being emotionally and cognitively 'in tune' with another person, in particular understanding what their situation is like for them.

We show who we are through our sense of self (autonomy) and through our relationships with others (connectedness). The paradox of human life is that we are both separate as individuals yet connected as part of a culture. We are individuals yet our fulfilment is found in relationships with others. Who we are is partly made up of the culture that we are in and the relationships we have formed. This dichotomy between self and others is reflected in two views of democracy, one identifying democracy with the freedom of the individual to pursue self interest, the other seeing individuals essentially as creators of communities. In any community there is a tension between the right to freedom, and the responsibility towards others. In a community of enquiry the right to freedom is shown in two ways, one in freedom of expression (even when you are wrong), the other is the right to silence, to pass, to listen and not to comment. Responsibility to others is shown through caring behaviour.

Caring requires the exercise of moral imagination, that is the ability to create and rehearse possible situations, to make 'thought experiments' such as putting oneself in the place of another. Caring combined with an understanding of how others think and feel is what we call empathy. This sense of interconnectedness, in which children realize they are one among many with interests and desires like others, is a necessary foil to prejudice and to thinking of people as stereotypes. The kinds of questions that exemplify empathy include:

- How would you (or that other person) feel?
- How would I feel if it happened to me (or to you)?
- What would it be like (or would you think) if you were the other person?
- Have I ensured (are we ensuring) equal opportunities for all?
- How do I show others I respect and value them?

Examples of teachers noting evidence of caring behaviour in discussion include:

Saeed did well to insist that everyone should have a turn to speak.

An example of the way Karen shows empathy was when she said, 'Imagine what it would be like to be that person . . .'

What was significant was the way everyone listened attentively to what others had to say.

Society and beyond

A third related element is the ability to 'decentre' from the self, to look at a situation as it were from above, what Mead calls 'the generalized other', what Singer calls 'the point of view of the universe' or what might be called 'transcendence'. This refers to the ability to transcend individual or group interest to think what would be right for anyone in a given situation. Transcendence relates to the awareness of the concept of justice and to principles of fairness. For some moral theorists, such as Kant and Kohlberg, the highest form of moral reasoning lies in the formulation of universal principles or duties. For others transcendence lies in seeking what is good, right or fair for people in a particular situation.

Transcendence points to an awareness of rights and values that transcend individual interests and desires. Transcendence looks beyond the self interest of individuals or groups such as friends and family, to include the wider society and ultimately a world-view. It is to be conscious of the relationship of human beings not only to each other but to nature, and to understand our duties to other species. The kinds of questions that exemplify a set of transcending values include:

- What would be the consequences of acting this way?
- What are the implications of behaving (or believing) that way?
- What is the right thing to do?
- Would it be right in every circumstance?
- What principle, value or moral, is involved?

Examples of evidence of awareness of universal moral values include:

Anne referring to the principle of doing to others as you would have them do to you.

I liked the way Kerry said if the rule was right for you it was right for everyone.

Paul did not just say it was not fair, he gave a reason why it was a fair rule and in what circumstances it should apply.

Qualities of a moral person	Principles of moral education	Key question
autonomy	thinking for oneself	What is right for me?
empathy	showing care for others	What is right for others?
transcendence	upholding principles of justice	What is right for all?

The link between creative thinking and moral thinking can be summed up in the need to encourage imaginative reasoning. As one child said during a discussion: 'Without an imagination you can't draw, you can't read ... without imagination you can't do anything.' The use of imaginative reasoning is necessary if children are to see themselves not only in relation to others in the present world, but also in the world that *could be*. With the help of others a community of enquiry can help children to transcend the present, to construct an understanding not only of what is but what could be. Participation in a community of enquiry aims to give children the tools they need to question their situation and to begin the search for constructive ways to change or transform it. As one child put it: 'We can make a better world ... the question is: Where do we begin?'

A community of *philosophical* enquiry is a group willing to discuss matters of importance, matters that relate to how they live and learn in their daily lives. During the process signs of change occur. Children learn how to object to unsupported claims and weak reasoning, they learn how to build on and develop the ideas of others, and they learn how to generate alternative world-views that challenge and extend their thinking. Because it is a philosophical enquiry, there is a focus on the underlying concepts of daily experience such as time, space, truth and beauty. As children probe these concepts they learn how to ask relevant questions, detect assumptions, recognize faulty reasoning and gain a sense of competency in their ability to make sense of the world.

Evaluating progress in a community of enquiry

A teacher evaluates the progress of her philosophy class of 6- and 7-year-olds:

Although it is impossible to separate the growth and maturation that has taken place in response to their work in other lessons I feel the children have responded positively to these sessions in a number of ways:

- their general behaviour in the sessions improved
- their readiness to listen to and engage with other children's thoughts increased
- they seem more willing to take risks with their thinking, and to share their thoughts
- they have more sophisticated opinions which they express more clearly
- several quiet or shy children have offered valuable contributions
- an increasing number of original thoughts were expressed in sessions
- the children seemed to become more in tune with each other as persons

Over the year I have become more and more convinced that philosophy for children would make a truly great impact if it were adopted as a whole school approach. In this way all the advantages I saw emerging in this class could be extended and multiplied.

As children begin to internalize the procedures of enquiry with the help of a good model they begin to take over responsibility for running and evaluating the sessions. The teacher's role becomes that of coach and participant rather than leader. In evaluating their own sessions children, in developing rules for running the session and criteria for judging the session, develop the capacity for self correction and self management. A community of enquiry provides a living model of a moral community in action.

One feature of growth in a community of enquiry is evidence of the move from second-order to first-order discourse. First-order discourse is about substantive issues that directly relate to our personal lives, and involve processes such as personal definition of concepts, personal meanings illustrated by personal narrative, and analysis of personal conceptual frameworks. Criteria for deciding if a discussion is first-order discourse include that of personal communicative relevance. The focus of first-order discourse is the development of personal understanding. Examples of this kind of discourse would include discussing personal definitions of friendship, or rules that relate to the way the classroom community operates. Second-order discussion primarily relates to discourse about the discourse of others, mediating the meanings of others rather than one's own meanings, for example by analysing given texts, views and definitions. The focus of second-order discourse is developing understanding of others, of other persons, situations and narratives. Philosophy for Children provides the opportunity for engaging in both first and second-order discourse.

Another feature is teacher involvement in the discussion. Evidence of a maturing community of enquiry is the changing nature of teacher intervention and the growth of autonomy and care in discussion shown by the students. The table opposite summarizes some of the features of the growth of a classroom community.[13]

Genuine values, like all moral points of view, are best created and tested through reflection and sustained enquiry. The community of enquiry provides a model of values in action as well as an opportunity to subject values to critical enquiry. It becomes a powerful means of moral education because values are embedded in the very procedures and moral routines of the enquiry. These are the rational passions or dispositions of critical thinking listed earlier (p. 9) without

Early stage of growth in community	Mature stage of growth in community
Teacher has control of procedures	Responsibility for procedures evenly shared between teacher and students
Teacher dominates the discussion, e.g. through questioning students	Students have increasing share in discussion, e.g. asking questions, building on discussion
Teacher introduces vocabulary of discourse, discussion and reasoning	Students use vocabulary of discourse, discussion and reasoning
Teacher evaluates student responses and quality of discussion	Students evaluate themselves, the contributions of others and progress of the group
Classroom discussion channelled through the teacher	Discussion channelled through more collaborative student–student dialogue
Stimulus materials focus on published stories and novels chosen by teacher	Stimulus includes broader range of materials, some chosen by students
Teacher relies on published materials for follow-up ideas and activities	Teacher creates own follow-up ideas and activities
Focus on whole class as community of enquiry	Use of more flexible arrangements, e.g. group work
Teacher is philosophically self-effacing, i.e. shows 'scholarly ignorance'	Teacher more involved in discussion as a co-enquirer, students show 'scholarly ignorance'
Philosophical discussion limited to lesson time	Philosophical discussion extends beyond lesson, e.g. through journal, homework etc.

which a community of enquiry cannot successfully function. Someone once said that education is what you remember when you have forgotten everything you have been taught.

Children in a community of enquiry learn as much through the act of participation as they do from what they say. As one child remembering his participation in enquiry the previous year put it: 'I remember how we talked and asked questions, and had to give everybody a turn and think about what people had to say in the philosophy class, but I can't remember now what was said.'

NOTES AND REFERENCES

1. MacIntyre, A. (1984), *After Virtue*, London: Duckworth, p. 244.
2. Singer, P. (1983), *Hegel*, Oxford: OUP, pp. 34ff. For an alternative reading which emphasizes Hegel's totalitarian views see Karl Popper (1945), *The Open Society and Its Enemies*, London: Routledge, Vol. 2, pp. 27–81.
3. Ferdinand Tonnies (1855–1936) wrote *Fundamental Concepts of Sociology*.
4. See Senge, P. (1990), *The Fifth Discipline: The Art and Practice of the Learning Organisation*, London: Random House; and Dryden, G. and Vos, J. (1994), *The Learning Revolution*, Aylesbury: Accelerated Learning Systems.
5. Habermas, J. (1990), *Moral Consciousness and Communicative Action*, Cambridge, MA: MIT Press, p. 66. See also Habermas, J. (1996), 'On the cognitive content of morality', Meeting of the Aristotelian Society, London.
6. Publications on moral education include: '*Education for Citzenship*' (National Curriculum Council, 1990) emphasizing the need for education for democracy, and more recently '*Spiritual and Moral Development: A Discussion Paper*' (Schools Curriculum and Assessment Authority, 1995, 1996, 1997).
7. Matthews, G. (1980), *Philosophy and the Young Child*, Cambridge, MA: Harvard University Press.
8. John Burningham's *Would You Rather* is a Penguin/Puffin picture book.

9. Mill, J. S. (1859), *On Liberty*, p. 186.
10. This argument is derived from Cam, P. (1994), 'A philosophical approach to moral education', *Critical and Creative Thinking*, Vol. 2, No. 2, Oct. 1994, pp. 19–26.
11. The Citizenship Foundation has published materials for social and moral education which provide good starting points for community of enquiry work. See Rowe, D. and Newton, J. (1994), *You, Me, Us!: Social and Moral Responsibility for Primary Schools*, London: Home Office/Citizenship Foundation.
12. Quinn, V. (1997), *Critical Thinking and Young Minds*, London: David Fulton.
13. For more on evaluating and assessing growth in community of enquiry see Splitter, L. and Sharp, A. M. (1995), *Teaching for Better Thinking: Community of Inquiry*. Victoria, Australia: ACER, pp. 148ff.

CHAPTER 4

Stories for Thinking: Using stories to develop thinking and literacy

A central thesis then begins to emerge: man is in his actions and practice, as well as his fictions, essentially a story-telling animal . . . a teller of stories that aspire to truth. But the key question for men is not about their authorship; I can only answer the question about 'What am I to do?' if I can answer the prior questions, 'Of what story or stories do I find myself a part?' . . . Deprive children of stories and you leave them unscripted, anxious stutterers in their actions as in their words. Hence there is no way of giving us an understanding of any society, including our own, except through the stock of stories which constitute its initial dramatic resources.

Alistair MacIntyre, *After Virtue*

I like discussing stories because it gives me a chance to share my thoughts with others.

Danielle, aged 9

Paul was a reluctant reader. At the age of seven he was struggling to read simple words. He would rarely look at a book voluntarily, and did not seem keen to be part of the new kind of lesson he was having called philosophy. When his turn came to read the next part of the story he said 'Pass'. As he sat listening to others discuss the story suddenly his hand shot up: 'Oh I get it', he said, 'we're not supposed to read the story we're supposed to think about it!' From that point on Paul became a participator in the Stories for Thinking lesson where reading was no longer just a matter of decoding the words on a page but thinking about what the words meant. Paul could now participate as a text user and text analyst, and practise skills characteristic of able and literate readers.

Stories have long been seen as a natural stimulus for discussion, investigation and problem-solving in schools.[1] Stories provide the most common starting point for philosophy with children, and a natural means for developing thinking, learning and language skills. To be full participants in a literate, democratic, multicultural society citizens of the future will require abilities to reflect, to think critically, to question the information they are given and to be flexible and creative in their approach to solving problems. If one of our purposes is to invite children into the club of critical thinkers and readers, then we need to show children models of critical reading, and introduce them to contexts where higher-order thinking is practised and valued. And we have strong pedagogical reasons for doing so. Studies of the most literate and able children show that they have aspects of knowledge and skills or competencies that less successful learners do not have.[2] These include:

- knowledge of literary forms, purposes and genre, including metalinguistic knowledge
- skills and strategies for processing literary knowledge, including the ability to question, interrogate and discuss narrative texts
- ability to apply and transfer their skills of narrative enquiry to other contexts

But how do stories help develop this metalinguistic awareness?

WHY USE STORIES?

Narrative comprehension is one of the earliest powers to appear in the mind of the young child, and is the most widely used way of organizing human experience. The power of stories resides in their ability to create possible worlds as objects of intellectual inquiry. Stories liberate us from the here-and-now, they are intellectual constructions but they are also life-like. They are intellectually challenging, but also embedded in human concerns. Stories provide a means to understand the world and to understand ourselves. No wonder they are the primary means of teaching in every human society.

All the great stories of humanity have the capacity to relate to the concerns and needs of people at different stages of development. They are 'polysemic', that is they have within them layers or levels of meaning and significance which we become aware of as we grow in experience and insight. We can turn to them again and again, for fresh insight about the basic philosophical questions about what we know and believe, about right and wrong, about human relationships and the self which are of relevance to people at all ages and stages of life. One reason we relate to stories is that they provide metaphors for our own life. As Anne, aged 7, says, 'a story is something that might happen to you.'

Human life can be regarded as a story, a narrative structured in which everyone has a part. In existentialist terms the fact of death gives narrative structure to life. To understand the narrative structure of stories, or of human lives, requires more than the exercise of human reason, it requires what Egan calls 'the other half of the child', namely imagination. When Dewey argued for education through experience, he envisaged such experience should include imaginative experience gained from stories. But what is a story, and what experience should be gained from stories?

Egan argues that a defining characteristic of a story is that it is a 'linguistic unit that can ultimately fix the affective meaning of the events that compose it.'[3] In a well-crafted story our affective responses are orchestrated by the events in the narrative. It is this 'affective meaning' that Egan sees as the unique characteristic of a story plot.[4] One reason why stories have this affective power is that stories have, as Egan says, a crucial feature which life and history lack, that they have beginnings and ends and so can fix meanings to events. Stories are in a sense 'given' in a way that life, with its messiness and incompleteness, is not. Unlike the complexity of everyday events stories end. What makes them stories is that their ending completes (in a rational sense) or satisfies (in an affective sense) whatever was introduced at the beginning and elaborated in the middle. As Kafka said: 'The meaning of life is that it stops.' As the Greeks had it: 'Call no man happy until he is dead.' Or in the words of Abigail, aged 8, 'In stories you don't know what happens until the end, but you know you are going to find out.'

What Egan is referring to is the simple traditional story form. His analysis works less well, and needs to be supplemented, when considering both more complex narratives which mix historical and other elements in fictional/factual forms, and also the attenuated narratives of Lipman's philosophical novels. However, the affective response can be seen to be characteristic of story, and of every aesthetic experience. A good story evokes what Pierce called an 'intellectual sympathy, a sense that here is a feeling that one can comprehend, a reasonable feeling'. Bettelheim said of fairy stories that a child's choices are based, not so much on right versus wrong, as who arouses his sympathy, and who his antipathy. For Egan the affective power of stories lies in the binary opposites such as love/hate, life/death, hope/despair, good/bad, true/false embodied in the most powerful of stories, such as traditional myths and fairy tales. These binary opposites act as structural devices, syntactical elements in the underlying grammar of stories and provide reference points for meaning.

Stories are not only powerful in the affective domain, but also provide potentially complex challenges for cognitive processing. Since a story contains many different elements, objects and relationships, which unfold in a specific sequence of events, for a young child it can be the most complex object of thought in their experience. To grasp and digest a story requires repeated acts of focal attention and efforts of understanding. The child's assimilation of the story requires a complex labour of attention and thought, and is the product of innumerable acts of focal attention to the story as a whole and its different parts, and to the child's affective responses to the story. For the young child the story is a piece of reality on which the child can rely, which is perhaps why getting the story right and hearing it repeated is so important. Later the child learns that stories can be made, changed and recreated in different forms. This issue of re-telling and re-constructing stories is one way of using stories for philosophical discussion. Part of the cognitive challenge comes from not only making sense of the narrative elements of the story but also the various possible relations between the story and reality. Through interrogating a narrative we can come to learn more about the story, but in a philosophical sense we may also come to learn more about the world and about ourselves. A teacher was reading *Winnie the Pooh* to her class and reached the point where Piglet's grandfather is said to have two names 'in case he lost one'. The teacher paused and asked 'Can you lose a name?' There was a pause for thought and a shaking of heads. Suddenly a hand went up, 'You could if you forgot it!'[5]

One of the chief benefits of using story as a stimulus for thinking in the classroom is that a good story arouses the interest and involvement of the child. For Whitehead[6] this was an essential first stage in what he argued should be the 'Cycle of Learning', whose stages he identified as follows:

Stage 1: *Romance* – involving arousal of interest and learner involvement

Stage 2: *Precision* – where attention is given to the details of what is being learnt

Stage 3: *Generalization* – where what is learned is applied and used

What stories for thinking should provide for young children is *romance*, an engagement of the learner in a narrative context, a motivation to be involved and to find out more. In stories there is an important link between memory, emotion and imagination. If a story is worthy then the children will be emotionally committed to it. If children are affected by the story-line their engagement will ensure a pathway to accessing its content, and its potential for thinking and learning.

Stories for Thinking: what they provide

Stories for Thinking can be seen as a means of providing:

- a love of literature through exposure to familiar story forms
- a context for critical thinking and discussion on issues of importance
- a community of shared reading and enquiry
- an awareness of our multicultural heritage of stories and books
- a stimulus to imagination, to verbal and visual creativity
- a contribution to knowledge about language, its forms and uses at word, sentence and text level
- an opportunity to practise active listening and speaking skills

---

The fantasy element of stories allows children to reflect more clearly on real experiences through powerful imaginary experience. Donaldson observes that there exists 'a fundamental human urge to make sense of the world and bring it under deliberate control'. She argues that this urge for children to make meaning is best served in contexts not totally 'disembedded' from their world of experience. Stories, when comprehensible to children, have the advantage of being embedded in human concerns such as characters, events and experiences, and yet offer the child the chance to 'decentre' from the immediacy of their own personal lives. They become able to look at themselves through looking at and thinking about others. The processes through which this is achieved can be summed up as:

- *questioning the story* – interrogating the narrative text or story
- *interpreting the story* – seeking precise meanings and giving reasons for judgements

- *discussing issues arising from the story* – finding answers to questions that have arisen

---

What sort of person was Jack? Thinking about character

The following example of discussion is from an enquiry into the story of Jack and the Beanstalk with a class of 6- to 7-year-olds:

RF:	What sort of person was Jack?
Faisal:	He was clever.
RF:	Why do you think he was clever?
Richard:	Because he climbed up the beanstalk.
RF:	Why did he climb up the beanstalk?
Chantal:	He was curious. He wanted to see what was up there.
RF:	What does being 'curious' mean?
Emma:	It means you want to find out things you don't know.
Paul:	I think Jack was curious and clever because he thought of a way to escape, and he was curious to see what was up the beanstalk.

(Later in the discussion, the class considered whether Jack was greedy.)

RF:	Do you think Jack was greedy?
Kelly:	Jack was greedy because he stole the giant's gold.
Leigh:	I disagree with Kelly. I don't think Jack was greedy because he was punishing the giant for killing his father. He is not being greedy, he's just doing what he thinks is right.
Jason:	I agree with Kelly and disagree with Leigh. It's not right to steal things, so he was greedy.

(The discussion ends with children taking turns to sum up their final thoughts.)

Alex:	Sometimes Jack was clever, sometimes he was curious and sometimes he was brave. Like most people really.

WHAT PROBLEMS DO STORIES POSE?

According to Eisner all learning requires the translation of human 'imagination into some public, stable form, something that can be shared with others'.[7] Stories and narrative texts are human constructions. What makes narrative problematical is that unlike logical or scientific constructions which can be tested against standards of empirical verification or logical necessity, narrative constructions can only achieve 'verisimilitude' to reality. Because stories and texts are human constructions they require an act of translation, of critical reading and questioning if they are to be made meaningful by the hearer or reader. The meaning of a story is not transparent, it must be re-constructed in the mind. There are several elements to narrative constructions that are open to interrogation.

An enquiry into a story progresses, like the application of thought processes to any body of material or experience through the formulation of questions. It is questions that focus attention on, probe and establish the significance of things, and through which one becomes not simply a passive onlooker but a witness able to report on experience. Kierkegaard, writing in 1837, argued that the procedure for story-telling to children should 'as much as possible, be Socratic, one should arouse in children a desire to ask questions'. But what kinds of questions?

Different sorts of questions that can be used to interrogate a text include:

1. *Factual or text-explicit questions* – where features of the text are explicitly questioned, usually requiring naming and information at the literal level. Such questions are often begin with 'What . . .?'
2. *Reasoning or text-implicit questions* – which question the hidden meanings, reading 'between the lines', and requiring inferences to be drawn. Such questions often begin 'How . . .?' or 'Why . . .?'
3. *Open or opinion questions* – which do not necessarily call for reasons but for judgements, where for example opinions or feelings about the text are being sought, or where readers

101

are reading 'beyond the lines' to question their own or others' experiences.

Researchers in classrooms have observed a predominance of factual rather than reasoning or open questions in lessons such as English, history, RE and maths. Only in science did they find reasoning questions predominant.[8] Factual questions are often useful as an opening for reasoning, and should be woven into a longer process of enquiry. Since every utterance is embedded within a context of discussion which includes previous utterances and subsequent utterances it follows that questions can only be fully understood within extended dialogue.[9] In looking at examples of interrogating text through dialogue we need therefore not to look at isolated exchanges but more at 'epistemic episodes' within the dialogue (see p. 260 for more on ways of analysing classroom discussion).

What is crucial in determining the use of function of a question is the response it evokes. What philosophical enquiry aims to achieve is a text-implicit open investigation through the use of discussion, evoking a pattern of responses which provide evidence of shared enquiry and reasoning. The overall sequence of this shared enquiry, however, does not rely solely on open or reasoning questions. A variety of questioning forms include rhetorical questions, such as: 'Why is that character saying that?', and statements can have an implicit questioning function during a discussion. A statement that proposes a hypothesis, such as: 'Every rule they say has an exception', may be an invitation to a judgement, e.g. 'Can you think of an exception?'

Why is it that in many learning situations it is the teachers who ask the questions, and the learners who should have most to ask remain silent? Is it because children lack the ability to formulate questions, or because they lack the authority of sanctioned knowledge, or because questioning is not what is expected of them? Questioning can require intellectual courage, my question may be silly or inappropriate, so it is better if I wait to see if it is articulated by another student or by the teacher. We need therefore to offer children discourse practices which legitimate and facilitate their practice in questioning, and provide models of enquiry that students can internalize and apply for themselves. More on the use of questioning will be found in the next chapter, what concerns us here are the problematic features of story that we want students to be aware of and to interrogate through the questions they ask.

What is a story?

Discussion plan for an enquiry into stories:

1. Stories often begin 'Once upon a time' – what does that mean?
2. Do all stories have a beginning, a middle, an end?
3. Could a story have no beginning, only a middle and end?
4. Could a story have no end, or more than one ending?
5. Are some stories true, and some make-believe?
6. How can you tell if a story is true or make-believe?
7. Are some stories good, and some not good – what makes a good story?
8. Are all stories made up by someone?
9. Does everything have a story, e.g. your desk, home, family?
10. Can a story have a story?

(From *Stories for Thinking* by Robert Fisher, p. 101)

Because stories are human constructions they require an act of translation if they are to made meaningful by the hearer or reader. The meaning of a story must be re-constructed in the mind. There are several elements to narrative constructions that are open to reflection, interpretation and discussion.

The following are some of the problematic features of a story:

- contexts
- temporal order
- particular events
- intentions
- choices
- meanings
- the telling

Contexts

What kind of world is this?

Matthew, aged 10

A story is set in a fictional context that aspires to the reality of a possible world, albeit an imagined world. All stories are related in some way to the human experience of time, place and society. Some stories, such as Aesop's fables, exist in a world of ordinary events that appear almost timeless. But even these may contain in their telling elements of particular social, historical and cultural contexts. What is unique to any story is when it happened, where it happened and to whom it happened. The characters will have uniquely personal experiences, but also be functioning in particular social, cultural and political contexts and be holding shared views derived from their particular cultural context. The narrative context, about who is in the story and what happened, will require an understanding of the story at a literal level, but will also need to be further interrogated and interpreted if all the implicit meanings and messages are to be fully understood.

Questions to help children understand the contexts of a story include:

When does the story take place?	(historical context: time)
Where does it take place?	(geographical context: place)
Who is in the story? Who is the story about?	(narrative context: society of characters)
What is the relationship between the characters?	(social context: relationships/ interaction)
What did the character feel, think and believe?	(experiential context: individual view)
What did they *all* feel, think or believe?	(cultural context: shared view)
Who has the power and authority in the story?	(political context: who has power?)

A key question in relation to all these contexts is:

How was it different in that time, place or society?	(compare the story context with your own)

Temporal order

> I wonder what happened before the beginning of the story?
>
> Christopher, aged 9

All stories exhibit what Bruner calls 'narrative diachronicity'. They all express a unique pattern of events over time. Sometimes these events are chronological, but they occur in 'human time' rather than in 'clock time', that is time made significant by the human meaning of events which it encompasses.[10] There are many conventions in which temporal order can be expressed, for example 'Once upon a time . . .', flashbacks, flash-forwards and so on. To ask children to reconstruct the temporal events of a story is to do more than merely to exercise their memory, it is to provide the challenging task of narrative reconstruction and meaning-making. And as anyone who has asked a group of children to do this with a familiar story knows, it can provide a stimulus for much argument and debate. All stories express a unique pattern of events over time. Sometimes these events are chronological, but they occur in 'human time' rather than in 'clock time', that is time made significant by the human meaning of events in the plot.

Questions to help children comprehend the temporal order of a story include:

What does 'Once upon a time' mean?
Who remembers what happened in the story?
What happened in the beginning/middle/end?

Particular events

> 'Why do things happen the way they do?'
>
> Dawn, aged 8

Stories are governed by what Bruner calls the principle of 'particularity', that is they take as their ostensive reference particular happenings. These particular events fall into patterns that become story types and genre. Each particular event, and groups or patterns of events are open to interpretation. The usual locus of the drama of a story is trouble or conflict of some kind. And of particular relevance in any story are precipitating events, which cause as it were an imbalance or disharmony, and where the problematic nature of life becomes apparent. It is in the comprehending of particular problems through interpretation that the educative power of stories lay, and not simply an understanding of what Kermode calls the 'consoling plot'.[11]

The events in a story constitute the genre, that is the loose but conventional way that generic aspects of the human situation are represented in narrative. The genre of the text may be open to question, indeed any text may relate to a number of genres. A genre is not just a property of the text but is a way of interpreting and coming to understand the text. It follows that there can be different versions of any text or event. Indeed there may be competing versions of a story or any event within a narrative, and the negotiation between different narrative versions is essential in social understanding and in understanding the nature of fiction. This process of developing understanding about the nature of narrative is gradual, but it can be helped by reflecting on and interpreting the particular events that make up stories.

The following questions can help encourage interpretation of particular events in stories:

What kind of event/episode/story is it?
Why did this event happen/what caused it?
What exactly happened?
What could have happened?
What should have happened?
What could/should happen next?

Intentions

Why did she say what she said?

Rajiv, aged 9

Stories are about people (or animals, robots, magical beings etc.) with intentional states such as beliefs, desires, theories, values and so on. Problems arise because it is not always clear what a given character's intentional states are, and even when they are clear the intentional states do not necessarily determine events. Because the links between intentions and actions are loose, narrative accounts do not offer complete causal explanations. Human intentionality presupposes some element of choice or freedom to choose. We can only interpret by reflecting from our own experience how a character feels or what s/he perceives in a given situation and the reasons for things happening as they do in the story. In a sense every outer adventure has an inner adventure, which is represented in the hidden mental processes of the characters.

The importance of such interpretative dialogue is relevant not only to knowledge about texts but also to the child's understanding of other minds. It therefore has a metacognitive function, as well as a philosophical function to aid thinking about thinking.

Such interpretative discussion could be informed by questions such as:

What does X believe?
What does X want?
What does X think . . .?
What does X want others to think?
What reasons would X give?
What does X think that Y should do?
Why does X think that?
What does X hope will happen?

Choices

Did they have any choice?

Anthony, aged 9

Part of the power of a story lies in its 'narrative drive', the anticipatory pleasure we have in wondering what will happen next. This is partly because we know events in stories as in lives are unpredictable, and partly because in any human life or narrative choices have to be made. All plots have decisive moments, which may involve a character making a choice or decision that alters the path of the story, perhaps in response to an invitation, a threat or a challenge. Should the hero set out on the quest? Should the parents of the princess in Sleeping Beauty tell her of the witch's curse about pricking her finger, or simply keep her away from spinning wheels? Where decisions spring from human intentions the actions will have moral consequences. There may also be unforeseen consequences. So any story can become a vehicle for moral or ethical enquiry. What moral questions or dilemmas does the story pose? Who is responsible for what happens? What consequences were there?

Questions to focus attention on decisions or choices in the story include:

What is the decisive moment in the story?
What choices or decisions have to be made?
Who has to make the choice(s)?
What could they do? What alternative choices or decisions are there?
What should they do? What choice would you make?
What choices were made? What were the consequences?
Were they the right choices? Why?

After reflecting on the moral contexts of a story we might want to ask whether these relate in any way to our own lives and whether any moral message could be drawn from the story.

Meanings

What does the story mean?

Holly, aged 7

A successful story is a whole, it has coherence, and like any construct can be studied as a whole. Bruner uses the term 'hermeneutic composability' to refer to the meaning or function of the text as a whole.[12] Unfortunately the word 'hermeneutic' implies that a story or text is a construct through which somebody is trying to express a meaning, or from which some 'message' can be extracted. However, there is no method of assuring the 'truth' of a meaning assigned to a story, or any way that logically or empirically the constituent elements of a story can be said to compose a meaning. There is as Bruner says a textual interdependence in any story between the whole and the parts both in construction and comprehension. The more complex a text in terms of constituent elements the more opportunity there is for textual or referential ambiguity.

This is not so with all stories. Barthes contrasts 'readerly' texts which are part of a well-known and well-rehearsed canon, such as stock kinds of folk-tale, e.g. 'tall stories', and 'writerly' ones that challenge the reader to interpret ambiguous elements in trying to make meaning of the narrative.[13] However, there is in the most readerly text a meta-discourse relating to the intentions of the author – why the story is told, and the contextual issue of politico-social conditions – background knowledge of where and when the story was created. Every story inhabits a world. How is this world like or unlike our world?

Other questions to help children interpret the meanings of a story might include:

What kind of story is it?
Who do you think wrote/told it first?
Where does the story come from?
Can you think of a/another title to the story?
What would you say the story was about?
Is there anything puzzling about the story?
What does this story tell us . . .?
What does the author/story not tell us?
What is the message (or moral) of the story?
In what ways is it like/unlike other stories?

The telling

Who is telling the story?

Asim, aged 8

Another element of narrative analysis is the distinction between the narrative plot, and its mode of telling.[14] A genre is not only a form of plot, but is also a style of telling. In a sense there are only a basic number of plots, but infinite ways in which they can be told. It has been argued that 'the function of inventive narrative is not so much to "fabulate" new plots as to render previously familiar ones uncertain or problematical.'[15] The storyteller or writer's task is in a sense to make the ordinary strange, to challenge the reader into an interpretative response. Any story is heavily influenced by narrative traditions, but good stories exhibit creative innovation, go beyond conventional scripts, leading people to see things in fresh ways. This can be in terms of the twists of a plot, or in the style of telling. This involves evaluation not only of the plot – what happened in the story – but also why it was worth telling and how it was told. Some accounts are poorly told, they are not story-like and are said to be 'pointless'. Others involve innovation of content or style – a breach of expectations – to create something that is unique and rewarding.

Questions to aid interpretation of the telling might include:

Was there anything special about the story?
Was it a well-told story?
Have you heard other stories like this?
What was different about this story?
Could you tell this story in a different way?
How would you change the characters or events?
If you told the story differently would it be the same story?

Reading and listening to stories create a mental space for thinking. But it is the quality of thinking that should concern us. Likewise all good fictions stimulate mental acts such as supposing, guessing and judging. If we restrict children to the inner voice of their own private judgements then we limit the opportunities for mental response that good texts offer. Reading is not over once the text is read, but continues through reflection, interpretation and discussion. Any story or book that children read can become a story for thinking if a teacher or reading partner follows the story up with questions for discussion. Many of the best questions will come from the children themselves.

By interrogating a text in a community of enquiry children learn that a story usually contains many more questions or problems than they first thought, and that questions (and answers) beget further questions in a dynamic and potentially endless process of enquiry. Through offering children discourse practices which legitimate and facilitate questioning, children learn how to question any kind of story or text.

But which stories or texts to use? Do some kinds of story have a richer potential for enquiry?

WHAT STORIES TO USE? – STORY MATERIALS AND TEXTS SUITABLE FOR PHILOSOPHICAL INQUIRY

A wide range of stories and texts can be used to stimulate philosophical discussion with children at home or school. The following kinds of narrative material were used as a stimulus for philosophy with 6- to 12-year-old children in the recent Philosophy in Primary Schools (PIPS) project:

* philosophical novels
* traditional stories
* children's fiction
* picture books
* curriculum-based narrative
* poetry
* pictures and photos
* artefacts and objects
* drama, role play and first-hand experience
* music
* TV and video
* factual narrative

Philosophical novels

The most popular philosophical novel used with primary-aged children is Lipman's *Pixie* which is well suited for work with children 8–10 years old. The first philosophical novel that Matthew Lipman wrote was *Harry Stottlemeier's Discovery*, published in 1974, which became the foundation for his Philosophy for Children curriculum. It remains the most popular of his texts for use with children for children aged 11–13 years. Other philosophical novels have been written for use with children, including Jostein Gaarder's best-seller *Sophie's World*, for 14- to 16-year-olds, which combines a story with a history of philosophy for teenagers but which has been used successfully to stimulate discussion with children as young as seven.[16]

Lipman identifies three requirements he considers essential for texts suitable for philosophical inquiry – literary

111

acceptability, psychological acceptability and intellectual acceptability. Of literary acceptability Lipman suggests that the literary quality of the text should be 'passable'. Judged by this criteria many teachers and students involved in the PIPS project felt that Lipman's novels provided good starting points for philosophical discussion but lacked sufficient literary merit to sustain student interest over time. Lipman argues that it is the lack of discursive literary elements which gives the novels their clear intellectual focus. He looks forward to a time when major writers would consider it a challenge to write textbooks for children.

Psychological acceptability is seen by Lipman to relate to the age-appropriateness of the story. He says of psychological acceptability that the response to the Philosophy for Children programme shows that children of all ages find complex ideas such as true, fair, good, right and person interesting as issues to discuss.

Intellectual acceptability relates to the problematic nature of the text. For Lipman a dialogical text, made up of constructed conversations, can contain ambiguity, innuendo, irony, and many other qualities that other prose lacks. Constructed conversations, as Plato and other philosophers have found, provide opportunities for intellectual challenge. Lipman's novels are special for they provide models of conversational inquiry and thoughtfulness, seeded with philosophical puzzles. Can other kinds of narrative material provide similar kinds of intellectual challenge?

Traditional stories

The telling of folk tales and fairy tales is a communicative act that crosses the boundaries of time and culture. Their function has been to entertain but also to educate as a vehicle for culturally shared knowledge, feelings, thoughts and imaginings. Fairy stories have a key role to play in children's social cognition and developing theories of mind, particularly in certain tales like Rumpelstiltskin which is quite complex in terms of its recursive structure, in its internal state vocabulary and its metacognitive language. Characters often do not know what other characters are thinking, and many entertain false beliefs about what other characters are thinking and feeling. Simple tales can contain complex and ambiguous psychological themes, which is of course why they can be powerful as narratives.

The purpose of literature, like the purpose of education, should be to help us find meaning in our lives, in particular to answer questions that are essentially philosophical – 'Who am I?', 'Why am I here?', 'What can I be?' Fairy tales offer new dimensions to the child's imagination. The message of fairy tales can be summed up as: if you have courage and persist you can overcome any obstacle to achieve your heart's desire. Discussing the obstacles and problems encountered by characters in fairy tales can help children understand and overcome the obstacles and problems they may face in their own lives. But it can be argued that traditional stories contain messages that entertain children rather than liberate them. A mode of oppression is built into many traditional stories, such as those of Grimm and Anderson, which limits imaginative thinking. This oppression takes the form in many stories of children experiencing some form of abuse – such as being kidnapped, abandoned or persecuted. Feminist critics argue against the stereotyping of girls in traditional tales, and that the passivity of female characters provides poor role models. Stories like Cinderella, it is argued, perpetuate stereotypes of passive, housekeeping females waiting for a charming prince to make their lives worthwhile. What critics of fairy tales alert us to is the need to develop a critical response to traditional tales – and to broaden the range of children's literary experience.[17] Critical discussion in a community of enquiry can help children to become aware of and to question traditional roles and stereotypes.

The content of many traditional tales may be problematical, and strategies that involve simple storytelling may not encourage children to think critically about the stories and the messages they contain. Stories pose problems of interpretation, and in a sense reading is never completed, but is constantly under review and open to change. Stories are ideal for critical and dialogical inquiry, and as a way in to the criticism both of narrative and of cultural forms. Many modern stories and picture books challenge cultural stereotypes and conventional adult views of the world. A community of inquiry may provide the framework children need to encourage attention to linguistic meanings, and to a search for general principles to explain specific events in the narrative and to challenge the story stereotypes being offered. Teachers do this by asking, and encouraging children to ask questions about: what does the story say (literal meaning), and what do the messages of the story say (symbolic interpretation)? Traditional tales and other forms of fiction can provide a good stimulus discussion which can help even very young children become philosophically sensitive to the complexities of stories and of life.

When 5-year-olds were asked whether fairy godmothers were real or not real, one child replied: 'In the world fairy godmothers are not real. But in stories they are real.' Older children too can respond to the complex themes in traditional stories with interesting questions for thinking and discussion.

What questions could you ask about the story of Cinderella?

The following are some 'thinking questions' suggested by a class of 10- to 11-year-old children to help younger children reflect on the Cinderella story:

Why did the sisters dislike Cinderella?
Why were they jealous?
Why were they so horrible?
What did the sisters think?
What did they say?
How did Cinderella feel?
What would you do if you were Cinderella?
Why has the prince not married?
Why does the king want the prince to marry?
Was it a good idea to have a ball? Why?
What is a fairy godmother?
Why did the fairy godmother go to see Cinderella?
How did she do her magic?
Is there really such a thing as magic?
What would you wish for if you had a fairy godmother?
Why did Cinderella have to leave at 12 (midnight)?
Why did the prince fall in love with her?
Why did the sisters pretend they could put the shoe on?
How might the story have ended?
Did they live happily ever after?

Some philosophical ideas to explore in Cinderella

What do words mean like being 'jealous'?
What do people think? Can we know what they think?
What do they feel? Can we know what they feel?
Why do they think, feel and say that? Do we know why?
Why do people act the way they do?
What do they believe? Why?
What do they want? Why?
What would it be like being someone else?
Is it right that they should behave like this?
What (philosophical) questions could you ask about this story?

Children's fiction

Lipman argues against the use of existing children's literature when teaching philosophy to children. He distinguishes between children's need for literal meaning (scientific explanation), symbolic meaning (the kinds to be found in fairy tales, fantasy and folklore) and philosophical meaning which is neither literal or symbolic but is essentially metaphysical, logical or ethical. Children's fiction is suitable, he suggests, for literal and symbolic meaning, but not for philosophical inquiry, which is best facilitated through 'philosophical novels'. However, much of the best of children's fiction includes metaphysical themes such as time, space and human identity; logical themes to do with informal reasoning and the interpretation of meaning; and ethical themes to do with the rightness of actions and moral judgements. It may be that Lipman's novels express these themes in a more expository way, but at the expense of the motivating and imaginatively nourishing qualities of the best of children's fiction.

There is a sense in which any fictional text can serve as a basis for philosophical discussion. At its best reading a story involves wondering what might happen, asking 'what if' in the open dialogue of speech, or the inner dialogue of imagination. Reading creates a mental space for thinking. But it is the quality of thinking that should concern us. To read is to think about meaning, but as any reader of Enid Blyton or Agatha Christie can attest such a process can be enjoyed at a fairly automatic and unreflective level. If to read a book is, in a sense, imaginatively to recreate or rewrite it then we need to expose children to the most challenging forms of fiction. We also need to invite them to become critical thinkers by providing opportunities to discuss and extend the meanings to be found in texts.

Narrative and argument are inter-dependent. Stories often contain hidden argument. To understand a Sherlock Holmes or Agatha Christie we need to go through the reasoning behind the events in the story to explain the conclusions to ourselves.

What questions would you ask about *Metamorphosis* by Kafka?

Some questions about a Kafka story that a teacher devised to share with her class of 12- to 13-year-olds:

Think about what is strange or puzzling about the story.
Write down as many questions as you can in response to the story.
Think about the *categories* into which you would put these questions.
Do some questions fit several categories? How and in what ways?
Which questions do you think are literal (about features of the text) and which philosophical (about contestable concepts and general issues)?

Here are questions from a list prepared by a teacher which she categorized as philosophical:

- How did he know that he still was not dreaming?
- What caused him to change?
- Why didn't he change completely?
- Can you change completely?
- Is there a difference between change and metamorphosis? (Why call it 'Metamorphosis')?
- Does loving someone mean allowing them to change?
- Is change a state of mind?

Note: The first part of Kafka's story can be found in *Stories for Thinking* (Fisher, 1996), p. 33. An excerpt from a classroom discussion with children appears below on p. 126.

Likewise all good fictions stimulate mental acts such as supposing, guessing and judging. If we restrict children to the inner voice of their own private judgements then we limit the opportunities for mental response that good texts offer. Reading is not necessarily over once the text is finished, but can continue through reflection, interpretation, discussion and creative activity. Text talk should aim to deepen understanding both of what is read, and of the world. Discussion in a community of inquiry can help make reading a social event, a publicly shared thinking about reading. But can fiction not written for philosophic purposes be used for philosophy? If so, what fiction is suitable?

Both classic children's fiction like *Alice in Wonderland*, *The Wizard of Oz* and *The Happy Prince*, and modern fiction like *The Iron Man* by Ted Hughes or *The Pearl* by John Steinbeck can be used to generate thinking and philosophical discussion with older children. One way to begin is to choose part of one of your favourite stories and prepare some questions about it to share and discuss with children.

Picture books

Lipman's novels contain no pictures. He explains that he has resisted putting illustrations in the children's books because he feels that to do so is to do for children what they should do for themselves, namely provide the imagery that accompanies reading and interpretation. It is true that pictures in a book can seem discontinuous with the text. This may be because the verbal and the visual are two distinct forms of intelligence, and need to be processed in different parts of the brain. This discontinuity may, as Lipman suggests, be due to the illustration being an impoverished representation of what we can visualize in our 'mind's eye'. However, pictures that are of quality and well-integrated in the text can add dimensions of meaning to a story.

One reason why philosophers, including Lipman, eschew illustration is that pictures are non-propositional. Pictures do not contain within them propositional units of meaning the way sentences do. But meaning is not something that only words and sentences have. Pictures demand interpretation, and the active construction of meaning. Meanings are not 'given' but must be re-constructed in the mind of the viewer (as in a different medium the meaning of a text must be created in the mind of the reader). In a picture book such as *Would you rather...?* by John Burningham the text shows one kind of meaning and pictures another. The combination of two kinds of interpretation creates its own challenge. Many picture books prise open the gap between the words and the pictures, forcing the reader/viewer to work hard to forge a conceptual and narrative relationship between them. Picture books without words can provide a powerful incentive for visual thinking and for the translation of the visual into the verbal. 'I can see what I mean,' said Sarah, aged 7, 'but I find it hard to put it into words.' Or as Brendan, also 7, says: 'I can see more than I can say.'

For young children, and for occasional use with older students, picture books, particularly classic books like *Not Now Bernard* (David McKee) or *Where the Wild Things Are* (Maurice Sendak) can provide a powerful stimulus for philosophical inquiry.[18]

Curriculum-based narrative

All curriculum subjects contain narrative elements which can provide a stimulus for philosophical discussion. The *Stories for Thinking* material includes stories related to themes in history (such as the story of Catherine Howard in Tudor times), art (such as the story of the Willow Pattern design), and religious education (such as the Christian parable of the workers in the vineyard). More on the use of curriculum-based material to stimulate philosophical enquiry can be found in Chapter 7.

Poetry

'Poetry begins in delight and ends in wisdom' said the American poet Robert Frost. Poetry has the benefit of concision. Metaphors, meanings and images are often compressed. If poems comprise 'the best words in the best order' the challenge for the reader remains: What do the words mean? What story is the poem telling? What problems does the poem pose?

One element of the *Stories for Thinking* programme is *Poems for Thinking* (1997), a book which offers poems and guidelines for critical discussion in a community of inquiry. Further discussion of the role of poetry for philosophy will be found in Chapter 7 (p. 206).

Pictures and photos

Works of art, or reproductions of works of art such as photos from colour magazines, and popular art forms such as cartoons can serve as a basis for community of inquiry. As with litera-ture a work of visual art can be interrogated in terms of meanings, intention and content. Using pictures, photos and art objects in a community of enquiry can enrich personal aesthetic experience through shared communication and enquiry. As one child said of a picture he was studying with a partner: 'Sometimes I don't really know what I think about it until I talk about it.'

In terms of art education the practice of art is not sufficient to gain a full experience of art. Children need to take on the dual roles of practising artist and critic. The uncritical assimi-lation (or rejection) of visual information and the unthinking application of skills are not enough. Pupils need to think for themselves, deeply and personally, about their aesthetic expe-riences; what they are hearing, seeing, and doing. As a child said after experiencing discussion of artwork in a community of enquiry: 'I didn't know *how* to talk about art until we talked about it together. All I could say was "Yes, I like it" or "No, I don't like it." Now I can say why.'

Teachers need to provide sessions solely for discussion of artworks, and the *Stories for Thinking* programme will include a *Pictures for Thinking* resource to add to the growing litera-ture on ways to help children engage in close observation, interpretation and critical discussion about works of art. For more on the link between philosophy and art see Chapter 7 (p. 228).

Artefacts and objects

Any object or artefact can be of narrative interest to the enquiring mind. Someone once said that if you were to know everything there was to be known about any one object you would come to know everything there was to be known about every object. Any object, either natural or designed, can become an object of intellectual inquiry. What questions can be posed about a chosen object? Which of these questions is philosophical?

Any object, products or artefacts could be used as a stimulus for reflection and inquiry. One group of 6-year-olds sat in a thinking circle in the middle of which the teacher placed a cauliflower. 'What questions' she said, 'could you ask this cauliflower?' The children made a number of comments and questions, including 'Can a cauliflower think?', 'Does the cauliflower want to say anything?' and 'What is it like being a cauliflower?' The discussion that followed centred on the ways in which human beings and cauliflowers are similar and different. The children may not have come to any deep metaphysical insights during the session, but perhaps never viewed a cauliflower in quite the same way again!

A teacher with 9- to 10-year-old children passed a football around her thinking circle and said 'Here is Fred. When he is passed to you can ask him a question.' Because the class were used to community of enquiry methods, almost all had a question to ask about the football. These questions were recorded and formed the basis of the ensuing discussion. 'I want my children to be able to question stories, pictures and poems,' said the teacher, 'but I also want them to think about and to question everyday objects around them.'

Drama, role play and first-hand experience

Drama, role play and first-hand experience, such as a visit or the witnessing of an experiment can be a stimulus for reflection and inquiry. One teacher used a visit to a local church as a special time for reflection on the meaning and value of the experience. Having explored the interior of the church she asked the children to sit with their eyes closed and asked them: 'What do you think?', 'What do you feel?' and 'What sounds can you hear?' After they had sat for a while in silent contemplation the children were asked to record their comments, thoughts and questions in their notebooks. After the visit these questions would form the basis of their community of enquiry. This process of experience, reflect, question and discuss can be applied to other special times, places and events.

Drama brings the possibility of thinking with the whole person, and of active engagement in the narrative from a multiplicity of possible viewpoints. Children who have not only read the story of Pandora's Box, but have enacted the feel of the box, the lifting of the lid and an enactment of the Spites that come flying forth have an immediacy of experience that mere hearing alone may not match. The activity of drama without time for reflection and discussion is soon forgotten. A community of enquiry can offer an opportunity to reflect on the active experience of drama and role play. The role of drama in expressing and embodying thought is explored further in Chapter 7 (p. 206).

Music

Research is currently being undertaken in London schools on ways of teaching music through critical inquiry and discussion, exploring personal and narrative responses to music. Research is currently being undertaken by Sara Liptai at Brunel University on ways of using music for thinking and aesthetic inquiry. The role of community of enquiry in music education is further discussed in Chapter 7 (p. 231).

TV and video

TV and video provide an endless diet of unreflective entertainment. The use of video clips can be a stimulus for critical discussion with children in communities of media study, with the aim of helping children to be active interrogators, not only of educational film and video, but also of the dominant forms of popular culture, such as adverts, TV 'soaps' and popular films. Questions that act as triggers for enquiry of any video

---

What is a philosophical story?

Some 6- to 7-year-olds (Year 2) have been asked to find a 'philosophical book'. One child shows the philosophical book she has brought in to the class:

RF: Who has found a philosophical story to show us. What is it?

Fran: It's called 'Owl at Home'. *(Child shows* Owl at Home *by Arnold Lobel)*

RF: Can you tell us what the book is about?

Fran: It's about an owl. It's stories about an owl.

RF: I see it's got different stories. Can you tell us about it . . . one of the stories?

Fran: It's about an owl. Funny things keep happening to him and he doesn't know why.

RF: Can you give us an example?

Fran: The wind blows his door open and he doesn't know who it is. He sees bumps in his bed and doesn't know what they are. He is sad and he fills his teapot full of tears. In the end he makes friends with the moon. *(Showing the book to the class)*

RF: Why do you think it is philosophical?

Fran: Because strange things are happening and he doesn't know why.

RF: What does he have to do when these strange things happen?

Fran: He has to think about them.

(Later a child sums up what he thinks a philosophical book is . . .

RF: Who can say what they think a philosophical book is?

Ross: A philosophical book is where people in it have to think about things and there's a question or problem that's difficult to answer.

---

clip include: 'What does it say?', 'Why is it saying it?' and 'What can you ask about it?'

Factual narrative

Various non-fiction forms of narrative can be of philosophical interest, for example popular accounts of the Great Mysteries of the World, and newspapers provide items of news and 'stories' on a daily basis which are ripe for enquiry and interrogation. Investigating the way two newspapers have reported the same story will provide plenty of scope for questioning at both the literal level and at the more general level about knowledge, belief and the moral contexts of human affairs. As one teacher says of the 'News Board' she has permanently on display with changing items of news: 'I want the children to question what they read and hear. They will only do that if they get practice at it. There's no better way of starting a community of enquiry than questioning the news of the day.'

Any story or book that children read can become a story for thinking if a teacher or reading partner follows the story up with questions and themes for discussion. Many of the best questions will come from the children themselves. 'Philosophy lessons are good,' said Sundu, aged 10, 'because you can think of your own questions, and try to answer other people's questions.'

INVITING CHILDREN'S QUESTIONS

Once the story has been read or retold invite the children to think about it. Ask if they found anything puzzling or peculiar in the story. Is there something in the story that made them think? Is there a question anyone would like to ask?

As questions arise write them on the board, numbering them as you go, and adding the child's name to their question to acknowledge their contribution. Sometimes children may prefer to make a statement rather than a question. If the child cannot turn it into a question record it as a statement which may need to be discussed. The following were questions raised by a Year 3 and 4 class (7- to 9-year-olds) having their first Story for Thinking session, after reading the story of Gelert (*Stories for Thinking*, p. 21). The first contribution was a comment:

The story doesn't sound too good if you're a vegetarian. (Luke)
Why is the story so miserable? (Robert)
Why is the story so bloodthirsty? (Kayleigh)
How did the baby fall out of its cradle? (Kevin)
Why didn't Prince Llewellyn look around the room for the baby? (Francis)
Why didn't the baby wake up? (Eleanor)
Why was the story made up? (Luke)
What is the point of the story? (Sara)
Why did the prince kill the dog before looking for the baby? (Alex)
Why are there different versions of the same story? (Daniel)
Where were they in the castle? (Harpreet)
Why did the prince jump to conclusions? (Michael)
Why did the prince have to go hunting? (Darrenjit)
What was he hunting for? (Harpreet)
How did the wolf get inside the castle? (Ricky and Brett)
Why did the prince kill the dog if it was his favourite animal? (Robert)
Can you bring people (or dogs) back from the dead? (David)

The questions are fairly typical for this age group. On this occasion about half the class asked a question, some children asking more than one. The teacher might then have asked the children to choose, e.g. by voting, which question they wished to discuss. On this occasion the teacher chose what she thought was the most interesting and philosophical of the questions, Luke's question: 'Why was the story made up?' She began by asking Luke to explain why he asked this question. As the discussion progressed the children discussed the difference between stories, myths and legends, they talked of people who made up stories and what makes a good story, and how you might find out whether a story is true. Towards the end of the 45-minute session the children chose Michael's question: 'Why did the prince jump to conclusions'. Michael explained why the question puzzled him: 'Why do people jump to conclusions without thinking first?', and the class began debating the motivation behind the actions of the central character, and examples of when they acted without thinking. They came to agree that 'Stop, and think' was a useful rule to remember, but hard to put into practice. By the end of the lesson there were still many more questions to discuss. These were displayed in the class for another time, and these and other questions became the subject of their writing in their Thinking Books.

As the children get more experienced in the process they will ask more questions, and their insights in discussion will delight and surprise you. The following are examples of the 26 questions raised by a class aged 9–11 years after hearing the story of The Willow Pattern (*Stories for Thinking*, p. 33). Almost every child in this class had a question and the teacher stopped writing questions when he ran out of board space! Here are some examples:

Why is the daughter so important to the father? (Gaurav)
Why was the Willow Tree so important? What did it stand
     for? (Faizal)
If the father loved the daughter so much why did he make her
     unhappy? (Chetan)
Could someone really change into a bird? (Ben and Bobby)
Shouldn't you be allowed to marry who you want to?
     (Stacey)
Is it a true story or not? (Ronald)
Who were the gods, and what did they look like? (Anil)
Who is telling the story? (Asim)

Any one of these questions, and many others suggested by the children, are likely to prove fruitful for discussion. In the early stages it may be better for the teacher to choose a promising question from the board for discussion. From the above lists of children's questions which would you choose as a starting point for discussion?

In the following enquiry the question chosen for discussion was a question that could be asked of any story.

WHAT IS THE POINT OF THE STORY?

The following questions were raised by a class of 13- to 14-year-olds after shared reading of the beginning of *Metamorphosis* by Franz Kafka:

 1. How do we know it wasn't really a dream?
 2. How did it happen?
 3. Why is it only his body has changed and not his thoughts and feelings?
 4. Why was he not bothered that he was a bug?
 5. How does he still have a human voice when his features were like a bug?
 6. Why is he a bug and not something else?
 7. How do we know he is a bug?
 8. How can he put his clothes on if he is a bug?
 9. If it was a dream how do we know he is awake now?
10. What is the point of the story?
11. If he is a bug, why is he such a big bug?

After voting, the class chose question 10 as their topic for philosophical enquiry. The following are excerpts from the discussion of this question:

RF:	The question that you chose was: 'What is the point of the story?' It was asked by Randiv. Before we see what answer you would give to the question I'm going to ask Randiv why he asked that question.
Randiv:	We've just read the story, and I wondered what the point of it was.
Jasminder:	Someone's written a story about a person changing into a bug. Why write about a person changing into a bug?
RF:	OK. Thank you.
Monica:	Maybe the point of the story is to make us realize what the point of the story is.
RF:	OK . . . Yes?
Sonal:	I think the point of the story is specifically for this, to make us think, to make us confused and to ask questions like 'What was it all about?'

RF:	Thank you. Anybody agree or disagree with that? (*Pause*) Do you think that the point of the story may have been, as has been suggested, to confuse, and to get people to question?
Steven:	Maybe to get people to question, but not just to confuse you . . .
RF:	So what is the difference between getting you to question something and confusing you?
Manish:	If you question something you are not immediately necessarily confused, in the first place you ask a question.
RF:	So what is the difference between being confused and asking a question?
Rahim:	Being confused is not knowing. Questioning is trying to find out what you don't know.

* * *

RF:	How many different questions do you think we could have asked about this story?
Matthew:	Millions.
Vinay:	Infinity.
RF:	An infinity that we could ask about this particular story?
Sonal:	A lot more! (*Laughter from the group*)

* * *

RF:	That's an interesting comment: 'If we knew how the world would end we wouldn't ask so many questions.' What did you mean by that?
Jasminder:	If you did know how the world would end you would still be asking questions. Like why would it end?
Shahir:	Like why would it end and how would it end, and if there was anything we could do to prevent it anyway. So we're still going to be asking questions.
Arun:	It's pointless, we're never going to find out how it's going to end anyway.
Chantelle:	Because we'll be gone. So there won't be anyone to answer our questions.
RF:	I think the question is not whether we would find out how the world is going to end but if we know

	how the world is going to end, that in a sense
	means there are no questions to ask.
Mandip:	Not that many.
RF:	Can you explain what you mean?
Mandip:	You wouldn't go after things as much as you do.
	You go after things now because you don't know
	how they will end. If you knew how they'd end
	there would be no point in asking questions.

   'A philosophical discussion will often tack back and forth,' says Lipman, 'like a boat going into the wind, but there's a forward movement.'[19] The person who leads (or facilitates) the discussion has an important role in ensuring this forward movement.

LEADING A DISCUSSION

A story can be interrogated in different ways, for example through using questions that focus children's attention on:

1. Thinking about the story – to explore children's under-standing of the narrative features of the story, and to encourage critical and creative thinking about the story
2. Thinking about a key theme of the story – to explore children's understanding and to encourage critical and creative thinking about the theme

'I think the discussion is good when it makes you think of good reasons, and it gives you a turn to think of good ideas,' says Gabby, aged 8. Thinking is for Gabby a holistic activity, but it includes a number of important elements that a leader can model and encourage to provide forward movement in a discussion. The leader is there to provide positive cognitive interventions that help take the discussion forward. During the course of a discussion a leader needs to be aware of opportunities to focus attention on the key elements of thinking. These include:

* *questioning* – asking good questions to provide a focus for enquiry

- *reasoning* – requesting reasons or evidence to support argument and judgements
- *defining* – clarifying concepts through making connections, distinctions and comparisons
- *speculating* – generating ideas and alternative viewpoints through imaginative thinking
- *testing for truth* – gathering information, judging evidence, examples and counter examples
- *expanding on ideas* – sustaining and extending lines of thought and argument
- *summarizing* – abstracting key points or general rules from a number of ideas or instances

A number of questions have been found useful in the classroom for injecting intellectual rigour into a discussion with young children (for further discussion on the role of questioning see p. 154). They aim to move it away from children simply giving an answer, from anecdotal comment and unsupported observations to a style of discussion characterized by the giving of reasons and the formulation of argument. They try to encourage children to take responsibility for their comments and to think about what they are saying. The aim is that such questions in time become internalized and come to be asked by the children themselves.

Research suggests that children's reading and comprehension skills can be improved by philosophical enquiry as part of an overall approach to language and literacy (see p. 198 for more on findings from research). The benefits of using stories as a stimulus for philosophical discussion identified by teachers in the Philosophy in Primary Schools project include the following:

- 'It is good training for children in raising questions, not only English but science relies on children generating questions – a skill they find hard.'
- 'Children have learnt to respect others, and have developed the confidence to put forward their own opinions and beliefs.'
- 'Answering questions by putting forward theories and hypotheses is not only intellectually stimulating, it is also psychologically "safe" for them, when they do it in a community of inquiry.'

129

Some questions to stimulate philosophical enquiry	
Questions	Cognitive function of questions
• What happened? What did they do?	Identifying facts in the story
• How did they feel in the story? What did you feel when you read that?	Responding to experience
• What did they think in the story? What did you think about it?	Reflecting on personal and social issues
• What choices did they have? How might the story have been different?	Exploring moral decisions
• Why do you say that? Can you give me a reason?	Reasoning
• What do you mean by . . .? Can anyone explain that to us?	Defining/analysing/clarifying
• Has anyone got another thought/idea/example? Who else can say something about it?	Generating alternative views
• How could we tell if it was true? How do you/we know?	Testing for truth
• Who agrees/disagrees with . . . (child's name)? Can you say who/what you agree or disagree with?	Why? Sustaining dialogue/argument
• Who can remember what we have said? What are the ideas/arguments we have said?	Summarizing

One teacher reflecting on changes brought about by lessons using *Stories for Thinking* identified the following changes in her class:

- *self esteem* – children are proud of their ability to discuss important and difficult issues seriously
- *listening skills* – children are more prepared to listen to and respect each other
- *higher order thinking* – children enjoy the challenge of discussing difficult questions
- *questioning* – children are more willing to ask questions in all lessons, and to seek answers to problems
- *communication* – children are more willing to talk and contribute to discussion and build on each other's ideas
- *literacy* – children are better able to use inference and deduction in reading and writing

What do children think they learn from using stories for philosophy? Responses of course will vary, from Tom (aged 12) who said 'Philosophy is a good exercise, it is like doing PE for the mind', to Jake (aged 15) who responded 'Philosophy is the missing element in the curriculum because it is the only subject that helps you to think better in every subject', and Paul, the reluctant reader we met at the beginning of this chapter, who said 'I think philosophy makes you think more because it gives you time to think'. It is this time to think that we all need, as adults and as children.

NOTES AND REFERENCES

1. See Cather, K.D. (1919), *Educating by Story-telling*, London: George C. Harrap & Co., Ltd. and more recently Egan, K. (1986), *Teaching as Storytelling*, London: Routledge.
2. For more on the link between literacy and metacognition see Garner, R. (1987), *Metacognition and Reading Comprehension*, Norwood NJ: Ablex; and Wray, D. (1994), *Literacy and Awareness*, Hodder/UKRA.
3. See 'The story form and the organisation of meaning' in Egan, K. (1988), *Primary Understanding*, London: Routledge, pp. 96–129.

4. Egan, K. (1978), 'What is a plot?', *New Literary History*, IX (3), pp. 455–73.
5. Fisher, R. (ed.) (1987), *Problem Solving in Primary Schools*, Oxford: Blackwell, p. 42.
6. Whitehead, A.N. (1932), *The Aims of Education and Other Essays*, London: Benn.
7. Eisner, E. (1985), 'The role of the arts in cognition and curriculum', in Costa, A.L. (ed.) *Developing Minds: A Resource Book for Teaching Thinking*, Alexandria, Virginia: ASCD, pp. 169–75.
8. For more on research into classroom questioning referred to see Barnes, D., Britton, J. and Torbe, M. (1990), *Language, the Learner and the School*, Portsmouth, NH: Boynton Cook-Heinemann; Mitchell, S. (1992), *Questions and Schooling: Classroom Discourse across the Curriculum*, University of Hull; and Van der Meij, H. (1993), 'What's the title? A case study in questioning reading', *Journal of Research in Reading*, 16, 1, pp. 46–57. Van der Meij found that most questions (60 per cent) about texts used in classrooms tend to be text-explicit (factual).
9. Barnes et al. (1990) found a discrepancy between the linguistic structure of utterances such as questions, and the function they serve in an extended piece of dialogue. Bakhtin (1981) makes a distinction between 'an utterance's neutral signification' and its 'actual meaning'. In dialogue actual meaning for the listener is created in their active understanding by means of the reasons, connections and inferences drawn from the utterance. Actual meaning is not present in the utterance, it is a potential to be explicated by the minds that read or hear the words. Actual meaning can only be understood 'against a background of other concrete utterances on the same theme, a background made up of contradictory opinions, points of view and value judgements' (Bakhtin, 1981). To fully understand the meaning relies on an understanding of the context in which the utterance was made. In a continuous exchange aspects of the dialogue are contained within each utterance. A closed question can for example serve the function of recalling a child's wandering attention back to the discussion. A student may, as Mitchell (1992)

observes, in supplying a factually correct answer within a particular context, be asking herself, 'Why am I being asked that question?' An open question is not identifiable by its linguistic structure alone but needs to be checked against subsequent utterances and the epistemic tenor of the dialogue within which the exchange is framed.

10. On the relationship between time and narrative see Bruner, J. (1991), 'The narrative construction of reality', *Critical Enquiry*, 18, 1, pp. 1–22; and Ricouer, P. (1988), *Time and Narrative*, translated by K. Blamey and D. Pellauer, Chicago.

11. Kermode, F. (1966), *The Sense of an Ending*, Oxford: Oxford University Press.

12. Bruner (1991), op. cit.

13. Barthes, R. (1985) *The Responsibility of Forms: Critical Essays on Music, Art and Representation*, New York: Scribner.

14. This distinction derives from the work of Labov. See Labov, W. and Waletsky, J. (1967), 'Narrative analysis', in Helm J. (ed.), *Essays on the Verbal and Visual Arts*, Seattle: University of Washington Press, pp. 12–44.

15. Bruner (1991), op. cit.

16. *Workbook: Sophie's World* by Peer Olsen (1995) has been published in this country by Green Submarine Ltd, providing a worksheet approach to the study of Gaarder's book.

17. See Bettelheim, B. (1976), *The Uses of Enchantment: the Meaning and Importance of Fairy Tales*, London: Thames & Hudson, for a classic account of the value of fairy stories. For a more critical view of the nature of fairy tales see Zipes, J. (1994), *Fairy Tale as Myth/Myth as Fairy Tale*, Lexington: University Press of Kentucky, and (1995) *Creative Storytelling*, London: Routledge. Zipes argues that storytelling can oppress children as well as help them find their own voice.

18. For ways of using picture books to stimulate philosophical discussion with 5- to 11-year-olds see Murris, K. (1992), *Teaching Philosophy with Picture Books*, London: Infonet Publications; Sprod, T. (1993), *Books into Ideas: A Community of Enquiry*, Victoria, Australia: Hawker Brownlow;

and de Haan, C., McColl, S. and McCutcheon, L. (1995), *Philosophy with Kids*, Books 1–3, Melbourne: Longman.

19. Quoted from the video: *The Transformers: Socrates for Six Year Olds* (BBC, 1991).

THE STORIES FOR THINKING PROGRAMME

Developer:	Robert Fisher
Aim:	To develop thinking, language and learning skills across the curriculum, through philosophical discussion
Sample skills:	Concept-formation, enquiry, reasoning and communication skills, thinking for oneself and in cooperation with others
Assumptions:	• Teaching thinking through philosophical discussion can enrich all areas of the curriculum • Teaching thinking is best achieved through creating a community of enquiry in the classroom • Stories and narrative material can provide a stimulus for philosophical discussion across the curriculum
Intended audience:	Children aged 7–14 years
Process:	Teacher/children read and discuss a narrative stimulus such as a story, poem or picture. This is followed by discussion of questions and issues raised by children or teacher. Extension activities review and relate the discussion to curriculum goals
Time:	One or two hours per week
Publications:	*Stories for Thinking* (1996), *Games for Thinking* (1997) and *Poems for Thinking* (1997). Other resources in preparation. Published by Nash Pollock Publishing, Oxford, England
Source:	Centre for Research in Teaching Thinking, Brunel University, 300 St Margarets Road, Twickenham TW1 1PT, England

---

CHAPTER 5

Socratic Teaching:
Facilitating philosophical discussion

The unexamined life is not worth living.

Socrates (in Plato: *Apology*, 38a)

Who was Socrates and why was he famous as a teacher? One child reflecting on the life of Socrates wrote: 'Socrates was a teacher who went round asking questions in the street, like "Are you mad?" In the end they made him take poison and he died.' Another child wrote: 'Socrates asked people questions like "Are you still alive? How do you know?" Another wrote: 'Socrates was always asking questions, and we are still looking for some of the answers.'

For Socrates there may be many ways of life worth living, but the unexamined or unquestioned life was not one of them. What did he mean by this? What he seems to have meant is that a characteristic of a human life is to be critically aware of what we believe and what we do. And if we are not reflective or critical we will lead unfulfilled lives, our thinking becoming a prey to prejudice and conflict, and 'there is something disastrous about allowing our everyday ideas to remain in a state of unresolved conflict.'[1] Part of the point of education for Socrates is to make us aware of our ignorance, of the conflicts of ideas and of current problems, and to show us that there is a method of dealing with these. This method exemplified by Socrates in the writings of Plato has a long history,[2] and in recent years there has been a revival of interest in the philosophical[3] and educational[4] ideas of Socrates. But what is Socratic teaching, and is it relevant today? This chapter looks at the way Socratic teaching can help develop philosophical thinking.[5]

As we have seen philosophical thinking is a matter of thinking about thinking, and as such it has both a cognitive and metacognitive content. The cognitive, or conceptual, content includes the exploration of the most basic ideas and problems of everyday life, such as:

• Who am I?
• What is the world really like?
• What should I believe?
• What options do I have?
• How should I live my life?

The metacognitive content is about the process of improving one's own thinking and reasoning, so that one has a better understanding of oneself as a thinker and better tools with which to examine whatever subject matter is under review.[6]

People believe in many things, but their beliefs are often egocentric and unconsidered habits of mind. Some of these beliefs are spontaneously formed, some are derived from the beliefs of others such as parents and teachers. What these beliefs have in common is that they are rarely raised to what Piaget called 'conscious realization'. They remain unarticulated, unsynthesized, prone to vagueness and contradiction, unless students are encouraged to express them freely in a mutually supportive environment. Open discussion allows students to articulate their thinking, but it does not necessarily provide the cognitive challenge for students to extend their thinking.

One of the reasons that philosophical enquiry is needed in learning is that intelligence alone is not sufficient to realize the potential in discussion for developing thinking and self awareness. Articulate people are not necessarily successful at thinking and learning. They may fall into the trap of making instant judgements, of jumping to conclusions, without taking time to think about or to explore alternatives. They may close off the opportunities to think and learn more. This impulsivity, or tendency to premature closure, is a characteristic of under-achieving children at all levels of intelligence. Thinking is defined by de Bono as 'the operating skill with which intelligence acts upon experience'.[7] One of the characteristics of skilful thinking is exploration, the ability to explore a situation before making a judgement – to expand consciousness so one can see more in any situation, more viewpoints and more options. Widening the range of response so that one opens up more potential paths of exploration is the heart of creative thinking and living. These thinking skills are not automatic, but they can be developed. Laura, aged 10, says 'Philosophical questions can come out of anything.'

One class used an apple as a stimulus for Socratic enquiry. What questions could they ask that would help them understand more about an apple? The following is an excerpt from the discussion:

Is an apple dead or alive?

An excerpt from a discussion with a class of 7- to 8-year-olds about life, death and apples:

RF:	Can you tell us if this apple is dead or alive?
Rachel:	It's dead.
RF:	Why do you think it's dead?
Rachel:	It's been plucked from a tree. When it was on the tree it was part of the living tree. Now it's broken off it's dead.
RF:	Who agrees or disagrees?
Leo:	I disagree.
RF:	Why? can you give a reason?
Leo:	I think the apple could still be alive. We don't know it's dead.
Gary:	I agree with Leo. Part of the apple is still alive. The pips inside are still alive. They can grow into a new tree, if you planted them.
Holly:	They wouldn't, they wouldn't you know Gary. I

	disagree. They wouldn't grow into a tree, not if the apple's dead.
Melissa:	I once planted a pip and it started to grow. So it wasn't dead.
Darren:	Because it's got pips it doesn't mean to say it is still alive. If you leave it there it will just shrivel up, just like someone dead.
Ellie:	I agree with Melissa. If part of something is still alive it's still alive . . . like the pips.
Susan:	I think it's partly alive and partly dead, because its been broken off the tree. That's why it will slowly wither up, unless you eat it.
Leo:	It will be alive then because it would be part of you.
RF:	So what does being dead or alive mean?
Justin:	To be alive you have to be part of something living like an apple on a tree . . .

We become creative when we are able to look at things from a new perspective. Einstein, who believed that the key to learning was flexible thinking, said 'To raise new questions, new problems, to regard old problems from a new angle requires creative imagination, and makes real advances.' According to Piaget, 'To understand is to invent.'[8] We make knowledge our own by reconstructing it through some creative operation of the mind. The mind, according to Oliver Wendell Holmes, 'once stretched by a new idea, never goes back to its original dimensions'.

Torrance suggests that creativity is 'a process of becoming sensitive to problems, deficiencies, gaps in knowledge, missing elements, disharmonies, and so on; identifying the difficulty; searching for solutions, making guesses, or formulating hypotheses about the deficiencies, testing and retesting these hypotheses and possibly modifying and retesting them; and finally communicating the results'.[9] This is also a good definition of philosophical enquiry. But how is it achieved in practice?

A number of creative thinking techniques and teaching strategies have been found helpful in developing divergent thinking. One of these, the Socratic method of teaching through questioning and dialogical enquiry, aims to support sustained creative effort in thinking. But what is the method and how is it best used?

WHAT IS SOCRATIC TEACHING?

One of the reasons that Socrates remains of enduring interest is that he is an enigma. He left no writings of his own and our knowledge of him derives largely from the writings of Plato. In the Platonic dialogues Socrates plays many roles, and it is not clear that his approach can be summed up as one method. Some have seen Socrates the educator as 'in some ways the greatest of good men and certainly the wisest'[10] but others have criticized him for his arrogance, directiveness and dominance in discussion.[11] The contradictions in Socrates' character mirror the contradictions characteristic of many teachers – a mixture of patient listening and preaching, of humility and arrogance, of kindly tolerance and aggressive persistence, a profession of ignorance and a jealous rivalry with fellow teachers. What then was the nature of the pedagogy that Socrates developed in the agora and open spaces of Athens?

It is clear that Socrates saw an intellectual and moral vacuum in the society that he lived in. The old order of social and moral custom was breaking down, and the new education that was replacing it, inspired by the sophists, was worldly and materialistic. Perhaps there are parallels here with our society and its preoccupations today. When the sophist teacher Protagoras was asked whether he believed in the gods, he is said to have replied: 'The question is complex and life is short.' Man (or human needs) was to be the measure of all things. Socrates did not believe he knew the measure of all things. He was not a sophist or teacher in the sense that he presented himself as a learned or all-knowing person. He was a philosopher in the true sense of the word, as 'one who loves wisdom'. As a teacher what Socrates was trying to establish was a new moral and intellectual discipline founded on reason, and a method of enquiry through questioning. The marketplace for Socrates was more than a place for making money, it was a space for thinking, for asking questions and for developing one's creative judgement about important and complex human problems.

To ensure that our lives are properly examined we should not merely accept the views of others, or rely on our own solitary meditations. We must engage in discussion. By listening and responding to what others think we come to learn what it is to think for ourselves. In articulating, sharing and modifying our ideas through the process of dialogue we come to take responsibility for what we say and think, and 'empower others to do these things too'.[12] To educate, for Socrates, could not simply be a question of transfer of knowledge. Education was an activity of mind, not a curriculum to be delivered. To be involved in learning in a Socratic sense is to be involved in a personal drama, for it depends both on making rational choices and emotional commitments. It has both a rational and a moral purpose, it exists to engender virtue through thinking that engages and develops the learner as an individual and as a member of a learning community.[13]

Socrates uses questions as a means of approaching truth through the use of reason in a shared enquiry. Socrates believed that a wise person, or teacher, is one who has recognized their own ignorance and uses it as a spur to better understanding. This may have been little more than the debater's trick of showing 'scholarly ignorance', but it was the peg on which he hung his philosophy of education.

This philosophy can be roughly summed up as:

- knowledge can be pursued, and can lead to an understanding of what is true
- the search for true knowledge is a cooperative enterprise pursued through dialogue
- questioning is the primary form of education, drawing out true knowledge from within rather than imposing knowledge from outside
- knowledge must be pursued with a ruthless intellectual honesty[14]

For Socrates the search for truth is also a moral enterprise. It is to do, in D.H. Lawrence's words, with the 'wholeness' of a person 'wholly attending'.[15] At the centre of Socrates' moral concern is the *psyche*. This is generally translated as 'soul', but it encompasses under a single head the life-principle, intellect and moral personality. His mission he said was to persuade people 'first and foremost to concentrate on the greatest improvement of your souls' (*Apology*, 30). One element of this, and one function of teaching through dialogue, was to gain self-knowledge.

What does it mean to 'know yourself'?

'Know yourself' was the advice given by the oracle at Delphi in ancient Greece, and became an aim of Socratic teaching. What did it mean?

The following lines entitled 'Know Thyself' come from the Elizabethan poet Sir John Davies:

We seek to know the moving of each sphere,
And the strange cause of th' ebb and flow of the Nile
But of that clock within our breasts we bear,
The subtle motions we forget the while.

We that acquaint ourselves with every zone,
And pass both tropics and behold the poles,
When we come home, are to ourselves unknown,
And unacquainted still with our own souls.[16]

If there is one constant in the research into effective thinkers and learners it is that they know more about themselves as thinkers and learners. It is this metacognitive element in human intelligence that is a focus in the most successful thinking skills programmes and teaching strategies.[17] For Socrates the search for this kind of self knowledge through dialogue was linked to the paradoxical belief that virtue (*arete*), in the sense of 'goodness' and 'excellence', is knowledge. If I really and fully knew which course of action was best how could I fail to follow it? There is an ambiguity here about what 'best' means, between a narrowly ethical sense and a more general sense. What Socrates seems to be arguing against is the pragmatism of the sophists, and of relativists today, who claim that there can be no absolute standards of truth or goodness. Socrates believed that there was a goal towards which a dialogue, if it was to be philosophical, should be heading, which was a personal understanding of what was true and right in knowledge and action. It is because we don't know the truth that we need to talk.

The Socratic method of teaching is through dialogical enquiry facilitated by questioning. The teacher is to assist people in giving birth to their own ideas (Socrates likened his method to that of a midwife). The aim of education is to uncover, through discussion, what our personal understanding and knowledge are in order to discover the truth. This personal understanding is gained through trying to define more clearly the concepts we use in everyday speech, and so helping us to understand more about the world and more about ourselves, so that we become better able to lead a good and fulfilling life. This final point brings Socrates closer to the sophists of his day, and to a utilitarian view of education, in that Socrates tended to equate the good with the useful – so the Socratic method would also help develop intellectual and communicative skills – and also that these would be taught as much by the model of the teacher as the process of enquiry. But many argued then, as they do now, that the Socratic method is not a desirable philosophy of teaching, that what is needed is 'traditional teaching'.

HOW DOES SOCRATIC DIFFER FROM TRADITIONAL TEACHING?

Traditionally the contrast has been drawn between the 'Socratic method' and 'academic' traditions of teaching (from the Academy, which Plato founded). Below is a summary in simplified form of the main differences between these two traditions of education, both of which have had adherents throughout educational history, and have champions today:[18]

For Socrates philosophy was an activity, something you do, rather than a set of philosophical truths to be learnt. To become a philosopher you need to acquire philosophical skills, you need to know how to philosophize.[19] To acquire these skills you need to practise with someone more skilful than yourself. In the earlier dialogues Socrates made use of analogies with martial arts – you begin by sparring with a teacher, and later you become an equal. It was a process in which the

The Socratic method	The Academic tradition
Philosophy is an active process	Philosophy is a learned body of teachings
Philosophy is questioning	Philosophy is dogmatic
Philosophy is inductive	Philosophy is deductive
Philosophy is linguistic	Philosophy is conceptual
Philosophy is open to all	Philosophy is for the few
Philosophy is applicable to life	Philosophy is abstract truths
Philosophy is dialogue (oral)	Philosophy is written

teacher, professing ignorance, was also learning. Philosophy for Socrates was the highest form of cognitive apprenticeship, which benefited both teacher and learner, whereas for Plato it was a body of truths that had to be learned and understood. The teacher as expert fed the student with knowledge, and the student was a passive learner in the process. For Plato truth was an objective body of knowledge, for Socrates knowledge is obtainable but in practice needs always to be questioned.

The principal characteristic of the Socratic method, according to Aristotle[20] was the use of 'inductive' arguments, which is the process of reasoning from particular cases to general truths. The Socratic method was more than this for the particular case he started from was what other people said and thought. He believed people learned to become philosophers not by being instructed in philosophical concepts or by being given academic knowledge but by being drawn from their pre-philosophic state into a questioning and reflective awareness of what they believed and of the words used to express those beliefs. Philosophy is linguistic and the ways in which we seek to structure or mirror reality is in words. He wanted to find out what people meant by what they said. The problem in seeking truth through a search for true definitions is that any definition uses words which themselves need definition, which is why a genuinely Socratic dialogue often ends inconclusively.

Socrates believed that philosophy was open to all, and that philosophical skills could be developed by anyone who had the power of speech. Plato on the other hand argues that dialectic (philosophy) is an academic subject to be introduced after many years of training and to those who have reached the age of thirty,[21] and professional philosophers today have echoed this view arguing that philosophy is not 'an appropriate subject of study at school'.[22] There is no philosophy for children in the academic world of Plato, but Socrates saw philosophy as of benefit to everyone, including children (*cf* the dialogue with the slave boy in *The Meno*). Philosophy was of practical value – it would help you do your job better and make you a better person.

One of the major differences between the Socratic method and Plato's Academy is the Socratic view that the spoken word is superior to the written word. A dialogue is interactive, it forces on the participants the need to articulate thinking and personal understanding. The experience of participating in a Socratic discussion can never be the same as reading a dialogue. In the *Phaedrus* Socrates argues that writing and speech-making (lecturing) are poor instruments of education because they merely rely on rote memory, they do not express a lived process of mutual enquiry. Among the biggest changes set in motion by Plato's academy was the shift from open discussion to lectures and written texts, from oracy to literacy. This academic tradition persists in the emphasis in educational practice today on written examinations and coursework, and the emphasis on individual or private study. What the academic tradition recognizes is the value of the written word as a vehicle of thought, and the use of personal writing as a powerful means of encouraging students to make meaning and to express understanding. What is needed perhaps is a better balance between the Socratic and academic modes of teaching. We need people who are knowledgeable in a range of academic and practical disciplines, but who are reflective and critical about what they know, who can apply their learning creatively to practical situations, who are articulate in speech as well as writing, who can cooperate with others, who can see things from different perspectives, who are willing to revise their ideas and who are committed to lifelong learning.

There is a need at all levels of education to use talk more effectively for learning. This is seen in the problems that many students have in articulating their ideas, in the needs expressed by employers for improved personal skills in communication, cooperation and teamwork in their employees (see below), and in the needs of society for creative participants in the processes of democracy.

Personal skills sought by employers

1 = ranked most significant

1. Oral communication
2. Teamwork
3. Enthusiasm
4. Motivation
5. Initiative
6. Leadership
7. Commitment
8. Interpersonal
9. Organizing
10. Foreign language competence

Source: Personal Skills Unit, Sheffield University, 1991

There seems a strong case here for more Socratic teaching to develop the competencies and dispositions of articulate and creative thinkers. What then are the implications for teaching in the classroom? The discussions that Socrates had in the marketplaces of Athens were voluntary. How can we infuse Socratic teaching into the involuntary context of the classroom?

Socratic teaching today can be divided into two broad approaches:

1. *Socratic enquiry* – formal lessons of Socratic enquiry
2. *Socratic questioning* – the infusion of Socratic teaching across the curriculum

The following is part of a discussion using a Socratic question as a stimulus:

145

What is truth?

An excerpt from a discussion with 13- to 15-year-olds:

RF: Do you think things are true even if we don't know them?

Tom: Things are true if they really happen.

Jake: I wouldn't say that, because if no-one knew it was true then you couldn't say it was true.

Tom: But it would still be true.

Jake: No, but no-one would like call it true, because they wouldn't know about it.

Tom: No, they wouldn't know it was true, but it could *still* be true.

Jake: No, but you couldn't like say, 'This is true', if you didn't know about it.

Tom: I know, but it could still *be* true, in the real world.

Jake: It could potentially be true, but it wouldn't really be *true*, because no-one could say it was true.

Tom: What does that mean?

Jake: It would be true if we find out about it. It's possibly true. It might be true in the future but not now.

RF: Would you agree with that, Tom?

Tom: Yes.

RF: Does that mean you've changed your mind?

Tom: Yes I have, slightly.

WHAT IS SOCRATIC ENQUIRY?

The Socratic method of enquiry was not to tell but to seek the truth through a sequence of questions, a process called the *elenchus* (Greek for cross-examination). The elements of this method as practised by Socrates can be summed up as:

- scholarly ignorance, in which the teacher poses as someone who does not know in order to provoke, motivate and facilitate the thinking of students. It is characterized by the teacher showing a self-conscious display of curiosity and puzzlement rather than as the person who knows the 'right' answer. Socrates himself claimed to know nothing.

- through the posing of questions, which Socrates believed was a process as least as important as finding answers. Certainty closes the doors of enquiry, and stops the search for better answers. Hence the beginning of wisdom was to realize how little one knows for certain about some of the central concepts that structure our lives.

- the search for truth was to find out what words and ideas that we use and take for granted really mean. Socrates believed that you could not say you knew what you meant unless you could define it in words and were using words with consistency. This was not simply a concern with meaning, but a way to overcome ignorant and muddled thinking about concepts such as justice and reason so that we can come to a better understanding of ourselves and the world.

- we should attend to what we think and believe as this will have an effect on how we live. Improving how we think is for Socrates a moral mission, the goal of which is to increase human good and human happiness. Because what people believe will affect how they act, their beliefs should be subject to careful thought and the processes of reasoning. The cultivation of moral understanding and virtue, he believed, was best assisted by philosophical enquiry.

In this century a European tradition of formal Socratic enquiry has been inspired by the work of Leonard Nelson,[23] his disciple Gustav Heckmann[24] and by philosophers trained in the method, principally from Germany and the Netherlands but extending to Britain.[25] For Nelson the power of the Socratic method lies in '*forcing* minds to *freedom*. Only persistent pressure to speak one's mind, to meet every counter-question, and to state the reasons for every assertion transforms the power of that allure into an irresistible compulsion'.[26] The essential skill of the teacher is to give responsibility to the student, to give no answers, but to set the interplay of question and answer going between students. The aim of education for Nelson is 'rational self-determination'. This is not to be gained from learning the rules of logic *in abstracto* but by the learner exercising the faculty of judgement. The mere asking and answering of questions are not sufficient to exercise the faculties of judgement. The explicit aim is to help students find an answer to their questions but the implicit aim is to force participants through dialogue to express their thoughts clearly, to systematize judgements and to test their own beliefs against the arguments and views of others.

The method of Socratic teaching for Nelson lay not in the teacher giving answers but in asking questions, for example:

- *What do you mean by that?* – constant effort to define what we mean
- *Can you repeat that in your own words?* – constant battle against misunderstanding
- *Can you give an example?* – asking for statements to be supported by an example
- *What has the answer to do with our question?* – checking for relevance in argument
- *Who has been following?* – checking for understanding among participants
- *Do you know what you said a few moments ago?* – checking for consistency .
- *What question are we talking about?* – focusing on the question under discussion

As the last question shows, a characteristic of the European style of Socratic teaching is that the focus is kept on the question in hand, and the emphasis in discussion is on the experiences and thinking of the participants involved rather than on what they have read or experienced second hand. The aim is to reach some form of consensus or agreement between all participants. To create the optimum conditions for discussion a maximum of 12 participants is recommended for each enquiry.

Part of the process is a review or meta-discourse at the end of each session, in which students and the teacher write down their thoughts about the discussion. This provides an opportunity for quiet reflection, and helps participants to explore their own personal understanding of what was said. These reviews can provide a starting point for the next session, as an aide memoire or to introduce a new line of enquiry.

In America the tradition of 'Community of Enquiry' developed by Matthew Lipman, Ann Sharp and others was influenced by the philosophies of Socrates, John Dewey and C.S. Peirce. Lipman's Philosophy for Children programme[27] shares many similar features of pedagogic practice derived from the Socratic Method but there are some differences between the Philosophy for Children approach and the European tradition of Socratic Dialogue, as shown in the table below.

Philosophy for Children and Socratic Dialogue: some differences

Philosophy for Children	Socratic Dialogue
Philosophical story as starting point	**Philosophical question as starting point**
Free-ranging discussion	Focus on one question or problem
Expression of alternative viewpoints	Aim for consensus of opinion
Enquiry through dialogue	Dialogue includes a meta-discourse
Questions written before discussion	Questions/statements written during discussion
Oral review of discussion	Written review of discussion
Follow-up activities and exercises	Further dialogue

Philosophy for Children programmes consist of specially written philosophic novels and stories, supported by discussion plans, activities and exercises. In Socratic Dialogue no special educational materials need be used. A philosophical question is chosen by the facilitator for discussion, and an important element of the dialogue is the meta-discourse. The facilitator and participants are encouraged to think about how the discussion is being conducted and can voice at any time their pleasure or displeasure about the behaviour of others or the way the problem is being tackled. Meta-discourse allows for the feelings and frustrations that may arise during discussion to be aired, without affecting the content of discussion. In Philosophy for Children, questions are written down on a blackboard or flipchart to set the agenda at the beginning of a session, whereas in Socratic Dialogue questions and statements are added during discussion to provide an overview and to monitor progress.

The aim of Socratic Dialogue is to achieve consensus. The facilitator encourages participants to reformulate what they said earlier, and to include in their own words the views of others so as to focus on points of agreement in the subject under discussion. Philosophy for Children facilitators tend to emphasize 'dialogue across differences', where difference of viewpoint can be challenged and questioned. Socratic Dialogue is more directive. The facilitator keeps attention focused on the question being discussed, whereas in a Philosophy for Children enquiry the discussion moves indirectly forward, as Lipman says like a boat tacking in the wind, and may end up having debated a wide range of issues.

Despite differences of emphasis and practice, what unites these two methodologies is a belief in the formal practice of philosophical enquiry as a shared experience focusing on questions of importance for the participants, and in which the teacher or facilitator is 'philosophically self-effacing', adopting a role of scholarly ignorance. The focus is on what the students have to think and say rather than on what the teacher has to say. Indeed in Socratic Dialogue the essential role of the teacher is that of questioner and facilitator of discussion. The following are examples of this in practice taken from a discussion on thinking between a group of 11- to 12-year-olds:

RF: Do you think all the time or just some of the time?

Richard: It depends what you mean by thinking.

RF: What do you think it means?

Richard: When you're asleep you are not really thinking because you are not talking to yourself in your mind.

Mark:	You only think some of the time.
Toby:	You relax.
Nick:	You rest.
Alex:	You're not just relaxing . . . you can sleep.
Paul:	When you're asleep your mind is still working . . . like it is dreaming and stuff like that.
RF:	So thinking is different from your mind just working?
Sarah:	Thinking is talking to yourself in your mind. You say things to yourself, like you're talking.
Lucy:	And talking to other people.
Emma:	I think that thinking is talking in words.
RF:	Can you think without words?
Tom:	You can think without words . . . you can think in pictures as well.
Leonard:	I agree with Tom. You can think in words and pictures, like I'm thinking of a cartoon, and that's words and pictures.
RF:	Does everyone agree that you think in words and pictures?
Children:	Yeah.
RF:	Have we decided that we think while we are asleep?
Tom:	No, you've got to be conscious. You've got to know you are thinking otherwise you are not thinking.
Duncan:	I disagree with Tom. If you dream you are thinking . . .
Tom:	No because you can't change anything about it. You don't know what's happening.
Nick:	Thinking is your thoughts. Your thoughts is what you get when you think. I think, he thought . . .
RF:	Perhaps it would help to ask . . . Can you think without thinking of something?
Toby:	You can't think without thinking.
Helen:	You've got to think of something. If you don't . . .
Lisa:	You can't think of nothing.
Helen:	No. I agree with Paul, there is always *something* going on in your head. There's no time when there's nothing going on or you'd be dead. A dead head.

Richard:	What happens when you're unconscious?
Lee:	You are still thinking, but you don't know what you're thinking . . . if you're knocked out. That's what it means. You're out . . . you are out of your mind. (*Laughter*)
Nick:	You can think of nothing.
Tom:	But if you are thinking of nothing you are thinking of something. You can't think of nothing. If you are thinking of nothing, you are not thinking.
Toby:	If you have nothing in you mind you are still thinking of something.
Richard:	That's impossible. That's not how it works.
RF:	If you were thinking of the word 'nothing' would you be thinking of nothing?
Nick:	Yes that would be nothing. If you're thinking of nothing . . . it's nothing.
Ashleigh:	I disagree with Nick, because if you think of the word 'nothing' you are still thinking *of* something.

(After further discussion about the nature of thinking I tried to round off the discussion by seeking through a question a summary and consensus of the views of the students involved.)

RF:	What can you say now about the difference between thinking and dreaming?
Richard:	You can control your thoughts but you can't control your dreams.
Lee:	Yeah . . . dreams don't always make sense.
Gerald:	In the day you're thinking all the time. You have millions of thoughts . . . but only a few dreams, or no dreams.
Kirsty:	You can't control your dreams, but you can start thoughts by thinking of something.
Lydia:	Like we're doing now.
Annika:	You can't control your dreams . . .
RF:	Thank you. I think we'll have to stop now . . . can anyone think of any other questions about thinking we've not asked?
Henry:	Can you think in your Mummy's tummy . . . I mean, before you're born?
RF:	That's interesting, thank you. OK . . . Can you

write down any thoughts you've got about what we discussed, or any questions or ideas you've got ready for another time . . .?[28]

In this dialogue the facilitator has tried to model the Socratic method, using elements from both the European and American traditions during a session of philosophy with children, allowing the discussion to tack back and forth between the group, being non-judgmental, intervening with questions on the theme under discussion, and encouraging the children to do a review or 'thinkwrite' at the end of the lesson.

Formal discussions such as this are not the only way in which the Socratic method can contribute to education. Socratic questioning can be used as a teaching strategy in all curricular subjects. But what are Socratic questions?

WHAT IS SOCRATIC QUESTIONING?

There are many different sorts of question that can be asked of students, but the most common distinction is between open and closed questions.[29] Research studies show that the questions teachers use most often are closed, factual-type questions.[30] These are rhetorical questions in the sense that the teacher knows the right answer and is testing recall of knowledge. Open questions are genuine queries where the teacher does not know the answer, and is asking the child. They become Socratic when the question is a genuine invitation to enquiry, for example 'What do you think?' Socratic questions provide a stimulus for thinking and responding, and Socratic questioning differs from random open-ended questioning in that it follows a pattern, a progression of follow-through questions that probe reasons and assumptions and which take the enquiry further. Some questions, such as 'Why are we here?' may be an ordinary open question or a question that invites philosophical enquiry.

Socrates is said to have called education 'a festival for the mind', and philosophical enquiry is essentially a celebration of ideas. Socratic questions help us to focus on ideas or concepts as the basic ingredients of thinking. All ideas, elicited by questions, are to be viewed as potential sources of truth. Such questions invite us to attend to our familiar everyday experiences (Lawrence's definition of thought as 'wholly attending'), to look further into things, and to explore the wonder and mystery we find there. The questions urge us to 'dig deep', and to think clearly about the concepts we use to structure our thinking about the world.

Socratic questions are the kind that can add rigour to any discussion, whether the lesson is history, art, science or any curriculum subject – and at all levels of education, from kindergarten to college, in school, at home or in the marketplace of life. They help to move discussion away from the unstructured swapping of anecdotes, items of knowledge or unsupported observations to a discussion with purpose and direction. The eventual aim is for the questions to become internalized questions that students ask themselves. Indeed one criterion that can be used to assess the effectiveness of any enquiry is to compare the number of students asking questions compared to the number asked by the teacher. Research suggests that teachers should in general ask fewer but better questions. What are these 'better questions'? There is no fixed set of questions that are Socratic, but below is a summary list of questions that are open, Socratic and act as invitations to better thinking.[31]

Socratic questions	
1. *Questions that seek clarification:*	
Can you explain that . . .?	*Explaining*
What do you mean by . . .?	*Defining*
Can you give me an example of . . .?	*Giving examples*
How does that help . . .?	*Supporting*
Does anyone have a question to ask . . .?	*Enquiring*
2. *Questions that probe reasons and evidence*	
Why do you think that . . .?	*Forming an argument*
How do we know that . . .?	*Assumptions*
What are your reasons . . .?	*Reasons*
Do you have evidence . . .?	*Evidence*

| Can you give me an example/ counter-example . . .? | *Counter examples* |

3. Questions that explore alternative views

Can you put it another way . . .?	*Re-stating a view*
Is there another point of view . . .?	*Speculation*
What if someone were to suggest that . . .?	*Alternative views*
What would someone who disagreed with you say . . .?	*Counter argument*
What is the difference between those views/ ideas . . .?	*Distinctions*

4. Questions that test implications and consequences

What follows (or can we work out from) what you say . . .?	*Implications*
Does it agree with what was said earlier . . .?	*Consistency*
What would be the consequences of that . . .?	*Consequences*
Is there a general rule for that . . .?	*Generalizing rules*
How could you test to see if it was true . . .?	*Testing for truth*

5. Questions about the question / discussion

Do you have a question about that . . .?	*Questioning*
What kind of question is it . . .?	*Analysing*
How does what was said/the question help us . . .?	*Connecting*
Where have we got to/who can summarize so far . . .?	*Summarizing*
Are we any closer to answering the question/ problem . . .?	*Coming to conclusions*

The Socratic teacher takes on the questioning role as a model for the child. As they reflect upon their teaching they ask themselves, 'What is the central question (or questions) which are most basic and crucial to this subject?' In seeking answers to questions the teacher is aware that children have two sources for their beliefs:

- beliefs that derive from others, that is believing what they have been told
- beliefs that the child forms as a result of personal experience, thinking and interaction with the environment including their peers

The first are received beliefs, the second are what we might call operational beliefs. The source of the first kind of belief is other people's interpretation of reality. Children learn to verbalize these, for example by saying what they must or must not do, but they do not necessarily incorporate them into their set of operational beliefs. What they say they should do is not always what they would do. The first set of beliefs control their words, the second their actions. The first derives from what they do on behalf of others – 'because my teacher tells me to'. The second is what they do for themselves. They learn to live with two belief systems, and often may not recognize contradictions between these systems. Their beliefs may remain at an intuitive level, or be unformed.

The inner source of belief defines how the child really thinks about the world. It is the result of the child making sense of the world, and responding to the world in the light of their own feelings and self interest. These egocentric beliefs, often unreflective and unarticulated, become the foundation for the child's actions and responses. Some of these spontaneously formed beliefs are rational and reasonable; some are inconsistent with the beliefs of teachers and parents. As a result of this conflict with authority and received wisdom many of these beliefs may not have been raised to consciousness. They are part of what Socrates called 'the unexamined life' which he said was not worth living. Children may have developed all sorts of theories about the world and their place in the world, their own theories of psychology, sociology, science, language and other areas of learning, as well as ideas about themselves as thinkers and learners. These theories, beliefs and ideas may become stumbling blocks to learning and to a fulfilled life.

The Socratic teacher aware of this problem seeks to provide an environment in which students can discover and explore their own beliefs. Such teachers create opportunities for thoughtful discussion, and encourage the conditions in which operational beliefs can be brought to consciousness through reflective thinking. How do they facilitate such thoughtful discussion?

HOW DO WE FACILITATE SOCRATIC DISCUSSION?

Socratic discussion can broadly divided into three kinds, the unplanned enquiry, the investigation and problem solving.[32]

Unplanned enquiry

Philosophy begins in wonder.

Plato (*Thaetetus*, 155D)

Enquiry in a Socratic spirit can be conducted at any time anywhere. Wondering and enquiry are not confined to planned activity but can occur at any time. We should aim to keep our sense of wonder and curiosity alive. Some have said it is the secret of eternal youth. It can be sparked by something that is said, done or seen. When the poet Tennyson found a flower growing in a crannied wall he expressed his wonder in these words:

Flower in the crannied wall,
I pluck you out of the crannies,
I hold you there, root and all, in my hand,
Little flower – but if I could understand
What you are, root and all, and all in all,
I should know what God and man is.[33]

Spontaneous moments such as seeing a special flower, or hearing an odd comment or question from a child provide opportunities for raising questions on the spot about what this might mean. Unplanned Socratic discussions can prove particularly fruitful when they centre on a student's immediate interest. And although there can be no pre-planning for such events we can prepare ourselves to take advantage of questioning opportunities by becoming familiar with a range of Socratic questions and share our own wonder at the world with our students.

Philosophical investigation

> The more connections and interactions we ascertain, the more we know the object in question.
>
> John Dewey

A philosophical investigation is an exploratory enquiry. It is a process of coming to know something better by exploring connections and relationships. The enquiry can come through a question posed by the teacher, or from comments and questions from children. The enquiry into the nature of numbers (below) involved a teacher's question acting as a stimulus for children's questions.

One way is by having some open questions to investigate when appropriate. On one occasion, when a class discussion had come to a natural end I asked the exploratory question: 'How do you *know* I am Mr Fisher?' There was a silence. One child raised a hand, and said: 'How do *you* know you're Mr Fisher?'

Another way to stimulate investigation is to collect, and possibly display, children's questions. A Question Box, a Question Time, Question Board or Question Book are all ways in which teachers have encouraged curiosity, questioning and enquiry in their classrooms. The following questions were asked by 6-year-olds as possible starting points for enquiry:

> *If I have two eyes why don't I see two of you?*
> *How can we be sure everything is not a dream?*
> *Can flowers be happy or sad?*

The essence of investigation is problem posing. As the playwright N.F. Simpson once said: 'And suppose we solve all the problems it presents? What happens? We end up with more problems than we started with. Because that's the way problems propagate their species. A problem left to itself dries up or goes rotten. But fertilise a problem with a solution – you'll hatch out dozens.' Children need help in posing and recognizing problems, problems of interpretation and action, and there is no better way to help them become interrogators of their world than by engaging them in philosophical investigation.

Problem solving

> The problems are solved, not by giving new information, but by arranging what we have always known. Philosophy is the battle against bewitchment of our intelligence by means of language.
> Ludwig Wittgenstein (Philosophical Investigations, 1.109)

Philosophy can be defined as the application of critical and creative thinking to questions that are problematic. The problems of philosophy are often conceptual, requiring careful analysis of words and meanings, but they may also involve the seeking of practical solutions, to ways of leading a better life. One can think of conceptual analysis, the investigation of meanings and uses of language, as pure philosophy. For some modern philosophers it is the only kind of philosophy. But there is another more traditional branch which we might call applied philosophy. This kind of philosophy might involve investigation leading to greater understanding of a concept, but applies this understanding to a practical problem. For Socrates philosophy led both to better understanding and to practical virtue.

Life is intrinsically problematic. In any field of learning or human activity we can always ask: 'What is the problem?', and more generally we can ask 'What is a problem?'

A problem can be defined in at least three ways:

1. something hard to understand, to accomplish or to deal with, such as *it is hard to understand why children bully each other*
2. a difficult question requiring a solution, such as *how to prevent bullying is a problem*

3. a question to be resolved by calculation, such as a mathematical or logical problem

---

What are numbers?

The introduction to a lesson in philosophical enquiry with a class of 9- to 10-year-olds using 'think–pair–share:

Teacher: I want you to think about this question: 'What are numbers?' Don't put your hands up. I just want you to think. What are numbers? Why do we use numbers? Where have numbers come from? Did someone invent them? Where do they go? . . . How many doors are there in this room?

Child: Two.

Teacher: If I take away these two doors, so that there are no doors, where does that number 'two' go? I want to give you some thinking time, and just think to yourself: What are numbers? Why do we have numbers? Where do they come from? What are they? I'll just give you a couple of minutes to think about that.

(Two minutes' thinking time elapse.)

Now what I'd like you to do is to turn to the person next to you and talk about your ideas. Tell your partner says about what you've been thinking. Remember to listen carefully to what your partner says. Think how you're going to show you are listening to them. Everyone ready? Right . . . go.

(About three minutes' discussion time elapse.)

What I'm going to give you now is a piece of paper to write down some of your ideas. Number them if you want to, but you don't have to. Just put at the top 'What are numbers?' or 'What is a number?' Make sure you both agree what is written down, and know what is written down.

(Two minutes of writing and discussion time elapse.)

> Put a star by two statements or questions
> think are most important, most interesting or
> you'd like to share ... Now I'm going to ask you
> to choose one of those ideas with the group, and
> I'm going to write it up on the board, just to make
> sure it is accurate and it's what you've actually
> said ...
>
> (The teacher then scribes the comments and ques-
> tions from the children on the board, with the
> initials of the pair of children by their contribu-
> tion. She will ask the children to identify similar-
> ities or relationships between any of the
> comments, and then to choose one for sustained
> discussion.[34] For more on philosophical enquiry in
> mathematics see p. 207.)

A philosophical problem unlike a mathematical problem has
more than one possible solution, and resolving the problem is
a matter of exercising judgement. What a good question does
is to draw one's attention to the heart of the problem, which
is why analysing what a good question is can be so fruitful for
children. As they become used to asking questions and thinking about questions their questions will become more fluent,
more flexible, more elaborate and more original.

Strategies to extend and develop student thinking include:

- *thinking time* – Encourage pauses for thought or some
  quiet moments of meditation on a topic. Remember to
  provide at least three seconds thinking time after you have
  asked a question, and three seconds thinking time after a
  child has given an answer.
- *think–pair–share* – Allow individual thinking time about a
  question, invite discussion of the question with a partner,
  and then open up for class discussion.
- *ask follow-ups* – Help students to extend or clarify what
  they have said by asking questions that challenge their
  thinking, such as 'Why?', 'Do you agree or disagree?', 'Can
  you say more?', 'Can you give an example?', 'Describe how
  you arrived at that answer' (think aloud).
- *withhold judgement* – Respond to student answers in a

non-evaluative fashion, not saying whether you agree or disagree, for example by a positive but neutral response such as 'Thank you', 'OK', 'That's interesting', 'All right', 'A-ha', 'I see'.

- *invite the whole group to respond* – Encourage a response from the whole group, for example by having a survey of opinion: 'How many people agree/how many disagree with that point of view?' (Hands/thumbs up, or down), or inviting questions: 'Having heard that, what questions might we ask?'

- *ask for a summary* – Promote active listening by asking for a summary of what has been said, for example: 'Could you summarize Kim's point?', 'Can you explain what Jane has just said?', 'Can you tell me the arguments so far?'

- *allow students to nominate speakers* – Give students the responsibility to nominate the next speaker, for example by saying 'Lee, will you please choose someone else to respond?' or 'When you've made your point you can call on someone (with their hand up) to respond.'

- *play devil's advocate* – Challenge students to give reasons for their views by presenting opposing points of view, or by asking students to be devil's advocates: 'Who can think of a different point of view/an argument against that?'

- *invite a range of responses* – Model open-mindedness by inviting students to consider alternative viewpoints: 'There is no single correct answer to this question. I want you to consider alternatives.' Call on students randomly to respond, sometimes avoiding those students who always have raised hands.

- *encourage student questioning* – Invite students to ask their own questions, before, during and/or after the discussion: 'Think what questions you might ask', 'Has anyone a question about what has been said', 'What questions do you think still remain to be answered?'

A Socratic approach to questioning means taking seriously and showing a genuine interest in what children say and think, what they mean, and in what ways it is true or makes sense. If you are interested in the meaning and truth of what children say then your curiosity will be translated into probing questions. By sharing their wonder, teachers convey interest in and respect for student thinking and provide a model to inspire children to show the same curiosity about the meaning and truth of what they see and hear. The message is that we should take everyone's thinking seriously.

The strategy recommended for listening to readers is a good one to remember: pause – probe – praise: pause for thinking, probe for questioning and praise for serious efforts in contributions to discussion through speaking, listening and thoughtful response. To learn how to participate successfully in Socratic discussion one has to learn to listen carefully to what others say, to look for reasons and assumptions, to think about implications and consequences, to seek examples and analogies, to be aware of evidence supporting and objections against arguments, and to seek to distinguish what we know from what we believe.

Four kinds of question, argument or discussion

- *conceptual* – about meanings of words and ideas
- *empirical* – about evidence and matters of fact
- *logical* – about reasoning and what follows from what
- *evaluative* – about judgements of what is and should be

Enquiry, whether planned or unplanned, may contain four kinds of questioning, argument or discussion.[35] The first is *conceptual*, and is to do with the meanings of words. Disagreements and misunderstandings in life are often matters of having different understandings of words. An aim of any philosophical enquiry is to encourage the careful use and definition of words. One way to do this is to encourage children to make distinctions between similar concepts. For example what is the difference between 'love' and 'like'? Is 'art' the same as 'craft'? Is 'knowing' the same as 'believing'? What can be helpful here is the use of Venn diagrams, to show which words and ideas fall under each concept, and which relate to both concepts. These differences are not a matter of 'mere semantics' but are to do with the accurate matching of words with meanings so that we can be clear in our thinking and have some common criteria with which to judge the worth of reasons and arguments. Hence we can always ask after a question or during a discussion 'What do you mean by . . .?'

The second category is *empirical*, and is to do with matters of fact. We may agree or disagree about what is an example of something in real life, about what has or has not happened. When we ask a child to give an example that illustrates an idea, there may be a question about the truth or reliability of the evidence. Questions of evidence become very important in courts of law, and in a sense a Socratic enquiry is striving for the impartiality and rigour of a court of law. All claims of fact are open to challenge and the questions: 'What is your evidence?' or 'How do you know?'

A third category is *logical*, and is to do with checking on the correct use of reasoning. This may be through either deductive logic or inference. Deduction is when one idea follows logically, or is entailed by another. For example: All humans are mortal: The Queen is a human; therefore the Queen is mortal. In this argument the conclusion is entailed or logically contained in the first two premises. This does not prove the conclusion right, for the premises or assumptions it is based on may be wrong. It simply follows logically from the argument. Other kinds of logical argument are inferences where we draw conclusions from the evidence or reasons used. When Sherlock Holmes says he is using deduction, what he means is he is inferring from the evidence a conclusion. It is not necessarily true in a strictly logical sense, but is a justified belief which is true in the sense of being beyond reasonable doubt. We can, however, always ask the question: 'What reasons do you have?' or 'Can you prove it?'

The fourth category is *evaluative*, and is to do with the judgements we make about what is right, or to be believed. Here we may need to take into account the implications or consequences of an argument. 'If it is true, what then follows?' We are more likely to form better judgements if we take account of these different aspects of argument – the meanings of words we use, the evidence we have, and the reasons we use.

A Socratic discussion should be about argument and not a quarrel. A quarrel is a personalized argument in which the point of the exercise is to win, to score points and to establish dominance over the opponent. The motivation is ego-directed not rational, driven (and sometimes blinded) by emotion and not reason. The trouble with quarrels is that neither side can admit they are wrong. For some children the only kind of argument they see is quarrelling, whether it be in televized 'debate' or with family and friends. The goal of Socratic discussion is to be self-correcting and to teach the constructive resolution of disagreement. This is a challenge no less difficult and no less important today than it was 2500 years ago.[36] Through Socratic education, with its focus on questioning and on explanation, every learner also becomes a teacher, and plays a part in the continuing quest for understanding and for ways of life that are worth living.

NOTES AND REFERENCES

1. Fisher, R. (1990), *Teaching Children to Think*, Oxford: Blackwell, p. 183.
2. Spiegelberg, H. (ed.) (1964), *The Socratic Enigma: A Collection of Testimonies through Twenty Four Centuries*, Illinois: The Library of the Liberal Arts.
3. Gower, B.S. and Stokes, M.C. (eds) (1992), *Socratic Questions*, London: Routledge; Vlastos, G. (1991), *Socrates: Ironist and Moral Philosopher*, Cambridge: Cambridge University Press.
4. Abbs, P. (1994), *The Educational Imperative: A Defence of Socratic and Aesthetic Learning*, London: Falmer; Paul, R.W. (1995), *Socratic Questioning and Role Playing*, Sonoma, CA: Foundation for Critical Thinking.
5. See Cannon, D. and Weinstein M., 'Reasoning skills: an overview', in Lipman, M. (ed.) (1993), *Thinking Children and Education*, Dubuque, Iowa: Kendall Hunt, pp. 598–604.
6. For ways of helping children gain metacognitive under-

standing see Fisher, R. (1995), *Teaching Children to Learn*, Cheltenham: Stanley Thornes.

7. de Bono, E. (1992), *Teach Your Child How To Think*, London: Viking.
8. Piaget, J. (1948/1974), *To Understand Is to Invent: The Future of Education*, New York: Viking.
9. Torrance, quoted in Fisher, R. (1995), *Teaching Children to Learn*, Cheltenham: Stanley Thornes, p. 76. Torrance's books include: Torrance, E.P. (1962), *Guiding Creative Talent*, New York: Prentice Hall; and (1965), *Rewarding Creative Behaviour*, New York: Prentice Hall.
10. Castle, E.B. (1961), *Ancient Education and Today*, Harmondsworth: Penguin.
11. *Journal of Moral Education*, Vol. 23, No. 2, 1994.
12. Lipman, M. (1993), 'Encouraging Thinking for Oneself Through Socratic Teaching', in Lipman, M. (ed.) (1993), *Thinking Children and Education*, Iowa: Kendall/Hunt, pp. 435ff.
13. Sutcliffe, R. (1993), 'Is Philosophical Enquiry Virtuous?', *Aspects of Education*, No. 49, pp. 23–36.
14. Ferguson, J. (1970), *Socrates: A Source Book*, Milton Keynes: Open University Press.
15. See D.H. Lawrence's poem: 'Thought' in his *Complete Poems*, Harmondsworth: Penguin.
16. Sir John Davies' poem is from his set of philosophical poems *Nosce Teipsum* (1599), 'Know thyself'.
17. Fisher, R. (1995), op. cit.
18. Ross, G.M. (1993), 'Socrates versus Plato: the origins and development of Socratic teaching', *Aspects of Education*, No. 49, pp. 9–22.
19. Emmett, E.R. (1961), *Learning to Philosophize*, Harmondsworth: Penguin.
20. Aristotle, *Metaphysics*, M, 1078b, 17–19.
21. Plato, *The Republic*, 7, 537d.
22. Warnock, M. (1988), *A Common Policy for Education*, Oxford: Oxford University Press, p. 57.
23. Nelson, L. (1949), *Socratic Method and Critical Philosophy*, New Haven: Yale University Press.
24. Heckmann, G. (1993), *Das sokratische Gespräch*, Frankfurt: Dipa Verlag.

25. This chapter has benefited from the work of Karen Murris, a Dutch philosopher and teacher, who has introduced the European tradition of Socratic teaching into Britain. See Murris (1994), 'What is Socratic dialogue?', in *Classroom Philosophy*, May 1994, pp.2–7.
26. Nelson, L. (1992), *The Socratic Method*, reprinted in Lipman, M. (ed.) (1993), *Thinking Children and Education*, Kendall/Hunt, pp. 437–43.
27. Lipman, M. (1991), *Thinking in Education*, Cambridge: Cambridge University Press.
28. This dialogue formed part of the research project Philosophy in Primary Schools (PIPS) undertaken in west London schools 1993–6.
29. Fisher, R. (1992), 'Questions for thinking', *Multimind*, Vol. 1, No. 3, October 1992.
30. See research on teacher's use of questions in Alexander, P. (1992), *Policy and Practice in Primary Education*, London: Routledge. For more on research into questioning see Morgan, N. and Saxton J. (1991), *Teaching Questioning and Learning*, London: Routledge; Wragg, E.R. (1993), *Questioning*, London: Routledge.
31. For related lists of Socratic questions see: Lipman, M., Sharp, A.M. and Oscanyon, R. (1980), *Philosophy in the Classroom*, Philadelphia: Temple University Press; Paul, R. (1993), *Critical Thinking*, Santa Rosa, CA; Sprod, T. (1993), *Books into Ideas*, Victoria, Australia: Hawker Brownlow; Sharp, A. and Splitter, L. (1995), *Teaching for Better Thinking: The Classroom Community of Enquiry*, Victoria, Australia: ACER.
32. This account of Socratic discussion owes much to the work of Richard Paul. See Paul, R.W. (1995), *Socratic Questioning and Role-Playing*, Santa Rosa, CA: Foundation for Critical Thinking; and Paul, R.W. (1993), *Critical Thinking: How to Prepare Students for a Rapidly Changing World*, Santa Rosa, CA: Foundation for Critical Thinking.
33. For more poems as a stimulus for philosophical discussion see Fisher, R. (1997), *Poems for Thinking*, Oxford: Nash Pollock.
34. From a lesson given by a teacher researcher Debbie Pacey.

35. I am indebted to Victor Quinn for this analysis. See Quinn, V. (1996), 'Four arguments and a quarrel', in *If... then: The Journal of Philosophical Enquiry in Education*, February, pp. 26–31.
36. In Europe the phenomonal success of *Sophie's World*, by Jostein Gaarder (1995), London: Phoenix House, a history of philosophy in fictional form, provides evidence of a growing interest in philosophy. The book embodies both the Socratic tradition of questioning and enquiry, and the Platonic emphasis on knowledge of texts and theories.

CHAPTER 6

Philosophy in the Classroom: Reviewing and assessing progress

Philosophy is the cement that can help bind all the separate disciplines.

Matthew Lipman

Philosophy is useful in all lessons because it helps you think and learn.

Raheem, aged 10

Philosophical enquiry can help develop conceptual understanding in all areas of the curriculum. The use of discussion is essential for developing understanding of the structure of any discipline. If we deny learners opportunities to make meanings through dialogue then we are denying them the chance to communicate and to extend their understanding. The act of participating in discussions forces students to verbalize their ideas, to reconstruct their experience and to sort out misunderstandings and partially formed understandings. By pooling ideas in a community of enquiry the group will often find solutions to problems that individuals could not solve. By participating in a community of enquiry the student will be engaged on solving more problems than they would do as an individual working on their own. Sharing ideas in a group will help develop confidence and a sense of shared endeavour. 'Talking together,' said Kim, aged 8, 'helps me to think of things.'

According to teachers who engage their students regularly in communities of enquiry qualities such as self-esteem, courage in expressing a point of view, willingness to listen to others and openness to differences of opinion are developed through this special kind of discussion. For them a community of enquiry is a way students can be taught in any area of the curriculum to:

- develop curiosity, and the ability to raise questions for discussion
- become involved in dialogue on issues of importance
- explain, argue and reason about the topic in hand
- think for themselves, through developing their own ideas, views and theories
- share, consider and respond thoughtfully to the views of others

CREATING A THINKING CIRCLE

A community of enquiry can be described as a thinking circle. The seating of participants in a circle or its near-equivalent such as a horse-shoe shape allows for equality of position with maximum vision within the group. Once the setting is established the usual stages in organizing a community of enquiry can be summarized as follows:

- Community setting
- Presenting a stimulus
- Listing questions
- Choosing a question for discussion
- Facilitating the discussion
- Reviewing the discussion
- Extending the enquiry

The following figure shows how a circle can facilitate discussion across a group.

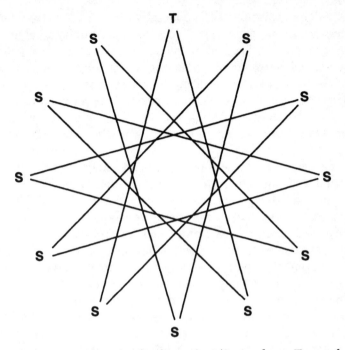

Figure 6.1   Socratic setting for discussion[2] (S = students, T = teacher)

COMMUNITY SETTING

Many classroom settings are not conducive to discussion. The physical setting is arranged for other processes and purposes. Children do not necessarily sit comfortably, or close enough for eye contact, and unstrained listening, in a room free of the distractions of movement and noise. Whatever the physical limitations of the setting, make the best of the situation available bearing in mind that each child should be able to see every other child's face. The ideal arrangement is to sit in a circle, either on chairs or sitting on the floor. Many teachers find that creating a physical setting that approximates to a 'thinking circle' helps to model and create a sense of community that encourages participation (see Figure 6.1).

There has been much research into the ideal conditions and numbers of participants for discussion.[1] Successful discussion can be achieved with differing group sizes, from 2 to 36 or more. The ideal number is generally around 12 to 16, which offers a good range of viewpoints and opportunity to contribute. Problems of large numbers can be overcome by dividing into two groups, or by including work in pairs and small groups during part of the discussion time. It is most important that every member of the class has the opportunity to enter into the discussion. As Cheryl, aged 10, said, 'It's good to know you can have a turn to talk even when you don't want to.'

Teachers use a variety of strategies to help create a special setting and ambience for discussion time. Some put a sign outside the door, such as: 'Do not disturb. Philosophy in progress', or find a special place in the school for uninterrupted discussion, such as the library, hall or studio. Others prefer the everyday setting of their classroom. One commented: 'Philosophical discussion is just part of good everyday teaching, it doesn't need any special setting.' Another said: 'Taking time to get the setting right helps to communicate the importance of what we are doing.' A third teacher said: 'The thinking circle should be a shared responsibility. I check with the children whether they think we have the best setting for our discussion.'

PRESENTING A STIMULUS

Philosophy is good because you don't know what you are going to have to think about.

Leon, aged 9

A stimulus is the presentation of a starting point for enquiry. The chosen stimulus should provide a kind of dramatic setting for the enquiry. It should provide what the philosopher Whitehead called Romance, that is something to stimulate the creative, critical or imaginative response of the student. The stimulus provides the challenging context for thinking. It aims to offer a positive cognitive intervention that will engage attention and stimulate enquiry. The starting point should be complex or challenging enough to repay close and focused attention.

One teacher described the criteria she used for choosing a stimulus as follows:

> I look for an example of something that is among the best in what has been created in that field, then I know that what I am offering is something of intrinsic worth. Sometimes it is quite new to the students, or it might be something familiar to some of them but which we are going to look at together in new ways.

Another teacher tries to choose something which interests her and to which her children will respond:

> I say to the children there is something here which I don't quite understand, and I would like you to help me to understand it better. It is true, and they often do!

In a typical philosophy for children session students begin the thinking process by reading a story or episode from a philosophical novel. If the stimulus is a text the community might be asked to share the reading, with individuals having the right to pass if they do not want to read. Each member could be invited to read a paragraph. Other forms of stimulus could include the presentation of one key question; reading student's own research, a poem, or other text; the close observation of an artefact or object of interest, or a picture; listening to a piece of music; viewing a video, or undertaking an experiment; or a shared experience such as a visit or field-trip. A very simple-seeming subject, like the words of a pop song, or a cauliflower placed in the centre of the circle, can provide a complex conceptual challenge. The stimulus could relate to any area of the curriculum, but should be of sufficient interest to arouse curiosity and to be sufficiently challenging to invite reflection and discussion.

There are many kinds of stimulus that provide suitable subjects for philosophical enquiry. The following letter reprinted from a newspaper has proved a challenging stimulus to discussion with older students and adults:

Dear Teacher,
I am the victim of a concentration camp. My eyes saw what no man or woman should witness: gas chambers built by learned engineers; children poisoned by educated physicians, infants killed by trained nurses; women and babies shot and burned by high school and college graduates.

> So I am suspicious of education. My request is: help your
> students to become human. Your effort must never produce
> learned monsters, skilled psychopaths, educated Eichmanns.
> Reading, writing and arithmetic are important only if they
> serve to make our children more human.
>
> Letter from School Principal to new teachers
> (*The London Tablet*, 10/10/92)

After the initial stimulus thinking time should be allowed so
that sufficient time is given for sustained attention and reflection. The stimulus might be repeated, or time given for students to process it themselves. At this point they should be
encouraged to ask themselves questions, and to think about
what was interesting, strange or puzzling about what they
have just seen, read or heard.

LISTING QUESTIONS

> *I like the thinking circle. It gives you the chance to think
> about and ask any question you like.*
>
> Rebecca, aged 10

A characteristic of a thinking circle is the experience participants get of having time to think, to reflect and to question.
Time for quiet and sustained thinking can occur at different
points in the enquiry, before the discussion starts, during the
discussion and at the end of the discussion. Thinking time
should always follow the experience of the stimulus for
enquiry to allow students time to reflect on what is interesting, puzzling or problematical about what was presented. This
is a time when students are invited to think of a comment or
question to share with the group. What is important here is
that the students are being asked to set the agenda for discussion. It is they who are interrogating, or learning to interrogate
the stimulus and their own thinking. Paper could be available
for students to note down their questions. These questions are
then shared with the class group, and listed on a board for all
to see.

The value of writing questions up on a board is that they
become visible, transportable and if necessary permanent
sources of enquiry. Students may be invited to write their own

questions on the board, or they may be scribed by the teacher
or another child. It is customary for the student's name to be
written alongside their question, both to identify the questioner and to provide public recognition of the contribution
that person has made to the enquiry through asking the
question. An alternative to the full name is to write the initial
of the student or students asking the question. It also means
that if the same, or very similar question is asked by different
students only their names need be added to the question on
the board. The listed questions provide evidence of enquiry
that can be displayed for all to see, can be added to over time,
and reflected on at a later time. Once questions from the group
are listed students can then choose which question or questions they wish to investigate.

CHOOSING A QUESTION FOR DISCUSSION

There are various ways in which one question from a list of
questions may be chosen. Students themselves may have a
preferred means for choosing which question to discuss. The
system for choosing questions should reflect community of
enquiry principles, which are that it should be reasonable, that
is founded on good reasons, and democratic, that is agreeable
to the majority of participants. The aim is to find a way of
choosing a question for discussion which meets with maximum approval and support. The methods for choosing may be
summarized as by:

- *lottery* – for example picking a question or number of the
  question from a hat
- *teacher choice* – choosing for example a theme to which
  most questions relate
- *individual pupil choice* – for example asking a pupil who
  has not spoken to choose
- *list order* – choosing the first question for discussion, then
  moving in order down the list
- *first past the post system* – the question with most votes
  being chosen

- *second round system* – with the two most popular questions being voted for again
- *multi-vote system* – where participants have two or more votes for chosen questions
- *transferable vote system* – in which members who did not vote for the leading questions are invited to re-allocate their votes
- *maxi-vote system* – in which anyone can vote for any and as many questions as they would like to discuss
- *progressive voting* – where members may vote for a question only if they give a reason for their choice

Choosing a question for discussion is an exercise in the procedures of democracy, aimed at respecting the majority or general will. What is recommended is that students in the thinking circle are given experience of different methods. The choice of any of the above methods can be supported by a reason. If for example a quick decision is needed then 'first past the post' might be the best option. What is important is that the members are clear which voting procedure is being used, and why. The problem with any democratic procedure is in safeguarding the interests of the minority. One way to overcome this is to organize for *all* the questions to be considered, for example by giving each question to a pair of students to discuss, or by giving out any questions not discussed to students to consider on another occasion.

Some of the best questions will arise during the discussion, such as in the following excerpt from discussion with children about a character in a story they read who had changed from being one kind of person to another. The group went on to discuss what it would mean to change into another person. What would change? If you swapped brains with someone would you be a different person . . .?

If you swapped brains with someone else would you be a different person?

From a philosophical enquiry with 6- to 7-year-olds:

Alex: If you swapped brains you would be someone else.

	You would do the things the other person would have done.
Nicola:	I disagree with Alex, because you would be the same person. You'd just have a different brain and different thoughts.
Alex:	Yes, but you would do something else that the other person wanted to do. You couldn't do what you wanted to because it wouldn't be your brain.
Richard:	You can't change your face, or your body or your brain.
Rebecca:	Your face would change as well as your brain.
Andrew:	Your voice would change.
Lisa:	You might be different or you might not. So I disagree with Alex.
Karen:	You would change because your brain makes your voice work, and you would say different things, and you would do different things and you would be a different person.
Sarah:	I agree with Lisa. Someone else might be able to do things you can't do, and you could do things that someone else can't do. Some things would be different and some things the same.
Kay:	You would change your age. You would have their age.
RF:	Would that make you a different person?
Rebecca:	If a teacher asks you something you would be thinking their thoughts. So you would be different.
Paul:	Yes, but no-one would *know* you were different. If the person thought of something, you might have the same thought. No one would know.
Alex:	I agree with Kay. If you were seven and swapped with a six-year-old, you would think you were their age. You would think you were them, so you would be different.
Emma:	It's your brain that tells you who you are.

You may find that the first three stages may take a whole lesson, and prefer to have the discussion, extension or review

activities in a second session. Lipman suggests that philosophical enquiry should take place twice a week, and this is the
preferred practice of many teachers. One of the benefits of this
approach is its flexibility. But whatever way it is planned the
core of the activity lies in discussion.

FACILITATING THE DISCUSSION

*You need to have someone to lead the discussion, but it
doesn't always have to be the teacher.*

Michael, aged 11

In facilitating a discussion the group leader's task is to encourage the expression of as many different ideas and opinions as
possible in the group, and to facilitate dialogue across these
differences.[3] Such discussion is no mere conversation. Facilitation of a successful community of enquiry is hard work.
If children find that 'the teacher will put up with aimless
discussion they will continue to ramble pointlessly until they
get bored.'[4] The function of the facilitator is to lead the group
through positive intervention in a philosophical direction
with the ultimate aim of some progress towards truth. This
is no easy matter. Many teachers report that this is the most
exhausting and challenging kind of teaching they have
engaged in. Persistence is needed to push for depth, not to be
content with the mere articulation of ideas but to ask continually 'Why?' 'What do you mean by . . .?' or to provide a
challenging counter-argument, can be gruelling work. When
it works well children will say things like 'We really had to
think hard!' When it fails to work well children make comments like 'It was a waste of time, we didn't get anywhere.'
As Susan Gardner points out: 'The fact that everyone has
something to say that is worth listening to does not mean
that everything that anyone says is worth hearing.'[5] Children's contributions can be repetitive, irrelevant, endlessly
anecdotal or simply reflective of a need to dominate the
discussion. The fact that much of what children say may be
without 'thought' (including their inner dialogue) is of course

a reason why philosophical discussion is so important. It is essential for the facilitator to keep the focus on thinking in the discussion, to ensure that students lay bare their thought processes and the reasoning behind their thinking. Children need to be made aware that this is an environment in which they must think before they speak, and think carefully about what is being said by others. Wittgenstein said: 'The philosopher's treatment of a question is like the treatment of an illness.' The approach is that of systematic, serious and sustained enquiry. But this intensive care and concern about precision in what is being said does not mean to say that the dialogue cannot be playful as in the following exchange between 11-year-olds:

Alan: If I had two brains I would be twice as clever.
Jenni: No you wouldn't, you'd just be in two minds all the time!

Students may be new to this way of working, and find it difficult to sustain reasoned dialogue as a group. Certain rules need to govern the discussion. A good way to start is to ensure these rules are understood and agreed at the outset. As Rebecca, aged 8, said: 'I think we need rules to help us remember what it is all about.'

RULES FOR ENQUIRY

An initial step that many teachers take towards developing the idea of a community of enquiry is to spend one session thinking about what rules would be useful for discussion sessions. A 'think-pair-share' approach often works well, where children think individually before exchanging their ideas with a partner or small group and before reporting back to the class. The process moves from inner talk (thinking), to oral expression, to written form. What is significant in developing sets of rules with different individuals, groups and classes is that although themes often recur, the sets of rules arrived at will differ and reflect the unique character of the individuals involved.

Here are examples of sets of rules for discussion created by individual 10-year-olds:

1. Listen to everyone's ideas and comments.
2. Give everyone an equal amount of time to speak.
3. Don't speak when another member of the class is speaking.
4. Listen to other people's ideas.
5. Try and put your partner's ideas into consideration.
6. Discuss all ideas.
7. Don't be scared to put your ideas forward.
8. Be kind to one another when you are in a group.

Donna, aged 10

After the rules have been created by individuals, they can be worked on in groups. One way to aid discussion is to ask the groups to make links between similar rules and try to agree in the best wording, and then to prioritize their agreed list of rules. Finally they can be developed through whole class discussion into a short list, incorporating as many ideas and suggestions as the children judge are of importance. The following is an example of a class set of rules having gone through this process:

1. Share your ideas with everyone.
2. Give everyone a chance to speak.
3. Take everyone's views into consideration.
4. Always listen carefully when someone is talking.
5. Be sensible, only put forward sensible ideas.
6. Discuss each other's ideas, but be careful not to interrupt.
7. Be polite, don't make rude comments about other people's ideas.

class of 10-year-olds

Rules such as these, agreed by the community, might be posted up for all to see as an aide-mémoire to the rules agreed to. During the discussion it may be the responsibility of all to monitor that the rules are being kept, or an umpire might be appointed with responsibility to check that the rules are being observed. This can be a particularly positive role for an otherwise disruptive child!

LISTENING AND RESPONDING

'What I like about the philosophy lesson is that you get listened to,' said Gary, aged 10. The skills of facilitation involve listening and responding. When we are listened to and we feel that we are speaking from our own experience we feel that who we are and the value of what we have to say are being affirmed. It is only when we have our current perceptions affirmed that we are ready to respond to wider perceptions and viewpoints. So when being a listener the more we show we are aware of the perceptions of the speaker the more likely is the communication to be effective. As the Greek philosopher Epictecus said: 'Nature has given one tongue, but two ears, that we may hear from others twice as much as we speak.'

Responsive listening is a skill as well as an attitude. Both we and our students need to practise it to get better at it. Responsive listening is marked by giving undivided and thoughtful attention in a way that communicates genuine acceptance and empathy. We all tend to see the world from our own point of view, coloured by our current feelings and expectations. The danger is that any of these factors can get in the way of hearing what is actually being said. An important task in responding to children is not to mix in our own ideas with what the child is saying, for example by paraphrasing. That is why checking on what the child is actually saying, without necessarily re-phrasing it, or when writing a child's comment or question on the board, getting the child's words right is so important.

Part of the skill of responding by the group leader will be the use of the kinds of Socratic questions which we have already discussed. Another way is to have a discussion plan prepared which focuses attention on a particular concept and explores it in greater depth than the students alone might achieve (see below for more on discussion plans). The role of the teacher or leader is crucial in providing a model – a model of seriousness, of attentive response and of keen interest in the ideas of others. As Patrick, aged 11, commented: 'A good teacher is interested in what you have to say, and tries to get you to say more.'

What is listening?

The following are some questions to consider:

- How do you communicate that you are giving full attention when listening?
- What factors might prevent you from active listening?
- During a discussion with children what are you actively listening for?

Questions to discuss with children:

- Is it easy or hard to listen? Why? Give an example.
- Is listening the same as hearing? In what ways is it similar and different?
- How do you know when someone is listening to you?
- How do you know someone understands what you say when you are speaking to them?
- Does listening need you to pay attention? Does it need patience? Is it hard work?
- What do you find really worth listening to?

LEADING THE DISCUSSION

In a community of enquiry the teacher is part of the circle, leading the group in a sharing activity. Experience in this large group provides a model for the norms we hope the child will follow in other, smaller learning groups.

The benefits that a teacher can bring to an inquiry or learning conversation include the following elements of mediation:

- focusing and maintaining relevance, e.g. by directing attention to important points, issues or factors in discussion
- seeking meaning, e.g. by asking for reasons, explanation or clarification of ideas
- expanding, e.g. by showing links between ideas, and links to new ideas for discussion
- discouraging the tendency of students to focus on their

own ideas rather than responding to and building on the ideas of others
- rewarding, e.g. by verbal or non-verbal expressions of positive response every positive contribution to the discussion

The aim is to enable group members to experience the many-sidedness of concepts that may be ambiguous and contestable and to achieve a better understanding of the topic under discussion through shared enquiry. One of the ways to achieve *shared* enquiry is to encourage children to talk and listen to each other, rather than for them to direct all their talk through the teacher. A useful rule to help children focus on what is being said is that no-one puts their hand up to speak until someone has finished what they want to say. Another possible rule to structure the discussion is that each participant must say who they are responding to, either by agreeing, disagreeing or adding to what they have said, e.g. 'I agree/disagree with Michelle because . . .' Speakers should also be encouraged to look at the person to whom they are responding.

In the early stages of discussion children may signal their wish to speak, or may simply speak when they have a chance to each other as in a conversation. The challenge for the teacher or leader is to ensure equality of opportunity as well as quality of dialogue. Problems that can occur include children interrupting each other, or not paying attention. One strategy for countering interruptions is to give each child an 'interruption card' (what one teacher calls a 'burning hand') that can be used once in the session by a child if they feel they have something important to say which can't wait. No other interruptions to a speaker are allowed. It can be helpful to give children note paper to write down what they want to say, perhaps noting who they agree or disagree with. Or a written task could be set during the discussion as a means of focusing attention. An effective method for discouraging dominant speakers is to give each member of the class five tokens. They must place one down each time they speak. When they have finished their tokens they must keep quiet! Another strategy to focus attention is to have half the group sitting outside the circle as observers (or participant researchers) noting the strengths and weaknesses in the discussion, then having the groups change places, so that each has a turn at discussing and as observers or reporters.

At the end of discussion there are various ways to provide a suitable sense of closure. The discussion will probably have tacked back and forth, and there may be a sense of incompleteness about the activity. This is partly inevitable since enquiry does not end with the discussion but is part of a continuing process of questioning, reflection and attempts to formulate better understanding of complex matters. This quest to understand the nature, and key concepts that structure any discipline, whether it be science, maths, history or art, is an ongoing process that has exercised and will continue to exercise the minds of experts in the field. However, certain strategies will provide a sense of psychological, if not philosophical, closure to the discussion.

One is through summary of the development of the discussion. With very young children this may be the teacher's summary, but the aim should be to help the children summarize the discussion for themselves. It may be helpful to track the discussion as it takes place by making notes of the main points, arguments, questions and issues on the board. Taping the discussion for later playback may help the group reflect on both the content and process. Asking students in pairs to try to reconstruct what they remember of the discussion can provide an interesting challenge.

Another strategy for closure is to provide an opportunity for 'last words' or 'final comments'. That is when each student has a final turn to say anything about the discussion which they have not said before or had a chance to say. They may pass or choose to say in a few brief sentences what they think. The rule here is that no-one is allowed to interrupt or respond. There is one turn each before the end of the session. These final words might be written, for example to note any ideas they thought were interesting or had not thought before, or to write any questions or comments they had not had a chance of saying.

A third way is to give students the chance to review the session. This element in the process is so important that it deserves to be regarded as a separate and key stage in the process. One of the marks of progress in philosophy is self-correction. Tell children that it is all right to change their mind, and part of the review process at the end might be to ask whose ideas have changed, or who has been given new ideas about the subject through listening to or thinking about the discussion.

REVIEWING THE ENQUIRY

Was it a good discussion?

Questions to aid review, evaluation and self assessment include:

- Did we ask many questions? What good questions did we ask? Why were they good?
- Did we listen well? Did everyone listen to what others had to say? Who listened well?
- Did we speak well? Did we explain well? Who spoke well?
- Did we take turns? Did we help each other to speak? Did we help their ideas?
- What reasons did we give? Did we think of different reasons? Were they good reasons?
- What ideas did we have? Did we change any of our ideas? Did we improve any ideas?
- What did we learn from the discussion? Did it help us understand anything better? What did I learn that I didn't know before?
- Was it a good discussion? Why?
- Was the discussion philosophical? In what ways?
- Did we make progress in the discussion? How could we make it better in the future?

Review is an important element in the process, as it helps to develop metacognitive awareness of the process, the content and the response of individuals. It aims to help children to identify what they have learnt from the experience, where they and others achieved success, and ways in which they or the group could improve in the future. This review can take place during or after the discussion. It can be undertaken as part of a whole group discussion, through paired discussion, in response to an evaluation sheet of key questions (see p. 262 for a sample of this) or through individuals doing a 'thinkwrite' in their notebooks or learning logs.

In analysing progress in a discussion it is important to have some success criteria against which to judge progress. In particular we need to reflect the two key aspects of philosophical enquiry, first the philosophical element: What makes a discussion philosophical? Secondly the enquiry element: How do we assess progress in philosophical discussion? (see pp. 193ff.).

EXTENDING THE ENQUIRY: EXERCISES, DISCUSSION PLANS AND GAMES

Teachers may wish to extend the philosophical enquiry through creative activity or exercises. Such creative activity might include writing a story, play or poem, doing some role play, making a model, or designing some artwork. It might include discussing, drawing or writing about certain aspects of the topic under discussion. A follow-up exercise might aim to promote accuracy and skill development related to curriculum application of the topic.

Exercises

A philosophical activity or exercise aims to extend thinking around a central topic or problem. It provides further opportunities for students to make judgements, for example in investigating relationships or making comparisons. What is similar? What is different? What is identical? (See Venn diagram task, pp. 33–4).

What is a friend? An activity which explores the nature of friendship.

Give children cards, on each of which are written one of the following definitions of a friend. Include some blank cards on which the children can write their own definitions. Ask children with a partner to look at the definitions, including their own, and to sort the definitions in order, starting with the one they agree with most and ending with the one they agree with least. When they have done this ask them to share their decisions with another, or the whole group.

A friend is someone you know.
A friend is someone who does what you say.
A friend is someone who is always on your side.
A friend is someone who agrees with everything you say.
A friend will always forgive you if you do something wrong.
A friend is someone you can share all your secrets with.
A friend is someone who helps you when things go wrong.
A friend is someone you meet every day.
A friend is someone of the same race and religion as you.
A friend is . . .

Discussion plans

A philosophical discussion plan usually consists of a group of questions that explore a single concept, relationship or problem. The questions may build on each other or focus upon the topic from different angles. Or the plan may consist of one central question, like 'What is fairness?'

Why use discussion?

The following questions could help frame your own thinking, or act as a starting point for discussion with colleagues or students.

1. What is a discussion?
2. Is every kind of talking together a discussion?
3. Do discussions need rules?
4. What good can come out of discussing things with others?
5. What do you like/not like about discussions?
6. Can you remember a good discussion? What made it good?
7. What things are best for discussion?
8. Are there some things you would not want to discuss?
9. Do you prefer to talk or listen in a discussion?
10. What would you like to discuss?

(from Fisher, R. (1995), *Teaching Children to Learn*, p. 50)

Games: activities to extend thinking

You play better if you think better.

Paul, aged 10

The essence of a game is that it involves actions undertaken for the purpose of enjoyment. But games can also have serious purposes. They can help us to practise skills, to develop concepts and strategies. They are particularly useful as 'warm-up' activities to enliven minds or to provide a motivating start to philosophical enquiry. They can be used as a closing activity at the end of a session, rounding off a period of work in an entertaining and challenging way. Thinking games can also become a focus for philosophical enquiry in their own right. Games can also function as the focus of a lesson, if they are 'games for thinking', that is games that have both curriculum relevance and cognitive content, by encouraging philosophical discussion between groups of children and between pupil and teacher.[6]

Thinking games give players practice in such skills as planning, questioning, reasoning, seeing things from different viewpoints and thinking of new ideas. In a sense every session of philosophical enquiry with children is a thinking game. A philosophical enquiry is a rule-governed activity, or should be (whether the rules are consciously agreed or internalized as conventions that are implicitly understood). The following are some of the critical thinking skills which thinking games can help to develop:

- analysing visual and verbal information
- applying rules
- categorizing
- checking and correcting
- communicating thoughts and ideas
- comparing and contrasting
- defining and describing
- divergent or lateral thinking
- estimating and educated guessing
- evaluating
- explaining
- forming conceptual links and associations

- formulating questions
- generating ideas and hypotheses
- giving and following directions
- identifying information needed
- logical thinking
- imagining
- making inferences
- making informed judgements
- memorizing
- non-verbal communication
- observing
- planning
- predicting
- problem posing
- problem solving, recognizing progress towards a solution
- reading for meaning
- seeing another's point of view
- sequencing
- spatial thinking
- strategic thinking
- synthesizing
- testing and improving ideas
- understanding cause, effect and probability
- verbal reasoning
- visualization
- writing and word skills

For example the game 'What if . . .' (see below) encourages players to create an original hypothesis or variation on everyday thinking that creates a new but possible world, and to consider what the consequences of that hypothesis might be. The 'What if . . .?' game is not simply an exercise in make-believe. It invites players to extend their thinking by considering the consequences of an imagined situation. 'What if . . .?' can be used to develop the four aspects of creative thinking:

- *fluency of ideas* – how many 'What ifs' can you think of?
- *flexibility of ideas* – what different 'What ifs' can you think of?
- *originality of ideas* – what 'What if?' has nobody thought of?

- *elaboration of ideas* – what are the possible consequences of a 'What if?'

What if . . .?

Aim of the game
The basis of creative or hypothetical thinking is the question 'What if . . .?' The aim of these games is to encourage creative thinking, through creating and thinking through the consequences of hypothetical states of affairs.

Players: Any number, playing in pairs, groups or as whole class
Age range: Seven to adult
Materials: Pen/pencil and paper

'What ifs?' provide possible starting points for discussion and writing, for example:

What if . . . plants started to walk?
you were turned into a frog?
no-one needed to go to sleep?
people discovered the secret of eternal life?
the oceans all dried up?
you were really given three wishes?
there were another Ice Age?
you won a prize of £1000?
you were given your own TV station to run?
you discover your best friend is a thief?

What do you think would happen and why?

These or similar 'What if . . .?' questions can be written on cards prior to the game, or can be written on a board during the game.

Here are some ways of playing 'What if . . .?' games:

1. What if – just a minute
Can you talk for one minute (or half a minute) on a given 'What if?' question?
Players play individually, in pairs or in team groups. A number of 'What if?' questions are written on cards, or on the board before play begins.

How to play
1. Each player, pair or team group is given, or chooses, a 'What if?' question to answer.
2. Players or teams are given a few minutes to prepare their answer, for example by brainstorming or noting ideas.

3. Each player, or representative of a pair or team of players, is then asked to speak for one minute in answer to their 'What if?' question.
4. Players win if they can 'beat the clock' by speaking without hesitation, repetition or deviation from the subject, for one minute (or half a minute if that is their target time).
5. The discussion can then be opened to other players, to question, comment or respond to the answer that has been given. After the discussion it is the turn of the next player to answer their question and to try to 'beat the clock'.

2. What if – questions
Can you make up your own 'What if?' question? How many 'What if?' questions can you make up? Which is the most interesting 'What if?' question?

How to play
1. Each player, pair or team group is asked to make up as many 'What if?' questions as they can in a given time.
2. Players, or teams, are given the agreed time to brainstorm and note down their ideas.
3. Each player, or representative of a pair or team of players, is then asked to share their 'What if?' questions. The winning players/teams are the ones who have listed the most questions, or who have reached a given target, for example ten 'What if?' questions.

Questions to think about
- Which do you think (from a list) is the most interesting question?
- Which is the most creative question?
- Which question(s) have you never thought about before?
- Can you think of a 'What if?' question that could *never* come about? Why?
- Can you think of a 'What if?' question that *could* happen? Why or how could it happen?
- When is it helpful for you to think 'What if . . .?'
- What helps you to have new ideas?
- Is it better to have many ideas or to have one idea? Why?
- Is it useful to think of consequences of what might happen? Why?
- What is imagination? What helps you have a good imagination?

Crucially in a thinking game the thinking is not over once the game has finished. Through questions and discussion players are invited to think carefully, broadly and purposefully about the game, and to reflect on their thinking through the game (what are the options and consequences?) and beyond the game (what have I learnt from playing the game?) A thinking game should encourage intellectual enquiry, and provide opportunities to exercise different aspects of players' intelligence, which might include the verbal, logical–mathematical, visual, physical, musical, intra-personal or social.

What are the benefits of playing thinking games? There is some evidence to show that when children play thinking games regularly over the span of a school year they improve in creative thinking skills and in their ability to participate in group problem-solving activities. Some teachers have reported improvements in verbal reasoning abilities and in mathematical ability, but it is difficult to prove that playing these games will automatically improve thinking and reasoning. It is likely that children will need to play thinking games over a number of years for there to be real and lasting benefits to their thinking and learning.

But the strongest reason for playing these games is not to improve the players' minds, or to improve their social skills, but because the games provide pleasure, challenge, what Yeats called 'the joy of what's difficult', and the joy of exercising one's human capacities in play. And it is a pleasure which can be used to enrich not only philosophy for children but any area of the curriculum.

At the end of an enquiry the group may have had a stimulus, asked questions, enquired into a topic (or number of topics), examined their thinking and been pushed for depth in the discussion, and reviewed and possibly extended the enquiry through an activity or exercise. The task now is to evaluate what has happened, and to use this assessment to inform future planning.

EVALUATION AND ASSESSMENT

I know that philosophy is good for you, but I can't say why.

Steven, aged 10

Questions that can help in the process of evaluation include:

- What happened?
- What did I learn?
- What did the children learn?
- What next?

In considering what happened in a philosophy session we need to answer the questions: *What makes a discussion philosophical? How do we assess progress in philosophy for children?* and *Does philosophy for children work?*

WHAT MAKES A DISCUSSION PHILOSOPHICAL?

The following are some elements to look for when evaluating a discussion or activity for its philosophical content:

1. Topics: content of discussion involves –	•exploring philosophical concepts (central, common and contestable)
2. Aims: learning intentions include –	•children learning to philosophize (posing/investigating/solving problems)
3. Process: teaching strategies include –	•a community of enquiry approach (a shared stimulus for philosophical enquiry) •students posing questions (setting their own agenda for discussion) •being given time to think (thinking as internal dialogue -Vygotsky)

- listening to and building on ideas (attentive listening, responding to others)
- following the enquiry where it leads (progressing towards truth or understanding)
- forming judgements based on reasons (giving reasons for beliefs)
- thinking about thinking (review and self-correction)
- developing positive attitudes (self-esteem, thoughtfulness towards others)

4. Learning outcomes: being able to –

- think for oneself (not relying on outside authorities)
- generate questions (speculate, hypothesize and interrogate)
- develop and build on ideas (being creative in one's thinking)
- communicate clearly (articulating one's thoughts)
- give sound reasons for beliefs (justifying beliefs, being critical)

The following is an example of philosophical discussion in the classroom with 13- to 14-year-old children. The stimulus for the discussion was provided by the following lines from the ancient Chinese philosopher Chuang Tzu (3rd century BC):[7]

Once Chuang Tzu dreamt he was a butterfly,
fluttering here and there.
Aware he was a butterfly.
Suddenly he awoke
and found he was Chuang Tzu.

Now he does not know
if he was Chuang Tzu

> *dreaming he was a butterfly*
> *or a butterfly*
> *dreaming he is Chuang Tzu.*

The question chosen by the group to discuss was 'Was the man dreaming?'

How do we know we are not dreaming?

An excerpt from a classroom discussion:

RF: How do we know we are not dreaming?

David: Dreams are just in your mind and not like anything real at all.

Chris: I disagree. You can dream you are swimming, and it's just like it's for real.

Naomi: I think imaginary things like dreams are just like real things. You can't always tell the difference.

RF: If you are imagining you are swimming and it feels real, how does it differ from the real thing?

Tom: If you're imagining it you're probably imagining it from real things you've seen and done, heard and smelt and whatever.

RF: What is the difference between really dreaming you are actually swimming, and feeling the cool water on your body and the spray, and the *real* thing of swimming?

Tom: Well, when you're dreaming it you can fall asleep and not die. In the water you can. If you're really in the water there's a risk of drowning and you've got to carry on. In dreams you're safe . . .

RF: If you're dreaming of being in the water, what's the difference between that and actually being in the water, because it *feels* the same.

Nick: Well I'd say that when you're actually in the water you can really feel it, but I'd say in dreams it's not completely real, there's something weird about, it's more imaginary, it's not like real life.

RF: So there's a difference in feeling, is that right?

Tom: It's like writing. In dreams you just write, but you don't know what you're writing, but in real life

195

	you have to think about it, and you know what you're writing.
Jake:	I disagree. I think it depends on how real the dream is. Some dreams seem more real than others.
RF:	So is there a difference in quality between a dream and real life?
Sarah:	In dreams you don't know actually what's happening or why. In dreams, I don't know how to describe it, you get an odder feeling. It's as if you're there and not there.
Tom:	It's like if there's a truck about to run you down you can't move. It's a kind of emptiness.
Emma:	Sometimes it feels more real in dreams than in real life.
Tom:	You can't really tell the difference. In dreams you're suddenly there, like you're swimming the 500 metres in the Olympics.
Nick:	I think most dreams are odd ones, are weird ones where you come out and a nun smiles, she's got green teeth and suddenly horns sprout out of her head . . .
Ben:	You remember the funny mad dreams, but you forget the boring ones.
Tom:	I agree, you remember the dreams that are out of the ordinary . . . strange, but the ones like ordinary life you don't remember much.
Jake:	You can never prove it, but you can be pretty sure it is a dream. In dreams you wake up, in real life you don't.

The discussion was philosophical in the sense it was about knowledge and belief (epistemology) and the nature of minds, but it was also in response to a poem so it was also in part a lesson in literature. Philosophical discussion can make an important contribution not only to English teaching but to other subjects across the curriculum (see Chapter 7). But before we look at its cross-curricular potential we need to consider the third phase in the planning–teaching–evaluation cycle – does philosophy in the classroom achieve significant learning outcomes? In other words, does it work?

DOES PHILOSOPHY FOR CHILDREN WORK?

If one learns from others but does not think, one will be bewildered. If, on the other hand, one thinks but does not learn from others, one will be in peril.
                                    Confucian Analects, 11.15

How do we assess progress in philosophical discussion?

There are two main ways of gathering evidence of progress in philosophical discussion either by the teacher/researcher analysing evidence of the discussion, or through self-assessment by the participants. Some ways of assessing and analysing transcripts of discussions will be found in Appendix 3.

Lipman's Philosophy for Children was initially designed as a programme of curriculum innovation to improve reasoning skills and thereby to improve the cognitive elements of academic performance. Philosophy for Children also appeals to educators in many countries not only as an intervention to raise educational standards through the development of thinking and reasoning, but also because it is seen as a way of fostering moral and social, particularly democratic, values. Philosophy in the classroom can therefore be evaluated across a number of dimensions that relate to many of the basic intellectual, moral and social aims of education.

The processes allowing for effective change when introducing any innovation in the curriculum are governed by five factors, or stages, which according to Fullan[8] can be summarized as:

1. Initiation of the programme
2. Implementation of the programme
3. Use of the programme
4. Impact and outcomes of the programme
5. Institutional response to the programme

Such a model can be applied to the introduction of Philosophy for Children within a range of institutional and social contexts. In Chapter 7 we look at Philosophy for Children within the wider context of the management of effective curriculum change in schools, but for now we will focus on research relating to evaluating impact and outcomes of the programme in the USA, in international and UK contexts.

The research evidence from a wide range of small-scale studies in countries across the world indicates that the Philosophy for Children programmes can make a difference to various aspects of a child's academic performance.[9] My own research and informal discussions with teachers and trainers from all parts of the world echo the findings of published research that:

- Philosophy for Children works best when teachers feel well motivated, supported and trained (Jackson 1993)[10]
- the benefits of Philosophy for Children in terms of quality of discussion accrue over time (Palsson 1994, 1996)[11]
- Philosophy for Children lessons within a Community of Enquiry format have positive effects on the quality of thinking, in particular 'dialogical, dialectical and argumentative' reasoning (Santi 1993)[12]
- Philosophy for Children is an effective programme for teaching democratic community values (Raitz 1992)[13]
- Philosophy for Children programmes have a positive effect in improving the self-esteem of students (Kite 1991, Sasseville 1994)[14]
- Philosophy for Children develops children's abilities in creative thinking (Kite 1991)
- Philosophy for Children programmes can help students obtain higher achievement scores in English and Mathematics (Williams 1993, Lim 1994)[15]
- Philosophy for Children programmes benefit from curriculum extension through the use of culturally modified and curriculum-relevant materials (Davies 1994, Holder 1994)[16]

Formative evaluations of these projects confirm that students enjoy philosophic discussion and find the community of enquiry approach motivating. Teachers generally feel that philosophical discussion adds a new dimension to their teaching and to the way students approach thinking. Students become more ready to ask questions, to challenge each other and to explain what they mean. Discussion in a community of enquiry requires the group to develop trust and the ability to cooperate, and to respect the views of others. They develop insight into the problematical nature of knowledge, and the need to subject what they read, see and hear to critical enquiry. Through this process they develop self-esteem as thinkers and learners. They can be expected to obtain higher achievement scores in tests of verbal and mathematical reasoning. They become more flexible and creative in their thinking. These effects are most powerful when philosophical discussion is extended across the curriculum. In the next chapter we look at ways of using philosophical discussion across the curriculum. As Jemma, aged 10, said: 'Philosophy can help in all your lessons, no matter what you're learning.'

NOTES AND REFERENCES

1. For a summary of research into the use of discussion in classrooms see Dillon, J.T. (1994), *Using Discussion in Classrooms*, Milton Keynes: Open University Press.
2. An analysis of seven settings for discussion is illustrated in Fisher, R. (1995), *Teaching Children to Think*, Cheltenham: Stanley Thornes, pp. 162–6.
3. For differing approaches to facilitating philosophical discussion see Sprod (1993), Cam (1995), Wilks (1995), de Haan et al. (1995) and Quinn (1997). See also Gardner, S. (1996), 'Inquiry is no mere conversation (or discussion or dialogue): facilitation of inquiry is hard work!', *Analytic Teaching*, Vol. 16, No. 2, pp. 41–51.
4. Lipman M., et al. (1980), *Philosophy in the Classroom*, Philadelphia: Temple University Press, p. 92.
5. Gardner, op. cit., p. 45.
6. For more on thinking games see *Games for Thinking* by Robert Fisher (Nash Pollock, 1997).
7. Source: Fisher, R., *Poems for Thinking*, p. 80.
8. Fullan, M. (1991), *The New Meaning of Educational Change*, London: Cassell.
9. Lipman, op. cit., pp. 217–24.

10. Jackson, T. (1993), 'Eualuation Report of Philosophy for Children in Hawaii', *Thinking*, Vol. 10, No. 4, pp. 36–44.
11. Palsson, H. (1994), 'Interpretative research and philosophy for children', *Thinking*, Vol. 12, No. 1, pp. 33–40.
12. Santi, M. (1993), 'Philosophizing and learning to think: some proposals for a qualitative evaluation', *Thinking*, Vol. 10, No. 3, pp. 15–23.
13. Raitz, K.L. (1992), 'Philosophy for children in Guatemala', *Thinking*, Vol. 10, No. 2, pp. 6–12.
14. Kite, A. (1991), *Teaching Thinking in the Classroom: A Case Study*, MEd thesis (unpublished), Edinburgh: Edinburgh University; Sasseville, M., (1994), 'Self esteem, logical skills and philosophy for children', *Thinking*, Vol. 11, No. 2, pp. 30–3.
15. Williams, S. (1993), *Evaluating the Effects of Philosophical Enquiry in a Secondary School*, Derby: The Village Community School Philosophy for Children Project. At secondary level a one-year project was undertaken at an inner-city comprehensive in Derby, involving 27 one-hour lessons with two groups of year 7 pupils, using a British version of Lipman's *Harry* novel in English lessons. One class had philosophy lessons with a trained teacher, the other had conventional English lessons. Overall the philosophy class showed greater gains in three measured areas than the control class, including a 'modest though reliably positive effect on the reading ability as tested by the London Reading Test, an improvement in intellectual confidence as measured by self-assessment on a 7-point scale, and teacher assessment using pre-determined criteria relating to cognitive and inter-personal performance' (Williams 1993). Lim, T.K. (1994), 'Formative evaluation of the Philosophy for Children project in Singapore', *Critical and Creative Thinking*, Vol. 2, No. 2, pp. 58–66; Lim, T.K. (1994), 'The Philosophy for Children project in Singapore', *Thinking*, Vol. 11, No. 2, pp. 33–7.
16. Davies, S. (1994), *Improving Reading Standards in Primary Schools Project Report*, Dyfed LEA. An 18-month research project studying the use of the Murris picture-books approach with Year 1 children, mostly bilingual, in six schools found gains in 'thinking and reasoning; listen-

ing skills; expressive language; discussion and debating skills; confidence and self esteem' (Dyfed 1994). Holder, J.J. (1994), 'Philosophy for Children in the Philippines project: Final Report', *Thinking*, Vol. 12, No. 1, pp. 41–4. These research studies show that philosophy for children improves standards of reading, particularly in reading for inference and meaning. It is hoped therefore that philosophy for children will have an important part to play in the new 'Literacy Hour' programmes for shared reading being developed in all primary schools in England and Wales.

CHAPTER 7

Philosophy across the Curriculum: Improving the quality of thinking and learning

One of the problems with philosophy is finding a place for it on the timetable.

Primary teacher

Philosophical questions can come out of anything.

Laura, aged 10

'Philosophy is fine,' said one teacher, 'it builds on what I want to do with the children, but where do I fit it into the curriculum?' Finding a place for philosophy in the curriculum is a problem many teachers face. One approach is to try to add it into an already crowded timetable. If we are serious about the need for children to question, to think and to discuss issues together in ways that offer them the highest intellectual challenge then a philosophy lesson will have at least as much justification as any other kind of lesson. If there is no time within the formal curriculum, some teachers choose to arrange philosophy sessions as an extra-curricular club at lunchtime or after school. A more common approach is to use philosophy within the given time-table, for example as part of English or Personal and Social Education.

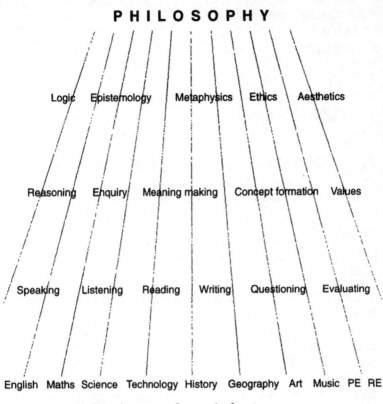

Figure 7.1   **Philosophy across the curriculum**[1]

This chapter will show how opportunities for philosophical enquiry can occur in any subject area of the curriculum. For many teachers the most natural home for philosophy is as an aspect of teaching English language and literature, but as language is a medium for learning across the curriculum, the philosophical uses of language can be explored through every subject area. Figure 7.1 shows how philosophy involves processes of enquiry that link to all areas of the curriculum.

This chapter explores some ways philosophical enquiry can enrich teaching and learning in the following subject areas:

- English: language and literature
- maths
- science

203

- design and technology
- history
- geography
- art
- music
- physical education
- religious education

ENGLISH: LANGUAGE AND LITERATURE

The limits of my language are the limits of my world.
                                        Ludwig Wittgenstein

A dictionary tells you what words mean but philosophy helps you understand what they mean.
                                        Jasbir, aged 10

Every lesson is a lesson in language, for language is, as Dr Johnson said, the dress of thought. Talking and writing are forms of thinking. At the same time they are activities through which thinking can be developed and extended. The common bond between philosophy and the teaching of English is that both involve a search for meaning. Both the philosopher and the skilled writer (or speaker) are concerned about the precise use of language to communicate meaning and understanding. Both are concerned with similar questions about the ways in which words connect with each other and connect with the world. Children who are engaged in philosophy are engaged in a language activity that will help them to become better language users. Vygotsky, a proponent of the prime importance of words for thinking, argues:

> Real concepts are impossible without words, and thinking in concepts does not exist beyond verbal thinking. That is why the central moment in concept formation, and its generative cause, is a specific use of words as functional tools.[2]

Every philosophical enquiry is a lesson in language, and meets many of the aims of English teaching. The National Curriculum prescriptions for Speaking and Listening in English (DfE 1995) could have been written with philosophy for children in mind. It states for example that 'pupils should be given opportunities to talk for a range of purposes, including; exploring, developing and explaining ideas . . . sharing insights and opinions.' The key skills it identifies are central to the aims of philosophical enquiry. Under 'Key skills for Key Stage 2 (grades 3–6)' we read that 'in discussion, pupils should be given opportunities to make a range of contributions . . . This range should include making exploratory and tentative comments when ideas are being collected together, and making reasoned, evaluative comments . . .' There is no problem in getting young people to talk. The problem is often getting children, especially in class, *not* to talk. Philosophy for children is a way to help them to make this talk constructive and meaningful, and through it to sustain intellectual curiosity.

About listening the National Curriculum says that 'pupils should be taught to listen carefully . . . They should be taught to identify the gist of an account or the key points made in a discussion, to evaluate what they hear, and to make contributions relevant to what is being considered. They should be taught to listen to others, questioning them to clarify what they mean, and extending and following up the ideas. They should be encouraged to qualify or justify what they think after listening to other opinions or accounts, and deal politely with opposing points of view' (p. 11). A community of enquiry is the ideal vehicle for developing attentive listening, to identify and question features of presentation and learn to modify ideas through listening to what others say.

In Reading the National Curriculum programme of study urges that pupils' reading should include texts with challenging subject matter that broadens and extends thinking. Literature for reading and response should also include a range of:

- modern stories and novels
- modern and classic poetry
- non-fiction texts from a range of media
- texts drawn from a variety of cultures and traditions
- myths, legends and traditional stories
- plays and texts for drama

We have seen in Stories for Thinking (Chapter 4) the way narrative materials can be used to generate higher-order thinking in speaking, listening and reading. Literature should be drawn from a variety of genres and include both poetry and drama. Using poetry as a stimulus for philosophical enquiry can help foster a love of poetry and at the same time enable children to become thoughtful readers able to pose questions, to discuss and to evaluate critically the texts they read. The following is a suggested sequence of activities for using a poem as a stimulus for a community of enquiry for one or more lessons:[3]

Using a poem for philosophical enquiry

1. The poem is read aloud. The poem may be read again by teacher or student.
2. Students read the poem to themselves and are given 'thinking time' to reflect on the poem.
3. After reading the poem, ask the students what they found interesting or curious in the poem, and to choose an idea they would like to discuss.
4. Invite students to ask questions. Their questions or comments are written on the board, with the name of the contributor written alongside their question.
5. Discuss the questions – which are 'literary', which 'philosophical'? Choose a question from the board, perhaps by voting, to form the basis of a discussion.
6. Begin the discussion by inviting the person whose question is chosen to say why they asked that question, and invite others to respond.
7. Extend children's thinking through asking further questions during or after the discussion.

Follow-up activities
Invite students to extend themes from the poem through other activities such as writing, drawing or drama.
Allow opportunities for students to review and share what they have learnt at the end of each session or unit of work.
Encourage students to find their own poems for thinking and sharing for a future enquiry.

Drama as performance or role play provides opportunities not only for children to read texts but to enter the narrative as participants. In drama there is a greater investment of the whole person and therefore the chance of a greater response. Drama brings the possibility of thinking with the whole person, with body, voice and mind. Through improvisation and role play children can explore their own and others' ideas. They can follow through their thoughts and feelings and consider the consequences. One way of responding to any story is through dramatic reconstruction or mime. Drama has the potential for putting children in touch with the very basic values of life. Nigel Toye gives an example of drama leading to philosophical discussion when:

> One class had been a mountain community and taken in a fugitive girl with her baby (derived from Brecht's *Caucasian Chalk Circle*). Some villagers were suspicious of her and when she was asleep one suggested searching her bag. As he reached to do that, a girl said, 'No, she is our guest. How can we take her in and then search her belongings? They are private to her.' This group of 9-year-olds then spent twenty minutes debating the issue of the morality of the act . . . and went on afterwards to look at the concepts of privacy, guest, host etc. as a full Philosophy for Children community.[4]

In all subjects there is a specialist vocabulary that students need to learn and use. If children use words as labels without understanding what they mean, then those words become like dud cheques in the currency of discussion. We know from classroom research that children can go through their school lives not understanding some of the key concepts used in lessons. An example of this occurred in a maths lesson on volume where 7- to 8-year-olds had spent much time experimenting with different containers and amounts of water and used worksheets to record their results. After the lesson I asked a child what volume was. He replied: 'It's the switch you use to turn the sound up or down.'

Helping children to understand technical and abstract terms, the tools they need for thinking and learning, is not easy but the focus on meaning and definition in philosophical discussion provides opportunities for developing accurate use of language in all areas of study.

MATHEMATICS

Numbers are the only things you can trust.

Tom, aged 14

'How are you at mathematics?'
'I speak it like a native.'

Spike Milligan

Plato had over the door of his Academy: 'Let no-one enter here who is ignorant of mathematics', and ever since philosophers have wondered whether the ultimate structure of the world was mathematical. Philosophical enquiry makes a contribution to mathematics by helping students to develop a better understanding of some of the basic concepts in maths, and to counter some any ill-conceived ideas they may have about the nature of mathematics.[5] Discussion in a community of enquiry can help children to reflect more deeply on the nature and processes of maths and on the processes of learning. It provides an opportunity to 'speak mathematics', an activity that many children find problematic.

The first puzzling question we might ask is: 'What is mathematics?' In considering the nature of mathematics we are asked to choose between two different metaphors. The first metaphor, derived from Plato, argues that mathematics is about discovery. A mathematician on this view is enquiring, like an astronomer who investigates the stars, into mathematical entities that are there in a realm of reality waiting to be discovered. The constructivist has a different metaphor, and argues that mathematics is about invention, and that mathematical enquiry is a creative pursuit, which involves making abstract constructions through the creative power of thought. Is a mathematician more like an astronomer or an artist, or like something quite different?

Traditional mathematics teaching can be regarded as a kind of Platonic activity, to do with the teaching of pre-existent knowledge, procedures and algorithms. Through a progressive set of exercises children learn how to do mathematics in the right way. Their answers are right or wrong and the pre-eminent need here is for accuracy. Or as one child put it: 'Maths is about getting things right or wrong, and you never know it until the teacher tells you.' Modern maths teaching tends to take a constructivist approach, arguing – as the proponents of philosophy for children argue – that children learn best when they are given opportunities to construct their own understanding of problems and to formulate their own hypotheses and solutions with the help of their peers. According to this view the objective of philosophical and mathematical education is not to impose a body of beliefs or truths, but to favour the emergence of understanding through a process of research and reflection. This reflective activity is best facilitated by discussion, or as a child said: 'I learn maths best when I have someone to talk it at.'

Maths teaching can be summed up as a series of dilemmas that reflect what is identified here as platonic and constructivist approaches. Each approach stresses complementary needs in maths teaching, including the need for:

Platonic	*Constructivist*
accuracy	exploration
drill and practice	investigation
skills development	conceptual understanding
typified by work in:	
maths scheme exercises	extension and problem solving work

Are mathematical entities, as Plato believed, real, independent objects of study about which discoveries (and mistakes) can be made? Or as constructivists believe is it we ourselves who construct what we talk about in maths?

Knowledge and accuracy in memorizing facts and procedures, through for example regular practice in mental arithmetic, are important in relieving the demands on short-term memory, and so enabling the child to engage in more higher level cognitive activity. Philosophical enquiry does not take the place of this kind of maths teaching, but can contribute to mathematical thinking by offering a research method for enquiry into the following important areas:

- *reflection on the nature of mathematics*, through discussing such questions as:
  What is mathematics? Who are mathematicians?
  Who are better at mathematics – girls or boys?
  Do you need a special talent to be good at mathematics? Is mathematics useful? Why study maths?

- *reflection on personal experience* in mathematics, developing metacognition, for example by:

keeping a learning diary or notebook to record ideas, feelings and problems

discussing experiences like being stuck, explaining, problem solving, testing, proving, etc.

having a help or question box where students can post any problems they have for later discussion

- *reflection on mathematical concepts*, developing a meta-language for mathematics, through discussing, for example: problematical concepts like number (see example below), infinity, abstract, zero, geometry, shape, cube, sphere, space, pattern, probability, definition, proof, existence, discovery, symbol, set, etc. in a community of enquiry

  discussing stories with a mathematical content

  discussing the lives and work of real mathematicians

- *reflection on mathematical processes* of investigation, for example by discussion of:

  ways of thinking mathematically about a given object, e.g. ask children to investigate a common object and find ten or more questions to describe it mathematically

  ways of interpreting a problem posed in words, or embedded in data (graphs, charts, etc.)

  a range of possible strategies for solving a problem

'Maths is a creative process rather than an imposed body of knowledge', said the Cockcroft Report, a major report on mathematics teaching, which argued that 'the ability to solve problems is at the heart of mathematics'.[6] Mathematical enquiry in supporting the creative process in coming-to-know has two aspects: reflection on content such as the concepts, problems and patterns involved; and reflection on the processes of learning. It means teachers of maths being perceived less as infallible experts and more as persons who like thinking and talking about mathematics. It means judging success in mathematics not only by those who score well in tests, but also those who work hard to further their mathematical understanding through effort and a striving for understanding.

What is mathematics?

Some questions to encourage reflection about the nature of mathematics:

- What is mathematics?
- Is mathematics useful? What does 'useful' mean? How is maths useful?
- Who uses mathematics? What is a mathematician? Are you a mathematician?
- What do you do to become good at maths?
- Can everyone succeed in maths? What does 'succeed' mean? Is success in maths the same for everyone?
- What makes maths a challenge (hard)? What is a 'challenge'? Is a challenge in maths the same as other challenges, such as in sports?
- Is maths invented or discovered? What does 'invent'/ 'discover' mean? What have you invented or discovered in maths?
- Does maths have a purpose? Does all maths have a purpose? What is the purpose (or usefulness) of what you have been doing in maths?
- How important is maths compared to other subjects?
- What questions do you have about maths?

We know that children's pre-conceived ideas about maths can hinder their approach to learning maths. There is a special problem with maths since many perceive it as being abstract, difficult to understand and divorced from human concerns. For these reasons many students develop negative attitudes to maths. They may believe that success in maths is due to some special talent that they do not and cannot possess. 'Maths is not for me, I'm no good at it', said one 7-year-old. Such attitudes serve as a pretext to justify failure, and a growing belief that effort will be useless. This is where a community of enquiry approach can help. By reflecting on their learning of maths in a community of enquiry students can be helped to a better understanding, and a more positive attitude. Becoming involved in dialogue about maths means becoming aware of the human and not just the mechanical and arithmetical side of mathematics. It means discussing the meaning and interpretation of concepts like proof, problem, answer, probability, estimation, pattern, line, infinity, sets and numbers. As Jill, aged 11, said: 'Maths means more to me when we can talk about it.'

SCIENCE

A theory can be proved by experiment; but no path leads from an experiment to the birth of a theory.

Albert Einstein

You need science to tell you what the world is, and philosophy to tell you why.

Jake, aged 16

Two important features about science have implications about the way it should be taught, and link it to philosophy for children. The first is that science is generative, in the sense it is about constructing meaning out of knowledge. Science is the product of the knowledge that people have. The construction of knowledge comes about through the need to assimilate, translate and accommodate knowledge into our schemas of existing ideas. Scientific claims depend not only on interpretations of events but also on our understanding of the concepts we use to describe phenomena. For example the scientific claim: 'All metals expand when heated' relies not only on the accumulation of evidence and observation and the ways these are interpreted, but also on our understanding of the concepts involved such as 'metals', 'expand' and 'heated'.[7]

Both philosophy and science involve systematic enquiry about the world. Science provides a means of understanding the natural, physical and technological world in which we live. It provides both knowledge about the world, and a method, the scientific method, for investigating, checking and finding out more. For many children, and adults, it is a long journey towards understanding. How can philosophy help in this process?

Philosophy is about conceptual enquiry, thinking about

concepts and ideas and about the processes of thinking. Science is about empirical enquiry into the physical and biological world. But it is not simply about the accumulation of facts, it is also about developing understanding and patterns of reasoning. Both fact and reason are the subject matter of science. The reasoning required in science and the skills developed through philosophical enquiry with children are closely related. One common kind of reasoning skill found in science and philosophy is analogical reasoning. What is time more like, an arrow or a wave? When two sets of information need to be related together then analogical reasoning is needed to analyse the similarities and differences in the two things. It is this process that helps us assimilate new information, and test the old.

Science and philosophy are both involved in the process of self-correction. We should for example be able to ask at the end of a scientific enquiry or philosophical discussion:

In what ways is what I think now similar to what I thought before?
In what ways is it different?
What are the reasons for this?

We need good reasons to alter our thinking. Learning what constitutes a good reason is a goal of both science and philosophy. This is important because science is fallible. The knowledge base of science is always changing. Many scientific theories, concepts, laws and methods are tentative. Students of science need to know how to work with knowledge, but also to be aware of its limits. Scientific explanation might not be the only kind of explanation and it may not be a complete explanation. No matter how certain we are from the evidence of experience there is always the possibility of doubt. As Gaarder says in *Sophie's World*:

> Although I have seen nothing but black crows all my life, it doesn't mean there is no such thing as a white crow. Both for a philosopher and a scientist it can be important not to reject the possibility of finding a white crow. You might almost say that hunting for 'the white crow' is science's principal task.'[8]

In the words of Bertrand Russell, 'The hand that feeds the chicken one day wrings its neck'. Science therefore involves epistemological enquiry. We can always ask: 'How do you know that?' 'Is it really true?' 'How can we be certain?' We need to qualify the claims that science makes by appeal to reasons and evidence.

Science developed as a branch of philosophy ('natural philosophy') and both share experimental and investigative methods of enquiry. The following is a list of common features of philosophical and scientific enquiry:

- *systematic enquiry*
  - asking questions such as 'How?', 'Why?', 'What will happen if . . .?'
  - having a clear focus for exploration and investigation
  - using both first-hand experience and secondary sources for information

- *investigating everyday life*
  - applying knowledge to explain and interpret common phenomena
  - relating their understanding to personal life and well-being
  - considering the protection of other living things and the environment

- *the nature of scientific ideas*
  - considering the evidence needed to test and support ideas
  - creative thinking to develop hypotheses and theories
  - recognizing that ideas and theories may change over time

- *communication*
  - using discussion to develop understanding of scientific concepts and vocabulary
  - using discussion to share and explain ideas and experiences
  - using a range of methods verbal and visual to present information and ideas

214

The community of enquiry approach is particularly useful in the planning and review stages of investigative science. Class discussion might begin in the pre-experiment planning stage to collect and consider the students' own ideas, suggestions and questions to be investigated. In this planning stage students should be encouraged to decide what evidence they need, to think about ways of making a fair test and to make predictions about what might happen.

The activity stage will be the time for students to collect evidence, through the recording of observations and measurements. Evidence is considered and conclusions drawn. Plenty of time should be allowed for the review stage, where the community of enquiry share and reflect on their experiment or investigation and try to come to a common understanding about the methods and ideas involved. A philosophical or 'thinking skills' approach will focus not only on the cognitive outcomes through asking students questions such as: 'What happened?', 'Why did it happen?', 'What does it mean?' – but also the metacognitive lesson, the thinking about thinking, through asking such questions as: 'What kind of thinking were you doing?', 'How did it help you find out/solve the problem?', 'What was scientific about your thinking?'

A philosophical approach can enrich science not only through the planning and review stages, but also in bridging science activities to other elements of the curriculum and to the world of everyday experience. Without this bridging or linking to meaningful activity in everyday life science will seem to have limited relevance, and instead of being something that helps them to make sense of their world will simply remain an imposed body of knowledge. Questions that can help in this bridging process might include some of the key questions of philosophy, such as:

What kind of reasons have we used? Where else might we use this kind of reasoning? (logical question)
Do we know this or believe it? How do we know? What kind of knowledge is this? (epistemological question)
What does this help us to explain or understand? What is there left to explain or understand? (possibly a metaphysical question)

215

How might this help us, or other people? Is it useful? (values/
   moral/ethical question)
*Was there anything strange, interesting or beautiful about
   this?* (aesthetic question)

According to the philosopher Peirce science 'rises from the
contemplation of the fragment of a system to the envisage-
ment of a complete system.' The following short conversation
shows the early stages of system building through group
enquiry with a group of 6- to 7-year-olds recorded by Vivian
Paley, a kindergarten teacher, and published in her book
Wally's Stories.[9] The theme of the discussion is the nature of
magic and science. It shows how a philosophically sensitive
teacher uses questions to help scaffold the spontaneous contributions of young children to help them engage in exploring
!meanings, suggesting hypotheses and making judgements.

What is magic?

Teacher:	A kindergarten boy once told the class he intended to become a mother lion when he grew up. He said he would do this by practising magic.
Thalia:	Magic doesn't make things that people want to be.
Teacher:	Is there any use for magic at all?
Thalia:	There are magic tricks. You can learn tricks.
Harry:	Well, he could put on a disguise and then there could be a tape recorder beside him of a lion and people would think that's a real lion.
Thalia:	But that would still be a trick.
Stuart:	Like the magic set my sister gave me. The balls don't really disappear. They're in the cup all the time.
Harry:	The only kind of magic there really is superhuman strength. Now *that* is really true.
Allan:	If you know how to do a magician's things, you do have to keep practising until you know how to do it real good.
Thalia:	But it's still just tricks, Allan.

Allan:	Everything isn't tricks, Thalia.
Teacher:	Even if you practised for years, could you learn to become an animal?
Allan:	No, but maybe something else.
Stuart:	My friend does this – it's not magic, but it's like magic. Like once he believed so hard his father would give him something and when that day came his father really gave him what he believed.
Teacher:	Is that like wishing?
Stuart:	No. He was just believing in his mind that his father would give him something.
John:	That boy in your class. It was just something he really wanted to happen but it couldn't happen. It was a fantasy.
Harry:	Scientists could work hard and make up a formula to make someone into a lion.
Thalia:	The only kind of magic I've heard of are miracles.
Teacher:	Is that something like Stuart's friend believing in something real hard?
Thalia:	A little different. Like you're wishing something will happen but you know it won't and all of a sudden it happens.
Sally:	I think there might be a potion some day. I don't think it could happen. I mean a potion to make someone a lion. But it might happen.
Harry:	They might be able to not make him into a lion but make him look like a lion with all the doctors working hard to do it.
Sally:	You mean to look like a lion but not talking like a lion. Not roaring or anything. But it wouldn't be magic. It'd be something to do with science.

(from *Wally's Stories*, pp. 198–200)

DESIGN AND TECHNOLOGY

When I am designing something I think with my hands.
child, aged 7

The word technology derives from the Greek *techne* which means the knowledge of how to do things and make things. It was used by Aristotle to classify anything deliberately made by humans, from *physis* or the natural order of things. Science is about developing understanding of physis, the physical world, whereas design and technology is about applying techniques to artefacts, systems and environments to achieve particular human purposes. What then has technology to do with the reflective practices of philosophy, which for the Greeks has *phronesis* or practical wisdom as its goal?

Technology challenges people to apply their knowledge and skills to solve practical problems. Technology is not simply a process of making things like cars or bridges. Rather it is about identifying and answering human needs, through generating ideas, planning, making and testing to find the best solutions. Technology is to do with capability, giving children the 'know how' to answer their own needs and the needs of others in a given context or environment. But it is also about developing a reflective understanding of issues related to how technology shapes and is shaped by society. These two aspects, the reflective and the active, need to work together if children are to come to grips with the problems of living in, and exerting influence on the technological world.[10]

The reflective and active aspects of design and technology capability are summarized in the table below:

REFLECTIVE	ACTIVE
homo sapiens – the human as thinker	homo faber – the human as maker
identifying needs and issues clarifying needs and issues detailing needs and issues 'knowing that . . .' using factual knowledge and understanding	proposing action developing proposals detailing plans 'knowing how . . .' applying knowledge to making things

The need to reflect on the nature and purpose of technology relates not only to designing and making but also to information technology. With the introduction into schools and homes of information technology such as computers, CD-Roms and the Internet, with its limitless potential for the exchange of information, there is an increasing need for children to respond to this flood of information in thoughtful and perceptive ways.

The following is a checklist of some of the skills that have been identified as necessary for students to cope thoughtfully with the growth of information technology:

- analysing
- categorizing
- evaluating
- explaining
- formulating questions
- making hypotheses
- making inferences
- observing
- predicting
- synthesizing

(*Source:* National Council for Educational Technology 1989[11])

This list of skills could equally describe the kinds of responses one would expect to find in a philosophical discussion with children. The skill of the teacher in promoting thinking skills through discussion about technology is to use both empirical questions about what things are and how they work and conceptual questioning that encourages concept building, definition and reasoning both about information and the kinds of technology being used for information handling.

The following is an excerpt from a discussion with a group of students about computers. The discussion included responses that reflected some of the thinking skills identified above.

What is the difference between humans and computers?

Excerpts from a discussion with a group of Year 9 and 10 students (aged 15 and 16):

RF: What is the difference between humans and computers?

Tom: Human beings can do some things without being told to whereas computers can only do things when they're told to.

Katy: Humans know who they are. They have names, computers don't.

Josie: My computer's got a name. I've given it one.

Tom: Yes, but your computer doesn't know what it is unless you tell it.

Katy: Computers are not aware of themselves but human beings are.

RF: How is a human similar to a computer?

Gerald: They both react to what they're told. Computers do what they're told . . .

Henry: Unless they've broken down.

Tom: Humans don't always do as they are told. They can choose.

Gerald: They both react to things along pre-set actions.

RF: What does that mean?

Gerald: Along actions or lines. So that you know what they're going to do. They have patterns that have been set for them . . . pre-set lines of action.

Tom: I disagree with Gerald. Humans don't always follow pre-set lines of action. You can't tell what I'm going to do next. You can with a computer, if you press the right button.

Tamara: Humans don't have buttons.

Katy: They do in a way. You only have to say something to some people and it starts them off . . .

RF: What human characteristics do computers have?

Jamie: They store knowledge.

Nick: They both have a memory.

Jamie: They can store knowledge in their memories.

Tom:	A computer only uses the knowledge it's been given.
Jamie:	So do humans, they only use the knowledge *they've* been given.

* * *

RF:	Could a computer ever be called a human being?
Lydia:	No.
Henry:	Not if it was called a computer.
RF:	Why?
Henry:	Because . . .
Tom:	Yes I think technology could make a computer that was just like a human.
Leroy:	You could have computer programs developed and programmed into them.
Katy:	Computers don't have arms or legs.
Leroy:	They could have.
Katy:	But they'd still be controlled by a computer. You couldn't call it a human being.
RF:	Does computer intelligence differ from human intelligence?
Tom:	A computer is intelligent but not clever or wise. It could do any IQ test if it were given the instructions.
Katy:	But it couldn't cheer you up if you were miserable.

* * *

RF:	What questions does the development of computers pose?
Daniel:	Are human beings kinds of computer?
Josie:	Might we never have to work again if they can build machines to do it?
Tamara:	Is it a good idea to create something more powerful and intelligent than human beings if given the chance?

HISTORY

Life can only be lived forwards, but it can only be understood backwards.

Soren Kierkegaard

I know what history is. When you're dead ... you're history.

child, aged 8

History began as story-telling, and stories told to preserve folk-memories have been told for thousands of years. History teaching as a discipline taught in elementary schools stretches back little more than a hundred years. It only became a compulsory subject taught in school in the early 20th century. As most teachers were untrained in the subject teaching history consisted mostly in memorizing little-understood historical facts and long lists of dates from textbooks. In more recent times subject matter has been balanced with historical method and genuine historical enquiry. However, until the advent of the National Curriculum history teaching in English schools has been judged by many inspection reports as often fragmentary and superficial in character. History became identified as the worst-taught subject in primary schools. What particular problems does the teaching of history pose, and might philosophical enquiry help?

It is important to distinguish between history and the past. History represents the systematic attempt to describe and explain the past through applying disciplined imagination to historical sources. The justification for history is that it is not only fascinating in its own right, but it has the power to help us to make sense of the present through an understanding of the past. As Santayana said, those who do not remember the past are condemned to relive it. The critical question in history, as in other disciplines, is an epistemological one: 'How do we know?' It follows that a central task of history must be to encourage children to weigh up historical evidence and to use it to make historical judgements. The purpose of historical enquiry is to 'ask and answer significant questions, select sources for historical enquiry, collect and record information and reach reasoned conclusions' (*History in the*

National Curriculum, p. 11). One way of coming to know is through critical thinking about sources of information, the ability to evaluate evidence and determine causal relationships in history. But where evidence is lacking we need creative thinking, in particular imagination and empathy to re-create a fuller picture of the past, to seek answers to such questions as: 'What did they think?' What did they feel?' 'What did they know?' This involves the capacity to generate ideas, hypotheses, to move beyond the egocentric self and to try to enter the thoughts and feelings of people in the past.

Finding out something about the past does not necessarily tell us what history is, just as doing sums doesn't necessarily tell us about mathematics or doing experiments tell us about science. We not only want children to *do* history, but to understand the concept of history and the nature of historical enquiry. 'What is history?' is a question that has occupied the minds of many philosophers. With a little prompting even 6 and 7-year-olds can say what they think history is. Jane for example said it was 'before a long time ago', for Paul it was what was meant by 'once upon a time', for Karen it was 'so long ago', while older children give more specific definitions all link it with what happened in time. With experience of philosophical discussion children tend to give longer answers, more elaborate answers, and will ask more questions to extend their understanding.

Children think history is about the past but their conceptions of time are ambiguous. For most 7-year-olds the past is 'a long time ago', many 9-year-olds think of the past as 'any time ago', by 11 many believe that the past could include significant events in their own lifetime. Research also shows wide variations in chronological awareness by 11-year-olds, some still defining history with the vague generalizations characteristic of 7-year-olds.[12]

Another feature of children's responses is that history is about 'important people and happenings'. Ben, a 10-year-old, makes a useful distinction when he says 'it is not about important things but things people think are important.' For Paula history is about 'something that has made a change in the world.'

Young children show a growing insight into the nature and

What is history?

Some questions to aid discussion with children about the concept of history:

- Is everything that happened part of history?
- Will you find everything that happened in history in history books? Why or why not?
- Who says what history is?
- Who decides what goes into history books? How do they decide what to put in and what to leave out?
- What are the most important things to find out in history?
- Is everything you read in history books true? Why? How do you know?
- Could history books be wrong? If so, in what ways?
- How could you find out if a history book was wrong?
- Does everyone agree about what happened in the past? Why, or why not?
- Do people have different points of view about what happened in history? Why is this?
- How do we know what happened in the past?
- Are there some things in history that we will never know? Why, or why not?
- Is the study of history useful? Why, or why not?
- Do you think the study of history is interesting? In what ways?
- Is history more interesting or important than other subjects, or less?
- What would you like to know more about in history?
- Do you have a history?
- How do you know about your own past life?
- Do you know everything about your past life. Why or why not?
- What were the most important events in your life? Why were they important?
- What evidence have you got of your past life?
- Do you think your memories about the past are all true? Why?
- Do other people know as much about your past as you do? Do they know more?
- When does history begin and end?

purposes of history. Children's concepts of time and of historical thinking can be extended through opportunities to reflect
on and discuss the concepts that underlie historical enquiry.

A group of children aged 8 were discussing the question of
evidence:

Child 1: Democracy was something invented by the
Greeks.
Child 2: How do you know?
Child 1: Everyone knows that. It's in the history books.
Child 2: It doesn't mean it's true.

Concepts of historical knowledge and time are not the only
problematical concepts in learning history. Children's understanding of political concepts, such as kingship, democracy,
revolution, parliament, freedom and laws is often hazy and ill-
defined. By the age of 11 children become more aware of the
abstract nature of government, and that political issues imply
moral judgements. Discussion in a community of enquiry
gives teachers the opportunity to discover how children interpret such key terms as government, laws, taxes, republic and
democracy. Ways of generating such discussion include inviting children to interrogate and discuss historical stories, pictures or artefacts. In this way children learn that history is as
much about asking questions as it is about finding answers.
Historians, like philosophers, ask questions about the past to
which there may be few right answers or final solutions. As
Kierkegaard said, life can only be lived forwards but it can
only be understood backwards.

GEOGRAPHY

Philosophy helps me to know where I am.
Anna, aged 10

G.K. Chesterton once sent a celebrated telegram to his wife:
'Am at Crewe. Where should I be?' We all have our private
geographies and mental maps which help us to understand
where we are. Sometimes, as in the case of Chesterton, they
let us down. The study of geography can help us make sense

of these private geographies through developing an under-standing of places and the relationship between places. Geo-graphical enquiry helps develop a sense of what places are, places that relate both to human society and the natural world. The contribution of philosophical enquiry is to help us and our students to explore in more depth what the relationships between human beings and their environment should be.

In the first issue of the journal *The Geography Teacher*, published 1901, Dr Benjamin Jowett issued the challenge: 'Can you teach Geography so as to make people think?' The devel-opment of geographical knowledge and skills should help us in thinking about some of the central problems facing the modern world, in particular issues facing the environment at both local and global levels. Our students are the future custodians of the earth. They will need to make important judgements about environmental issues. For this they will need knowledge, including the knowledge that traditionally has been the subject matter of geography. But they will need more. To think about environmental issues in any depth is to involve oneself in concepts like fairness, responsibility and rights; strategies like identifying consequences, imagining alternative possibilities and relating particular parts to larger wholes; and issues that are ethical and contestable. The dilemma was summed up by a child during an environmental discussion as follows: 'We know so much about the world, but we don't always do what's good for the world.'

When it comes to helping our students become aware of issues that affect the environment, to develop judgement and concern about the quality of the environment, our best pros-pect is to equip them with not only with a sound base of curriculum knowledge, but also opportunities to think and talk about environmental issues in a community of collabora-tive enquiry. As environmental dilemmas and crises bear down upon us through the global networking of news, we can invite our children to be participants in the kinds of philosoph-ical conversations from which in the past they have been excluded. As soon as questions move from how things are to how they should be we enter into questions that are no longer simply descriptive but ethical, they are to do with a moral vision of how things ought to be.

226

To 'value both the natural world and the man-made environment as the basis of life and a source of wonder and inspiration' (Schools Curriculum and Assessment Authority, 1996) will involve having to make certain judgements about our duties to human beings and to other species, defining certain key terms like 'sustainable environment', and deciding on priorities in preserving habitats and promoting human development.[13]

The following are some of the kinds of questions relevant to environmental enquiry:

How should we treat the environment?

- Should we consider what is best for ourselves, what is best for others or best for all (does 'all' include the unborn)?
- Should we consider what is best for humans or should we consider animals, plants, rivers and other aspects of the physical world?
- Who should we care for – our family, our friends, our local community, our country, our world? How should we show this care?
- What is the environment, and what is the place of human beings in the environment?
- What should our duty be to other species, can we ever know what an animal feels or wants?
- What is 'development', and what are the problems of modern development?
- What is good or beautiful about nature, why and how should we preserve it?
- What could we do to improve our local environment, what should we do?
- Should people in rich countries help people in poor countries, why and how?
- What kind of world do you want to live in, and how could you help create it?

Many geographical skills and attitudes are also characteristic of a good philosophical dialogue, for example the ability to 'observe and ask questions' (about geographical features and issues) and in trying to answer these questions 'analyse the evidence, draw conclusions and communicate findings' (*Geography in the National Curriculum*, 1995).

ART

> *I never do a painting as a work of art. All of them are researches. I search constantly . . .*
>
> Picasso

> *You have to think about art to really appreciate it.*
>
> Tom, aged 13

Philosophy through Art can be said to rest on two main principles. First that art requires thinking through. As Kant said, art is 'a representation of the imagination which induces much thought', and to be fully appreciated art requires activity of thought. Secondly art can help us to think better through being a focus for the enquiring mind, providing a stimulus for research and philosophical enquiry.

Through sensory appeal it invites thoughtful attention and the making of human connections. Art requires us to make a personal response. Art connects us to another life, that of the artist, and sometimes to another culture. Art challenges our feelings and judgements. A work of art also contains ideas, concepts, reasons, problems and questions. The meanings we make from a work of art are personal, but they can be shared. This sharing of perceptions in a group or community of enquiry can help us to refine our understanding, to think with more critical and creative insight. We can see more when we are helped to see through the eyes and work of others.

A work of art presents an intellectual challenge. It exercises the mind through offering us a game of speculation and ambiguity – a philosophical puzzle. Art offers the mind something to work on. It has been created to hold our attention, and encourages us to make rich human connections. Among these connections may be social themes, existential questions, puzzling forms and structures, personal anxieties and insights, historical cultural patterns. Art has emotional resonance, it appeals to feelings, to moods, and to responses that are difficult to capture in words. We are presented with gestures that are at once expressive and mute. Art is problematical because it has no words (other than a title). But we can supply the words through our capacity for critical and creative thinking.

A work of art is created twice – first by the artist and then by the viewer. It is continually being recreated in the eyes and minds of observers. A work of art invites interrogation – but we, the viewers, are also the ones who are interrogated. Art can be an opportunity for many kinds of cognition, including the sense of wonder that Aristotle said was the spur to philosophy.

The problem with art is that it is easy to slip into a 'look and see' mindset. We look and believe we see right away what there is to see. We tend to suffer from 'impressionism'. We go by impressions, we are hasty in our approach, we take things in too quickly. As with the television image, which lasts on average three and a half seconds, we come to rely on the ability of the brain to make rapid intuitive impressions. To gain a richer and more philosophical experience of art we need to strive against this natural impulse to categorize our first impressions. We need to slow down, to allow for looking time and thinking time. But how can we achieve this?

First choose a work of art you think might be worth looking at for a while. In my Philosophy through Art sessions participants are given a number of works of art to browse through, letting the eye wander (and the mind wonder) until an image is chosen. A rich image, such as Chagall's *I and the Village*, or Van Gogh's *Starry Night*, will repay close observation. Abstract images, such as Kandinsky's *Swinging* can equally feed the eye and the mind.[14]

Having chosen an image the following steps may help in using art for philosophical enquiry:

- take time to look, say 3–5 minutes, go on a mental walk around the picture, pause at significant details, avoid hasty interpretation
- look from varied perspectives, close-up and further away, odd angles and different points of view, let your mind seek meanings

- link what you see with what you know, and focus on what you do not know, look at space and negative space (the empty areas)
- think about the story or stories that may be embedded in the artwork, find words for the images, symbols and ideas
- ask questions, and let questions emerge, what feelings and thoughts arise from what you see?
- take notes, mental notes or scribbled notes of what you can see and what cannot be seen, what is curious, what surprises, what interests and what puzzles you
- share your questions, comments and responses with others – choose a problem or contestable issue as a focus for dialogue

Philosophy through Art can be an intimate personal experience, a dialogue in the mind. But as Walter Pater warned, we can become 'dwarfed in the narrow chambers of the individual mind'. An investigation of art with others in a community of enquiry can help to extend and enrich our understanding through a shared exploration of meaning. It can for example help us to:

1. *think about art*, through asking meta-questions such as:
   - What is art?' (For the artist Duchamp: 'It's art because I say it's art.')
   - What is beauty? (For Keats, as for the Greeks: 'Beauty is truth, truth beauty.')
   - What is truth? (Is the best art true to life? In what ways?)
   - In what ways can art help us to reach the truth? (Can a photograph be a work of art?)
   - How does art differ from life? (What is the difference between a person and a drawing of a person?)

2. *think in art*, through asking of any artwork:
   - What can you see?
   - What concepts (ideas) does the artwork contain?
   - What processes (techniques, materials) does the artwork contain?
   - What judgements (designs) does the artwork contain?
   - Can we translate the visual into verbal, all that we can see into words?

3. *think through art*, by asking for example:
   - What does this artwork say about life?
   - In what ways does it connect to our own lives?
   - What symbolic meanings does it have?
   - What story does it tell?
   - What questions or problems does it pose?

Through the shared interpretation of an aesthetic experience in a community of enquiry art becomes not only a source of visual thinking and a vehicle for understanding. According to Wittgenstein 'the true mystery of the world is the visible, not the invisible.' Philosophy through art provides an opportunity for thinking more about the mysteries of what is visible, both in art and in life.[15]

According to Howard Gardner's theory of Multiple Intelligences visual intelligence is a basic mode of intelligence characteristic of human minds, as is musical intelligence, and that understanding develops through experience, reflection and discussion. As Jane, aged 8, said 'Art is not just about painting, it's about seeing and saying what you can see.'

MUSIC

Music, by stirring emotion, causes the appearance of the hidden nature of man, a nature which is akin to the supersensual world.
al-Ghazali, Islamic philosopher, c. 1100

A piece of music is a series of choices in time.
W. H. Auden

Music is a kind of language that you can't quite understand, Sometimes talking about it helps you understand.
Amy, aged 10

Music is a source of metaphysical conundrums. What is music? What does it do? What does it mean? Like art, music raises questions that can provide a stimulus for aesthetic and philosophical discussion with children.[16]

There seems to be a special kind of human faculty which Howard Gardner calls 'musical intelligence'. This may have developed through an ancestral need to hear and assess sounds so as to be safe from predators in a hostile environment. We still need the skills of attentive listening to survive and thrive in today's busy world. Music makes use of this ability to listen and to appraise sounds in discriminating ways. Music is not so much concerned with our physical as with our spiritual and psychological well-being. Music binds us in a special way to our social and cultural context. It is a unique tool for arousing our physical, emotional and intellectual faculties.

Music starts with listening, yet we are so surrounded by noise that we block out much that we might listen to. We listen to significant sounds but ignore the rest. Children today are submerged in a sea of technological sound. They are not as adept at filtering out sounds as adults. Their only defence against a confusion of unwanted sound is to 'close their ears' to the sounds around them, rendering themselves functionally deaf at times. No wonder teachers report that young children find attentive listening so difficult to achieve.

Our first aim in teaching music is therefore to re-introduce children to the rich variety of sounds in their environment, including musical sounds, and to help them to think about these sounds. Philosophy for children can help by providing opportunities for attentive listening, and for discussing the patterns of sounds heard. Music can be used in a community of enquiry as a stimulus for:

- *aesthetic enquiry* – exploring the place and value of music in human experience
- *philosophical enquiry* – exploring intellectual and emotional responses to music
- *musical enquiry* – exploring musical sounds, providing opportunities to categorize, distinguish, describe, connect and compare different kinds of sound, and to develop musical concepts

Sounds and silence are the raw materials of music. Some children have little or no experience of silence. If philosophy is about developing thinking then children need to experience periods of quiet reflection. In terms of music education listening to silence is as important as listening to music. Composer Igor Stravinsky once said: 'Value your intervals like dollars.'

By that he meant that it is the pauses of silence that make music eloquent. A music or philosophy lesson should include 'thinking time', that is moments of quiet meditation. If children do not experience these with teachers at school, when will they experience them? As children regain their early childhood sensitivity to sound, they will become more appreciative of silence.

Music has the capacity to arouse the mind. There is some research evidence to suggest that playing music to students (in particular 18th-century classical music) prior to a challenging intellectual task, like a test or exam, will enhance their performance. It is no wonder then that music is incorporated in many accelerated learning techniques. Music is a powerful tool. The problem is that many teachers feel insufficiently equipped to teach music. A community of enquiry approach is useful since it relieves the teacher of the mantle of the expert, and can help the teacher's own musical development through the shared experience of exploring a musical stimulus.

Music is also a strongly cultural experience. We identify with and possess the music we like. For many children this is a strongly tribal experience. They know what they like, and it is often what the grown-ups don't like. We are all possessive of our preferred musical idioms. However a musical curriculum (such as *Music in the National Curriculum*) demands that children become acquainted with a range of musical styles and genres from different times and places. Children, and some adults, tend to reject the music they do not like as 'not music' or 'not music for us', so a philosophical approach can be very useful in challenging children to define their own terms and clarify their own thinking without having to merely accept the categories and values promoted by their teachers or their peers.

A community of musical enquiry can provide opportunities to share in a wide range of musical stimulus. It is important that all such discussions begin with a piece of music for the group to listen to. Unusual pieces of music make good starting points, since they require children to clarify for themselves which elements they regard as essential for calling something music. Music from different cultures and contemporary music which is in some sense 'problematic' provide good starting points for discussion.

What is music?

Some philosophical questions:

- What is music? What is not music?
- What are musical sounds and what are non-musical sounds?
- Can any noise be music or part of music?
- What does music do? What is the value of music? to you? to society?
- What kinds of music do you like? Why?
- Have your tastes changed? Why?
- Is there a difference between appreciating music and liking it?
- Why do people make music? What is the purpose of music?
- What is the difference between composing music and playing it?
- If you change one thing in a composition does it change the whole composition?
- Does music that is not written down exist?
- Does music exist when it is not being played? Where? How?

Philosophical discussion can help children clarify some of their basic musical concepts and values, and become aware that in any group there may be a range of opinions about the nature and purposes of music. Children can also engage in musical analysis in a community of enquiry. To stimulate such discussion it may be helpful to offer children two pieces of music to investigate, compare and contrast. The two pieces of music should come from contrasting traditions, and offer different solutions to the particular element of music under consideration, for example different kinds of percussion, violin or flute playing. The following are some questions to help musical analysis after hearing a piece of music, to help in developing understanding of different elements and expressions of music:

What can you hear?

Some questions about musical analysis:

- What can you hear that is making the music? instruments? voices?
- How do you know which instruments are being played?
- How many performers are there? Who do you think they are?
- What mood or feeling does the music communicate?
- Does it have pitch? melody? rhythm? harmony? tempo? timbre? texture? structure?
- Are there any patterns in the musical sounds? What are they?
- When and where do you think the music was created? Why?
- Compare this piece of music with another you have heard. Which do you prefer? Why?
- Compare two performances of the same piece. Which do you prefer, and why?
- What do you think would be the best title for the music. Why?

Children can easily be trapped in their own musical tastes and culture. Philosophy can be liberating when it shows other ways to think about and experience the world. Philosophical enquiry can free children from simplistic and stereotypical responses such as mindless response to 'muzak'. Music for thinking can include compositions by the children themselves, examples of spoken music, birdsong and sounds of nature. Begin by asking them to list what they can hear, list the questions and comments they want to discuss, or ask the key questions: 'Is it music? Why?' Another possible stimulus for discussion can come from combining art and music. Show two pictures and listen to two pieces of music and discuss: Which picture goes best with which music, and why?

The more we practise interpreting our aesthetic experience the better we get at it, and the more we can share it with others. This in turn will enrich our understanding not only of art but of other people. As Brian, aged 10, reported after an aesthetic discussion: 'Now we have talked about it I still don't like it but I can see why other people do.'

PHYSICAL EDUCATION (PE) AND SPORT

PE needs two things – thinking and doing.

Danny, aged 9

Another kind of intelligence identified by Gardner in his theory of Multiple Intelligences is that of kinaesthetic or physical intelligence, which is made up of both physical and mental skills. These physical and mental skills are closely linked, and are exemplified by such judgements as 'thoughtful move' and 'intelligent play'. Success in physical activity depends on intellectual skills such as concentration, judgement and close observation, as well as on creative skills in thought and movement. Philosophical enquiry can help encourage a thoughtful or 'mindful' approach to physical activity, including awareness of self and of others. This is important in an educational context since both success and safety in physical activity can be helped by a 'think first' approach.

In order to help children become reflective about physical activity they should be given opportunities to articulate and share any questions, comments or problems they face in relation to PE. There may be particular questions that children might want to raise in a community of enquiry about PE in school. There are also other more general conceptual questions that can be explored which lie at the heart of PE as a discipline.

What is physical education?

Questions to discuss include:

- What is physical education?
- Should we be taught PE or games in schools – why, or why not?
- What, if anything, do we learn through PE and games?
- What are the most important things we can learn through PE and games?
- Does PE or games make you a better person – why, or why not?
- What does it mean to play 'fairly', what is, and what is not, fair play?
- What is good sporting behaviour, and not good sporting behaviour?
- What is the difference between being an individual participant and a team player?
- What code of conduct should be observed by a player, or a spectator?
- How are success and failure to be judged?
- Should boys and girls play the same sports?
- Should *everyone* have to do PE and games in school?
- Is it better to play well in a game or to win?
- What mental qualities are involved in being successful in physical education or sport?

In order to develop positive attitudes children should be taught 'to observe conventions of fair play, honest competition and good sporting behaviour as individual participants, team members and spectators' (*Physical Education in the National Curriculum*, 1995, p. 2). They need to learn how to cope with success and failure and to be mindful of others and the environment. There are a number of issues here which need to be explored – both through physical and through mental activity. Philosophical discussion is one way to stimulate such mental activity. We need, as one child put it: 'PE for the mind', as well as PE for the body.

Sport is one of the most potent of human activities in its

capacity to give meaning to life, and in the creation of self-identity.[17] No understanding of current affairs is complete without some knowledge of the role sport plays in national and international events. For many people sport is as important as religion in their lives, indeed for some people, including children, sport is a kind of religion. It can certainly exhibit many of the characteristics of religion, including rituals, ways of life, worship, pilgrimages, holy places, the ability to give meaning and purpose to life and a self-transcending ideal. Although the comparison of sport to religion may be problematical, sport is clearly an important aspect of life for many people. It is surprising therefore that the concept of sport has received little attention from philosophers.

In the past sport has been regarded as a morally uplifting form of education, particularly by English public schools. Sport, it was argued, promoted the manly Christian virtues of initiative, self-reliance, obedience and loyalty. The notions of fair play, the striving for grace under pressure and the safe release of animal passions in a rule-governed environment added to the benefits of physical exercise. However, opponents of the morally educative view of sport argue that it detracts from rather than enhances moral education by encouraging dominance, a win-at-all-costs assertiveness and a tribal competitiveness that is fuelled by the greed and commercialism of professional sport. Whatever view we take of the moral benefits or otherwise of sport in education it is clear that sports studies can provide a source of serious intellectual enquiry.

One problem concerns its definition. What is a sport? How does it differ from a game? Must it have a winner or loser? In a classroom discussion about possible definitions of sport one child suggested that all sports posed some physical problem. Another child suggested every sport has a target that you must aim for. Another child built on this idea by suggesting that an activity could not be a sport if it did not require effort by the players: 'You cannot win if you don't try.'

Another contestable issue concerns the value of sport. Is it educational? What are the benefits and dangers of sport? How important is it compared to other areas of the curriculum? According to educational philosopher Richard Peters sport is not as intrinsically worthwhile as other subjects such as literary appreciation which 'contribute much to the quality of living'.[18] Others would argue that sports have much in common with the arts. They are creative pursuits, with an aesthetic appeal. The philosopher A.J. Ayer described football as a cross between ballet and chess. In a discussion on whether sport can be beautiful, one child said: 'Beauty is the winning goal.' Another countered: 'Not if you're on the losing side.' In some sports such as ice skating the aesthetic beauty of movement, 'artistic merit' is given a score. However, in skating, as in most sports, winning is the object of the game. If this is so, how far should one go to win a game? Would you cheat to win a game? Have you ever cheated to win a game? What counts as cheating?

Sports, like all human activities, give rise to moral and social questions. They provide a resource for enquiry that can be of benefit to both the sporting and the non-sporting child. As one girl said at the end of a discussion on equal opportunities in sport: 'I don't like playing games, but I like talking about them. I wish we could talk more and play less.'

RELIGIOUS EDUCATION AND SPIRITUALITY

Philosophy helps me to show my beliefs.
                              Muslim child, aged 10

Religions can be seen as protective systems of beliefs designed to transmit well-tested information about the nature of life and of human possibility. The spiritual seems a universal form of human intelligence, and like other intelligences can be developed through a variety of means, including philosophical discussion. The potential for spiritual development and preparedness for religion seem to have been wired into human nature through an evolutionary process. Why has the spiritual developed as a dimension of human existence? Possibly because it is essential for human flourishing. It can inspire and provides a feeling of transcendence, with the ability to rise above everyday to experience awe, wonder and mystery. It satisfies the human search for meaning and purpose, and provides a means through which people can recognize who they are, why they are, where they are and where they are going.

We are wired with the potential for religion but not for the specific contents of any particular religion. Religions change and so do religious beliefs. Many of our beliefs depend on accidents of time and place. Religions differ. They may arise out of a common spiritual hunger, but their beliefs, practices and world-views may be radically different. They can give rise to the highest forms of human creativity and moral action. They can also give rise to much intolerance, cruelty, bigotry and social repression. Because religion incorporates basic and powerful beliefs about the human condition it is important that children have an opportunity to articulate, share and consider these beliefs.

What is the difference between philosophy and religion?

William James was being teased by a theology student who said to him: 'A philosopher is like a blind man in a dark cellar, looking for a black cat who isn't there.' 'Yes,' said James, 'and the difference between philosophy and theology is that theology finds the cat.'

In a classroom discussion of this question, Ahmed aged 10 said: 'Philosophy helps me to think. My religion helps me to believe.'

The potential for spiritual development is open to all students, and is not confined to religious beliefs. Many children who do not come from a religious background are capable of spiritual dimensions of experience. It has to do with the universal search for human identity and significance. It has to do with relationships with other people and with the world, and for believers with God or the divine. It has to do with the way we respond to challenging experiences, such as death, suffering, beauty and encounters with good and evil. It has to do with meaning, purpose and the values by which we live.[19]

According to Paul Tillich the predicament of Western society is our loss of 'depth'. By this Tillich means we have lost touch with asking ourselves about the meaning of existence. We have lost depth by not questioning, wondering and reflecting on our nature and our ideals. This loss of depth can be recovered through philosophical discussion with children. If the religious or spiritual dimension derives from a disposition to wonder about and to question our existence and being, then philosophy for children has a clear religious dimension.

A community of philosophical enquiry provides the supportive context through which children can articulate their beliefs, to discover common ground with others and to explore differences. Thinking is not to be imposed on children as a set of dogmatic beliefs, but is in a sense a celebration of the free expression of ideas, facilitated and guided by the community. but as Santayana warns, 'although the essence of spirit may be merely to think, yet some intensity and progression are essential to this thinking.'[20]

The following are aspects of religious or spiritual discussion that can provide opportunities for depth and development in thinking:

- *beliefs*
  - articulating personal beliefs, including religious beliefs
  - becoming aware of the shared beliefs on which people base their lives
  - developing an understanding of how beliefs contribute to personal identity
- *sense of wonder*
  - being inspired by the natural world and human achievement
  - developing a sense of awe and mystery
  - the feeling of being moved by beauty or kindness
- *transcendence*
  - feelings that may express belief in the existence of a divine being
  - ability to rise above the self-centredness of everyday experience
  - awareness of the need to control or transcend certain emotions and feelings
- *search for meaning and purpose*
  - asking questions about life

- reflecting on the origin and purpose of life
- developing individual identity and self-respect
- *relationships*
  - recognizing and valuing the worth of each individual
  - developing a sense of community
  - ability to build relationships with others
- *creativity*
  - ability to express innermost thoughts and feelings, through discussion with others
  - ability to exercise imagination, intuition and insight
  - ability to express oneself through art, music, literature and other activities

Most children can relate to these aspects of the spiritual, but their experiences and the meaning they ascribe to them will vary. Philosophical enquiry helps them to become aware of and reflect on their experience through exploring their ideas and becoming aware of the ideas of others.

The sort of oral groundwork provided by discussion in a community of enquiry can lead to reflective explorations about the meaning of life and of human experience. The following is a reflection by a 10-year-old on why people are not perfect:

Why did God not make us perfect?

Some reflective writing after a philosophical discussion by a Anna, aged 10:

I know why God did not make us perfect, if he did we would simply be more angels. God wanted humans to be people who could make their own choices. *Not* saints who were so perfect that they obeyed his every wish. I think that God gives us life like a test. Like GCSEs. If you pass, you go to a higher level. If you fail, you take the test again. So, if you lead a good life, you are born again in a higher position. If you just aren't good enough, you stay in the same position. If you lead a wicked life, you are demoted to an animal or plant, and stay as that for a lifetime as a punishment, then you are given another go at the test. When/if you reach the highest level, and *still* lead a good life (which gets harder to do as you get richer and more important) you are admitted to heaven. That explains why there are so few angels that we know of.

CITIZENSHIP

This is a great discovery, education is politics! What a teacher discovers is that he or she is a politician, too, the teacher has to ask 'What kind of politics am I doing in the classroom?'

Paulo Freire (1987)

Everyone should have the chance to speak and say what they think

Ravinder, aged 8

One of the challenges children face today is how to make sense of the messages they receive, through the media, through school and home and through contact with others, about what they should think of themselves and of others, about how to behave, and about problems in the community. Children face a bewildering range of conflicting messages about the choices that face them. It is no wonder that many are confused about what they think and what they should do: 'It's because there are so many choices we don't know what to think', said Lucy, aged 9.

Children need help to meet these challenges by developing moral and social values. Social values are concerned with the good of society, the environment and global community. They create a vision of, and a commitment to, the sort of world we want to live in. Values that underpin a philosophical enquiry might include commitments to:

- truth, justice, freedom, equality and human rights
- respect for justice as fairness in rule and law
- recognition of the importance of care and commitment
- responsibilty as active participants in the democratic discussion
- concern for creating a better future

Philosophical enquiry aims to encourage children to think about social values and become aware of and involved in the life and concerns of their community and their society. Discussion of social issues in their community helps children build their capacity to become active and effective citizens. It increases their awareness both of themselves as unique human beings with their own needs, and also the needs of others. This growth of self awareness combined with awareness of others is at the heart of what philosophy develops – 'sophia' or wisdom. It is also the heart of 'emotional intelligence'.

According to Daniel Goleman there are two different kinds of intelligence, rational and emotional. How we do in life is determined by both – it is not just IQ but emotional intelligence that has an effect. Children have to explore their own emotions, and the emotions of others. Children need opportunities to think about and explore personal, moral and social values to help build the qualities and skills that develop emotional intelligence. They need to learn how to discuss and resolve through dialogue the emotional conflicts, problems and challenges of living with others. They need to learn how to effectively express their views to others, and be open to the views of others and how they can contribute in making a difference for the better. As Manesh, aged 9, put it: 'We are learning, so we can make a better people and a better world.'

Children do not learn to be active, participating citizens by being told about the world they live in by others, just as they do not learn to ride a bike or read by merely being told how to do it. The best way to learn about democracy is to practise it, even on a limited scale. There is no better way of learning to be an active citizen than in a community of enquiry. But how do you begin?

Newspapers provide good starting points for the discussion of values. Look at the news stories in today's newspaper. What are the social and moral problems involved? Choose a story relevant to the children's life concerns. Ask them to identify questions and problems and issues from the story. Use their comments and questions as stimulus for a discussion in a community of of enquiry (see below). Such discussion should show that real life is a complex affair, that there are many viewpoints to take into account and rarely are choices clear-cut.

Recognizing the plurality of viewpoints and developing the self confidence to take your own reasoned view are the key aims of such a discussion. If they do not learn from the errors of the past and the present our children will repeat those mistakes.

Here are some examples of themes for discussion with children prompted by recent stories in the news:

News Story	Theme	Key Questions
A racist murder	Racism	Why does it occur? Why is it wrong? What can be done about it?
Protests over foxhunting	Animal Rights	Why are animals hunted? Should it be allowed?
News of civil war	War	Why are there wars? What are the alternatives?
Drug-smuggling	Drugs	What are drugs? Is drug-taking bad? Why?
Children not in school	School	Should going to school be compulsory? Why?

(From Fisher, R. (2001), *Values for Thinking*

A democratic community develops

Are there specific issues and problems current in the news that are worth discussing? A democratic community develops through adapting to the individual needs of its members. Decisions in a democracy should always be open to review and reason. The process of democracy ensures this openness to change in response to the needs of the individual through embodying the rights of all to a voice and a vote.

A democratic community:

- embodies as a principle the freedom of
  expression of individuals
- makes critical reasoning, not convention, the arbiter
  of moral judgement
- is organic in the sense that its working procedures
  and values are open to adaptation
- ensures that all its members have the right to a voice
  and a vote.

Discussion plays a central role in the development of community. Learning to talk face-to-face with other members of one's community about questions of common interest is one of the most basic and most important of human activities. For children, it not only lays the groundwork for language and literacy development, but also boosts confidence in oneself as a member of a learning community, whether it be a class, a club or a family. Shared discussion helps to create and sustain the community, and also to solve community problems. Carol, aged 11, summed up the value of democratic discussion by saying: 'A democracy is when everyone has the chance to say what to do to solve a problem, and it's not just left to a few.'

The problem with any community, particularly a pluralist community where individuals come from differnt cultures and backgrounds, is that there may be many significant and potentially conflicting interests and opinions. Similarly, under the description of democracy there may be differences of interpretation and practice. Not everyone has the same understanding and experiences of life or of democracy. What is needed is engagement from an early age in practices that support democracy and the development of understanding the problems and conflicts in life through shared discussion. If children are to learn how to negotiate and make decisions they must engage in practices that support negotiation and decision making. The community of enquiry provides just such a forum of careful listening, constructive argument and collaborative discussion where individuals, whether they be children or adults, can find their own path to personal meanings and shared values. As Peter, aged 8, said: 'I have a lot of ideas but I don't much say them except in our "philosophy" lesson.'

Information-processing skills

These enable students to locate and collect relevant information, to sort, classify, sequence, compare and contrast, and to analyse part–whole relationships. They help build knowledge and understanding of the key concepts essential in becoming informed citizens, such as fairness, justice and democracy. They are to be developed through discussion of topical political, spiritual, moral, social and cultural issues, problems and events.

Questioning skills

These enable students to ask relevant questions, to pose and define problems and investigate ideas. Students develop and demonstrate these skills when they reflect upon and raise questions about personal, moral and social issues, and investigate the legal, political, religious, social and economic institutions that influence their lives. These skills enable pupils to learn about the issues that concern people in their local and wider communities.

Reasoning skills

These enable students to give reasons for opinions and actions, to draw inferences and make deductions, to use precise language to explain what they think, and to make judgements and decisions informed by reason or evidence. They are developed through helping students to engage in study, reflection and discussion of personal, moral and social issues that require the use of reasoning, argument and explanation. These skills aid participation in democratic discussion and decision-making.

Creative thinking skills

These enable students to generate ideas, suggest hypotheses, and supply imagination in looking for alternative and innovative outcomes. Citizenship and values education provide opportunities for students to develop creative thinking through the use of their imagination in considering other people's experiences and in thinking about views that are not their own. Pupils develop these skills when they contribute to exploratory discussions of problems, and seek solutions that are of use to themselves and others.

Evaluation skills

The link between thinking skills and citizenship education is summed up in the need to encourage imaginative reasoning. As Andrew, aged 11, said during a discussion: 'Imagination helps us to know what it is like for other people.' The development of imaginative reasoning is necessary if children are to see themselves not only in relation to others in the present world, but as citizens in a society that *could be*. As one ten-year-old put it: 'You need imagination to think how the world might be.' Citizenship is not only about what is but also about what might be. Can we imagine a better, fairer and more successful society? What would that world be like? How might it be created? We can make a better world and a better society. The question is, 'Where do we begin?'

CONCLUSION

Philosophy is important. It should be for everyone.
Kieron, aged 8

Philosophy begins in wonder. And at the end when philosophic thought has done its best, the wonder remains.
A.N. Whitehead

The teaching of philosophy for children is not easy, no matter what our level of experience and expertise might be. It is a challenging task, but one founded on a natural curiosity about the world and the human capacity to create and share ideas with others. We may not be prepared for where the ideas in a discussion may take us. When problems are open-ended we can no longer give the impression that we know all the answers - we don't. And neither do we know all the questions.

Certainly some of our children will surprise us with the questions they raise, like the 7-year-old who asked: 'If the world began with a bang, what happened before the bang?' They will surprise us too with some of the answers they give, like the 6-year-old who said: 'I know I am a person because when I speak to myself I always get an answer.' In a philosophical discussion we become pioneers alongside our children, thinking anew about what we so easily take for granted, and re-creating in ourselves what Buddhists call 'beginner's mind'. We are co-equals in the enquiry and will be as perplexed as our children about some of the questions and problems they raise. The philosopher Karl Popper called his autobiography *Unended Quest*, and our own search for philosophical understanding may also be unended. We can show children ways to start their own journeys of philosophical enquiry and we have a method for doing so, one that has worked well across the world, as successfully in village schools as in universities – the method of community of enquiry.

A community of enquiry is a method of mutual help for investigating issues and solving problems, encouraging students to be active participants in the learning process, making their own discoveries and facilitating their own understanding under the guidance of a discussion leader. It is an ideal method for promoting cooperative learning, and for motivating children to listen attentively to each other.[21] It provides a safe and supportive environment for experimenting with ideas. Its overall aim is to suspend judgement, to allow that our everyday thinking may be wrong or at least incomplete, and to develop a clearer understanding about what we think and mean. As Wittgenstein said, 'What can be said at all can be said clearly.'[22] However, as important as clear definitions are in aiding clarity of thought and reasoning, philosophy for children is about more than this. It is also about developing reasonableness and good judgement. A community of enquiry provides children with the opportunity both to create and to challenge the moral order. It recognizes that children have a right to express their thinking about questions, problems and issues that relate to their own lives and concerns. It provides an opportunity for children to talk about difficult things like the nature of infinity, why people die, or how they should live. It recognizes that philosophy can take place at different levels, that it need not be serious or hard work, it can be fun. As Ravi, aged 10, said: 'It can be fun playing with ideas, like thinking impossible things and wondering if they are impossible.'

The community of enquiry invites children into the club of critical thinkers, and treats them as thinkers and reasoners, even when sometimes they are not! It is based on the optimistic view that given appropriate encouragement, nurturing and reward children will come to act philosophically, in the sense of being able to discuss important and complex questions in a thoughtful way. Language is developed through use, and so is the ability to philosophize. Learning to think in many ways is like learning a mother tongue, it is developed through immersion in contexts that engage our response. If children can learn a new language, learn to play the violin or how to play chess at an early age, why should they not be introduced to philosophy? It is after all the best means we have of teaching thinking.

One of the advantages of doing philosophy with children is that it does not require expensive resources, although resources as we have seen are available to support this work in home or classroom. All it needs is an enquiring mind sensitive to philosophical questions, and willing to think about thinking. It exercises a form of intelligence that we all have (one of the multiple intelligences Howard Gardner calls existential intelligence'), but which we do not all use. As Carla, aged 10, says: 'We can all do philosophy if we try.' Some of the most important benefits of philosophy for children will not be quantifiable. During discussion there occur those magic moments whose value is beyond measure. How can you quantify that moment when a very inarticulate child sitting in the corner of the classroom thinking and not communicating very much suddenly has an idea and is able for the first time to articulate a very thoughtful contribution to a discussion? There are, however, certain outcomes that can be expected to be in evidence, developed over time through the practice of philosophy for children. Children engaged in philosophical discussion are likely to show evidence of being:

- more able to ask questions
- more active in classroom discussion
- more creative in generating ideas about a given topic
- more willing and able to give reasons or evidence to support opinions
- more reasonable and thoughtful in their behaviour
- more attentive to what others are saying
- more confident in themselves as thinkers and learners

Teachers experienced in leading philosophical discussion report a number of professional benefits including becoming more effective in their teaching through, for example, the use of discussion in the classroom. The success of philosophical discussion brings its own rewards, as with the teacher who said 'it has provided me with greater satisfaction in my teaching'. At the practical level of lesson planning philosophy with children provides teachers with some ideal resources and starting points for classroom discussion, in particular to develop critical reading skills and extend literacy. Many teachers report that undertaking philosophy with children has altered their perception of pupils' capabilities. As one teacher reported, 'I now think of children and the potential of children's thinking in an entirely different way. It has raised my expectations of what they can think and say.' Others speak of ways philosophical discussion has revitalized their interest in different areas of the curriculum, or as a means for whole-school development and its 'contribution towards the creation of a Thinking School'.

The following is an excerpt from an account by teacher Johanna Kiernon of her experience of introducing philosophy to children:

> They say that Philosophy begins in wonder. It was wondering how children think and learn that lead me to philosophy with children as a possible methodology to assist children to be more skilled listeners and articulate speakers. I found, however, that philosophy did more than this, it helps children to reason and think things out for themselves ... Philosophy offers the opportunity to enhance thinking skills and raise the child's self-esteem, and to increase children's tolerance and respect for each other. It is mind-expanding and fun... It is possible to observe progression when Philosophy is part of the regular time-table for a term or more. Initially the children are using comparisons, making distinctions and forming opinions. Later on they become practised in argument and logic, and gradually the thinking becomes more critical, more reflectve and sensitive to context. They are more tolerant of those who contradict them, and become better at seeking out evidence and giving evidence when questioned ... Last year I taught twenty 4-year-olds in a Reception Class... I now believe that even very young children can handle abstract concepts. They may not be able to define such concepts as 'jealousy', 'good' or 'lying' but they can explain why it is right to tell the truth and that it is unkind or unfair not to share. Philosophy has helped them explore the subtleties of their meaning, for example that a good person can do bad things... Even these very young ones enjoy Philosophy and will continue with a conversation at a deep level for 45 minutes or more. Philosophy in the classroom is regarded as fun, but it is as challenging for the teacher as it is for the child.

Philosophical discussion is an intellectual quest, an adventure in ideas. If you enjoy ideas then philosophy with children will bring its rewards, for them and for you. There are no people who are incapable of philosophical thinking. All people, including children of a young age, have the intellectual resources to do philosophy, all they may lack is the opportunity and the motivation.

Philosophy is more than an exercise in thinking skills, it is a way of life that helps you create a better life. A vital feature of philosophy is its interest in rearranging, shifting, displacing and reframing ideas and beliefs. Another feature is its attempt to exist in places of uncertainty, exploration, possibility and imagination (Haynes, 2002, pp 42). Philosophy, said Wittgenstein, 'is not a body of doctrine but an activity'.[23] There is no better way to understand more about it than to act upon it, either by facilitating some philosophical discussion, or by getting some further training in doing philosophy with children.[24] The philosopher Heidegger once said that a song only begins to be a song in the singing, and similarly philosophy only begins to be philosophy in the act of philosophizing. All we need is the confidence to begin and to involve others in the experience. This courage to begin, to take the first steps into what may be uncharted territory in philosophical enquiry with children, is something we all need. There may be setbacks when the discussion does not seem to be working, and every venture of importance must survive some setbacks, but there will also be unexpected rewards, as the children and teachers quoted in this book have shown, in doing philosophy with children. The courage needed to begin is for me well illustrated in the words of the following anonymous poem:

Appolinaire said
'Come to the edge'
'It is too high'
'Come to the edge'
'We might fall'
'Come to the edge'
And they came
And he pushed them
And they flew

NOTES AND REFERENCES

1. Adapted from Splitter and Sharp (1995), *Teaching for Better Thinking*, p. 117.
2. Vygotsky, L. (1978), *Mind in Society*, Cambridge, Mass: MIT Press.
3. Adapted from Fisher, R. (1997), *Poems for Thinking*, p. 13.
4. Toye, N. (1996), 'On the relationship between philosophy for children and educational drama', *Thinking*, Vol. 12, No. 1, pp. 24–6.
5. This discussion of philosophical enquiry into the myths of mathematics owes much to the work of Marie-France Daniel and her colleagues in Quebec. See Lafortune, L., Daniel, M.-F., Pallasco, R. and Sykes, P. (1996), 'Community of enquiry in mathematics for higher education', *Analytic Teaching*, Vol. 16, No. 2, pp. 19–28.
6. Department of Education and Science (1982), *Mathematics Counts*, the Cockcroft Report, para. 249.
7. Gazzard, A. (1993), 'Thinking skills in science and philosophy for children', in Lipman, M. (ed.) (1993), *Thinking Children and Education*, Dubuque, Iowa: Kendall Hunt, pp. 619–32. For more on cognitive intervention in science teaching see Adey, P. and Shayer, M. (1994), *Really Raising Standards: Cognitive Intervention in Academic Achievement*, London: Routledge.
8. Gaarder, J. (1995), *Sophie's World*, London: Phoenix House, p. 214.
9. A fuller discussion of this and other passages from *Wally's Stories* appears in Kennedy, D. (1996), 'Young children's moves: emergent philosophical community of enquiry in early childhood education', *Critical and Creative Thinking*, Vol. 4, No. 2, pp. 28–41.
10. For a collection of problem-solving challenges in design and technology see Fisher, R. and Garvey, J. (1994), *Investigating Technology*, Books 1 and 2, Melbourne: Longman Cheshire.
11. Quoted in Garvey, J. (1996), 'The value of post-computer work in discussion in promoting thinking skills', Brunel University: unpublished paper.
12. For more on the development of children's concepts in

history and other areas of the primary curriculum see Willig, C.J. (1990), *Children's Concepts and the Primary Curriculum*, London: Paul Chapman.

13. For a stimulus and discussion plan on environmental ethics see 'Who can buy the sky?', in Fisher, R. (1997), *Poems for Thinking*, p. 32.

14. Art images for thinking can be found in Fisher, R. (1994), *Active Art: Picture Pack*, Cheltenham, Nelson Thornes; and in Fisher, R. (in press), *Pictures for Thinking*.

15. For more on the relationship between aesthetics, learning and thinking see Perkins, D. (1994), *The Intelligent Eye: Learning to Think by Looking at Art*, Santa Monica, California: The Getty Center for Education in the Arts; and Abbs, P. (1994), *The Educational Imperative: A Defence of Socratic and Aesthetic Learning*, London: Falmer.

16. This section on music owes much to the research of Sara Liptai (Brunel University) in using philosophical enquiry to develop the music curriculum. See Liptai, S. (1996), 'A case for an aesthetic community of enquiry', *If... then: The Journal of Philosophical Enquiry in Education*, October 1996, pp. 16–24.

17. For more on sport as a subject of philosophical discussion see Cresswell, R. (1996), 'Demons, devils, dragons and flames: harnessing sporting interests in the philosophy classroom', *Critical and Creative Thinking*, Vol. 4, No. 2. For more on the social and political dimensions of sport see Allison, L. (1993), *The Changing Politics of Sport*, Manchester: Manchester University Press. For a discussion of the moral dimensions of sport see Arnold, P.J. (1994), 'Sport and moral education', *Journal of Moral Education*, Vol. 23, No. 1, pp. 75ff.

18. Peters, R.S. (1966), *Ethics and Education*, London: Allen and Unwin.

19. SCAA (1995), *Spiritual and Moral Development: SCAA Discussion Paper 3*, London: Schools Curriculum and Assessment Authority.

20. For more on the use of philosophical enquiry in religious education see Sharp, A. (1994), 'The religious dimension of Philosophy for Children', *Critical and Creative Thinking*, Vol. 1, Nos 1 and 2; and Mendoca, D. (1996), 'The religious

dimension in Philosophy for Children', *Critical and Creative Thinking*, Vol. 4, No. 2.

21. For more on cooperative learning see Fisher, R. (1995), *Teaching Children to Learn*, pp. 89ff.
22. Wittgenstein, L. (1922), *Tractatus*, 4.112, London: Routledge.
23. Wittgenstein, L. (1922), *op.cit.*, Preface.
24. The British society for training in philosophy for children is The Society for the Advancement of Philosophical Enquiry in Education (SAPERE). *www.sapere.net*

APPENDIX 1

Some questions and topics for philosophical enquiry with children

The following is a list of questions and topics for philosophical enquiry that appear in this book illustrated with discussion plans or excerpts of philosophical discussion with children.

APPENDIX 2

Discourse vocabulary: a checklist of some terms to use

One aim of philosophical enquiry is to develop a vocabulary of discourse to enrich children's understanding and capacity to engage in thinking, reasoning and discussion. The following is a list of some of the terms that could be used to help students at different ages and stages, from 5 to 16+ years, to identify and assess elements of philosophical discussion.

Stage/age (year)	Words/concepts
1. 5–7+ (yrs 1–3)	listening – speaking
	talking – discussing
	thinking – thoughts – ideas
	brain – mind
	knowing – believing
	imagine – imagination
	question/s – answer/s
	reason
	rule – rules
	agree – disagree
	example – decision
	view/s – opinion/s
	problem – solution

right – wrong
fair – unfair
true – untrue (lies)
real – not real
similar – different
mystery – philosophy

2. 7–11 (yrs 4–6)   accept – reject
compare – contrast
argument – quarrel
version – statement
reasons – supporting arguments
predict – assess
clarify – confuse
respond – reply
rule – exceptions
example – counter example
prove – disprove
evidence – example
explain – justify
relevant – irrelevant
meaning – definition
argue – persuade
fact – opinion
data – information
possible – probable – certain
cause – effect

3. 11–14 (yrs 7–9)   assumption
logic/logical – illogical
implications – consequences
analysis – classification
concepts (clear/fuzzy)
identical – contradictory
cause/effect relationships
definition – distinction (between words/ideas)
criteria (criterion) – judgement
assumption (implicit) – assertion
clear – ambiguous (vague/imprecise)
analogy – metaphor

empathy
objective/subjective
principle
dilemma – compromise
authority – evidence
prejudice (bias) – balanced view
observation – interpretation
paraphrase – summarize

4. 14–16+ (yrs 10–11)   consistent – circular argument
concise – verbose
simplified – over-simplified
premiss – conclusion
consistent – inconsistent
content – context
assessment – evaluation
infer – imply – entail
connote – suggest
reason – faith – intuition
fallacy – error
relevant – irrelevant
hypothesis/hypothetical – statement of fact
misrepresent – misdescribe
necessary – sufficient conditions
weak/strong argument – criticism
logical certainty – logical impossibility
explicit – implicit
plausibile – implausible
qualifying – refuting

5. 16+ years   *prima facie* (self-evident) – burden of proof
subjective – objective
begging the question (assuming what you have to prove)
fallacy – false alternative
contrary – contradictory – converse
equivocation (changing meanings mid-stream)

> *reductio ad absurdam* (reduction to
> an absurdity)
> slippery slope argument – the thin
> end of the wedge
> *ad hominem* (irrelevant personal
> attack)
> dichotomy – false dichotomy
> straw man – irrelevance
> valid/invalid inference
> generalization
> ends/means relationships
> identifying and using criteria

Further reading

Warburton, N. (1996), *Thinking from A–Z*, London: Routledge.
A useful reference dictionary of words to do with reasoning
and argument.

APPENDIX 3

Checklist of discourse skills

The following checklist is designed to aid assessment of group discussion. It is not a checklist of all the functional skills relating to discourse. It identifies various discourse features of language in an easily identifiable way, illustrating a small set of broad skills to form a manageable checklist for assessing some of the discourse skills central to philosophical discussion. The skills can be divided into four broad, related categories – personal participation (1), interactive skills (2/3), enquiry skills (4) and reasoning skills (5–10). The checklist can be used for assessment of individuals or groups.

1. *Participation*
   number of comments
   response to teacher
   response to another student
   extended utterances
   non-extended utterances
   response to agenda (building on the discussion)
   unclassified response (non-specific response)

2. *Organizing*
   identifying task (e.g. problem/question to be discussed)

planning (e.g. organizing discussion)
directing (e.g. asking for responses)
concluding (e.g. summing up, last words)

3. *Collaborating*
active listening (giving serious attention, allowing each speaker to finish)
agreeing (specifying with whom/what view you agree with)
encouraging (showing verbal or non-verbal responsiveness to others)
turn-taking (yielding turn to others)
self-correcting (moderating one's views during discussion)

4. *Questioning*
asking initial question (identifying a puzzle or problem for discussion)
identifying kind of question (is it factual/philosophical/ literary, etc?)
asking follow-up questions (seeking reasons, clarification, etc.)
self-questioning (rhetorical or genuine self-enquiry?)

5. *Initiating*
making initial statements (within a stage of the discussion)
setting new line of enquiry (introducing new problem or issue)
seeking justification (asking for reasons, proof, evidence)

6. *Extending*
developing the discussion (building on ideas, making connections)
adding detail (giving examples, evidence, instances, etc.)
translating (re-phrasing one's own or other's ideas or contributions)

7. *Countering*
raising objections (with reason, argument or counter-argument)
qualifying (clarifying, drawing distinctions, amending viewpoint)

self-maintaining (giving judgement or opinion without reason)

8. *Reasoning*
explaining (defining, clarifying, illustrating the meaning of . . .)
justifying (giving supporting reasons or evidence)
comparing (comparing or contrasting, drawing an analogy)
hypothesizing (suggesting a theory/explanation/possible consequence, etc.)
generalizing (arguing from a particular instance to a general rule)

9. *Recounting*
using anecdote (is it relevant? coherent? illustrating a point?)
paraphrasing (e.g. summarizing a text, event or an idea)
describing (giving an account of a situation, experience or idea)

10. *Reviewing*
reviewing (analysing progress of discussion or element of discussion)
monitoring (checking understanding of one's own or others' contributions)
evaluating (assessing quality of and contributions to discussion)
judging (critical judgement of discussion or element of discussion)
commenting (giving opinion on relevant features of context of discussion)

APPENDIX 4

How do we assess progress in philosophical discussion?

There are two main ways of gathering evidence of progress in philosophical discussion, either by the teacher/researcher analysing evidence of the discussion, or through self-assessment by the participants (see Appendix 5). The best way to analyse evidence is to record the session on video or audio tape, then to transcribe and analyse elements of the discussion. It can also be instructive for the group to see/hear and to review their taped discussion.

The following are some ways of analysing a transcript of philosophical discussions:

1. *track whole discussion*, analysing discourse or cognitive feature of each contribution (e.g. using a checklist of skills as in Appendix 3)
2. *track one discourse or cognitive feature* through whole discussion (e.g. how many examples of reasoning, questioning, extended utterances?)
3. *track one student* (or small group) through discussion, analysing their contributions
4. *track contributions of every individual participant* – who/how many spoke? who spoke most? what was the gender balance of contributions?

5. analyse *student/teacher ratio* of contributions to discussion (who dominated the discussion, students or teacher? what is the ratio of contributions?)

6. split whole discussion into *epistemic episodes* or segments of discussion that have a particular focus (e.g. topic or style of enquiry) – what were the turning points? what were the most interesting ideas? what does each episode show?

7. analyse *one epistemic episode* – the following questions may help:

- what was the focus, purpose or theme of the episode?
- what was its place in the flow of discussion?
- what comment initiated the episode (was it by teacher or student?)
- what sustained the episode (teacher, student or mixed contributions?)
- what were the turning points in the discussion?
- was there evidence of critical thinking (analysing), creative thinking (exploring), problem posing (enquiry), or problem solving (making reasoned judgements)?
- compare this episode with another – is there evidence of progression in individuals, or the group?
- what do you think individuals or the group gained from this experience?
- in what ways did the episode match, exceed or fall short of your aims?
- what have you learnt from the way you facilitated this episode?

APPENDIX 5

Evaluating philosophy for children

Some questions to help in evaluating a philosophical discussion:

1. Asking questions
   - Did we ask good questions?
   - How many questions?
   - What kind of questions?

2. Discussing
   - What did we discuss?
   - Did we try to answer the question?
   - Did we have a good discussion?

3. Listening
   - Did we listen to each other well?
   - Did we respond to what others said?
   - Did we show respect for each other during the discussion?

4. Speaking
   - Did we explain our ideas clearly?
   - Were there any good ideas? Did we build on these ideas?
   - Did everyone have a chance to speak? Who did most of the speaking?

5. Reasoning
   - Did we find any answers?
   - Did we give good reasons for our answers?
   - Were we willing to change our minds?

6. Thinking about thinking
   - What kinds of thinking did we do?
   - Did we learn anything from the discussion?
   - Did we improve our thinking? Why or why not?

The importance of evaluation is that it helps us to plan and improve our practice in the future.

Some questions to help in planning:
   - What would be good to discuss next?
   - What would be the best way to discuss it next time?
   - What do we need to remember?

Bibliography

A select list of books on philosophical enquiry in education:

Abbs, P. (1994), *The Educational Imperative: A Defence of Socratic and Aesthetic Learning*, London: Falmer Press.

Andrews, R., Costello, P. and Clarke, S. (1993), *Improving the Quality of Argument 5–16: Final Report*, Hull: University of Hull, Centre for Studies in Rhetoric.

Bakhtin, M.M. (1981), *The Dialogic Imagination*, ed. Holquist, M., trans. Emerson, C. and Holquist, M., Austin: University of Texas Press.

Cam, P. (ed.) (1993), *Thinking Stories: Philosophical Inquiry for the Classroom*, Sydney: Hale & Iremonger.

Coles, M.J. and Robinson, W.D. (eds) (1991), *Teaching Thinking: A Survey of Programmes*, London: Duckworth.

Costello, P.J.M. (2000), *Thinking Skills and Early Childhood Education*, London: David Fulton.

de Botton, A. (2000), *The Consolations of Philosophy*, London: Hamish Hamilton.

de Haan, C., MacCol, S. and McCutcheon, L. (1995), *Philosophy with Kids*, Books 1–3 and activity book, Melbourne: Longman.

Dillon, J.T. (1994), *Using Discussion in Classrooms*, Milton Keynes: Open University Press.

Fisher, R. (1990, 1992, 1995a), *Teaching Children to Think*, Oxford: Blackwell, 1990; Hemel Hempstead: Simon & Schuster, 1992; Cheltenham: Stanley Thornes, 1995.

Fisher, R. (1995b), *Teaching Children to Learn*, Cheltenham: Stanley Thornes.

Fisher, R. (1996), *Stories for Thinking*, Oxford: Nash Pollock.

Fisher, R. (1997), *Games for Thinking*, Oxford: Nash Pollock.

Fisher, R. (1997), *Stories for Thinking*, Oxford: Nash Pollock.

Fisher, R. (1999), *First Stories for Thinking*, Oxford: Nash Pollock.

Fisher, R. (1999), *Head Start: How to Develop Your Child's Mind*, London: Souvenir Press.

Fisher, R. (2000), *First Poems for Thinking*, Oxford: Nash Pollock.

Fisher, R. (2000), *Values for Thinking*, Oxford: Bloomsbury.

Fox, R. (1996), *Thinking Matters: Stories to Encourage Thinking Skills*, Exmouth: Southgate.

Gaarder, J. (1995), *Sophie's World*, London: Phoenix.

Goleman, D. (1994), *Emotional Intelligence*, London: Bloomsbury.

Haynes, J. (2000), *Children as Philosophers: Learning through enquiry and dialogue in the primary classroom*, London: Routledge/Falmer.

Lipman, M., Sharp, A.M. and Oscanyan, F.S. (1980), *Philosophy in the Classroom*, Philadelphia: Temple University Press.

Lipman, M. (1985), 'Thinking skills fostered by Philosophy for Children' in Segal, J., Chipman, S. and Glaser, R. (eds.) *Thinking and Learning Skills*, Vol. 1, Hillsdale, New Jersey: Lawrence Erlbaum, pp. 83–108.

Lipman, M. (1988), *Philosophy Goes to School*, Philadelphia: Temple University Press.

Lipman, M. (1991), *Thinking in Education*, Cambridge: Cambridge University Press.

Lipman, M., Sharp, A.M. *et al.*, *Philosophy for Children Programme*, children's novels and teacher's manuals for teaching philosophy with students aged 5–16+ years, Institute for the Advancement of Philosophy for Children, Montclair University, Upper Montclair, New Jersey, USA.

Lipman, M. (ed.) (1993), *Thinking Children and Education*, Dubuque, Iowa: Kendall/Hunt Publishing Co.

Matthews, G.B. (1980), *Philosophy and the Young Child*, Cambridge, MA: Harvard University Press.

Matthews, G.B. (1994), *The Philosophy of Childhood*, Cambridge, MA: Harvard University Press.

McCall, C. (1990), *Stevenson Lectures in Citizenship, 1991*, Glasgow: University of Glasgow.

McCall, C. (1991), *Laura and Paul*, philosophical novel for children, Glasgow: University of Glasgow.

Minnis, F. Overell, G. and Sutton, A. (1990), *The Transformers: the Art of Inspired Teaching*, London: BBC.

Murris, K. (1992), *Teaching Philosophy with Picture Books*, London: Infonet Publications.

Nelson, L. (1949), *Socratic Method and Critical Philosophy*, New Haven: Yale University Press.

Paul, R. (1993), *Critical Thinking: How to Prepare Students for a Rapidly Changing World*, Santa Rosa, CA: Foundation for Critical Thinking.

Portelli, J. and Reed, R.F. (1995), *Children, Philosophy and Democracy*, Canada: Detsellig Enterprises Ltd.

Quinn, V. (1997), *Critical Thinking in Young Minds*, London: David Fulton.

Rowe, D. and Newton, J. (1994), *You, Me, Us: Social and Moral Responsibility for Primary Schools*, London: Citizenship Foundation/Home Office.

Sharp, A.M. and Reed, R.F. (eds) (1991), *Studies in Philosophy for Children: Harry Stottlemeier's Discovery*, Philadelphia: Temple University Press.

Sharp, A.M. and Reed, R.F. (eds) (1995), *Studies in Philosophy for Children: Pixie*, Madrid, Spain: De La Torre.

Splitter, L. and Sharp, A.M. (1985), *Teaching for Better Thinking: Community of Enquiry*, Victoria, Australia: ACER.

Sprod, T. (1993), *Books into Ideas: A Community of Enquiry*, Victoria, Australia: Hawker Brownlow.

Sutcliffe, R. (1993), *Harry Stottlemeier's Discovery*, philosophical novel by Matthew Lipman adapted for use in Britain, Horsham: Christ's Hospital.

Wilks, S. (1995), *Critical and Creative Thinking: Strategies for Classroom Inquiry*, Armadale: Eleanor Curtain.

Journals with articles on philosophical enquiry with children include:

Thinking: The Journal of Philosophy for Children, IAPC (USA).

Analytic Teaching: The Community of Enquiry Journal (USA).

Critical and Creative Thinking: The Australasian Journal of Philosophy for Children.

Information on the Internet

The following are websites about philosophy for children and philosophical enquiry in the classroom.

Australian Philosophy for children
www.utas.edu.au/docs/humsoc/philosophy/postgrads/FAPCA.html
Dialogueworks: Resources and Training in Philosophy with Children
www.dialogueworks.co.uk
Robert Fisher's website
www.teachingthinking.net
Philosophy for Children (UK)
www.thinkingcap.org.uk
Philosophy for Children (worldwide)
www.p4C.net
UK Society for the Advancement of Philosophical Enquiry and
Reflection in Education
www.sapere.net
US Institute for the Advancement of Philosophy for Children
http://chss.montclair.edu/ipac/homepage.html

The following are some websites about teaching thinking and
thinking skills:

Accelerated Learning
www.alite.co.uk
Edward de Bono
www.edwdebono.com
Tony Buzan
www.mind-map.com
Cognitive Acceleration through Science Education
www.kcl.ac.uk/depsta/education/teaching/CASE.html

DfEE Standards on Thinking Skills
www.standards.dfee.gov.uk/thinking
Creativity Resources for Students
www. cre8ng.com
Emotional Literacy Organisation
www.antidote.org.uk
Daniel Goleman and his work
www.eiconsortium.org/members/goleman.htm
Harvard Project Zero (Howard Garner, David Perkins *et al.*)
www.pz.harvard.edu/Default.html
Carol McGuiness research report
www.dfee.gov.uk/research/re-brief/RB115.doc
National Emotional Literacy Interest Group
www.nelig.com
Northumberland LEA Thinking for Learning
www.ngfl.northumberland.gov.uk
Questions Publishing
www.teachthinking.com
Robert Sternberg and his research
www.yale.edu/pace/teammembers/personalpages/bob.html
Thinking Classrooms in Practice
www.thethinkingclassroom.co.uk
Thinking Teaching Journal
www.education-quest.co.uk
Thinking Together
www.thinkingtogether.com
US commercial resources
www.criticalthinking.com
US National Education Association
www.nea.org/helpfrom/connecting/tools/thinking.html#intro
US School Improvement Research
www.nwrel.org/scpd/sirs/6/cu11.html

Index

Gardner, H. 231. 236. 245
Gardner, S. 178
geography 225-8
Goleman, D. 271
Grimm brothers 113

Habermas, J. 61
Heckman, G. 147
Hegel, G. 57,58
Heidegger, M. 11, 247
history 222-5
    discussion questions 224
Holder, J.J. 198
Hughes, T. 117
Hume, D. 82

illustrations 117-18
impulsiveness 16-17, 136-7
individuality 11-12
indoctrination 73
inductive arguments 143, 164
information technology
    219-21
Institute for the
Advancement of Philosophy
for Children
(IAPC) 29
    see also Philosophy for
    Children Programme
Internet 271
Internet investigation 158-9

James, W. 240
Johnson, S. 204
Jowett, B. 226
judgement 10-11, 43-4, 137,
    164-5

Kafka, F. 97
    Metamorphosis 116, 126-8
Kant, I. 43, 72, 87, 228
Keats, J. 230
Kermode, F. 106
Kierkegaard, S. 101, 222
Kite, A. 198
knowledge
    and intelligence 16
    scientific 212-17
Kohlberg, L. 67, 68, 71, 75, 87

language 12-13, 28, 59-60
Lawrence, D.H. 140
Lim, T.K. 198
Lipman, M. 12, 23, 26-44,
    111-12, 115, 117, 128, 149,
    169
    *Harry Stottlemeier's
    Discovery* 30, 35, 44, 111
    Looking for Meaning 32, 33
    Pixie 32
Liptai, S. 121
listening skills 83, 181-2
'Literacy Hour' 20
Lobel, A. 122
logical analysis 164

MacIntyre, A. 54, 94
McKee, D. 118
McPeck, J.E. 41
magic 216-17
mathematics 207-12
Matthews, G. 72
Mead, G.H. 11, 87
metacognitive awareness
    13-15, 136, 215
meta-discourse 149-50

33134790